improvisations on butor

improvisations

Crosscurrents
Comparative Studies in
European Literature and Philosophy

University Press of Florida
Gainesville . Tallahassee . Tampa . Boca Raton
Pensacola . Orlando . Miami . Jacksonville

on butor

Transformation of Writing,
by Michel Butor

Edited, annotated, and
with an introduction by
Lois Oppenheim

Translated by
Elinor S. Miller

Crosscurrents:
Comparative Studies
in European Literature and Philosophy
Edited by S. E. Gontarski

Improvisations on Butor:
Transformation of Writing, by Michel Butor,
edited, annotated, and with an introduction by Lois
Oppenheim; translated by Elinor S. Miller (1996).

• • • • • • •

01 00 99 98 97 96   6 5 4 3 2 1

Library of Congress Cataloging-in-Publication Data

Butor, Michel.
[Improvisations sur Butor. English]
Improvisations on Butor: transformation of writing / by
Michel Butor; edited, annotated, and with an introduction
by Lois Oppenheim; translated by Elinor S. Miller.
    p.   cm.—(Crosscurrents)
ISBN 0-8130-1377-1 (alk. paper)
I. Oppenheim, Lois. II. Title. III. Series: Crosscurrents
PQ2603.U73I4813   1996
844'.914—dc20   95-30938

The University Press of Florida is the scholarly publishing
agency for the State University System of Florida, comprised
of Florida A & M University, Florida Atlantic University,
Florida International University, Florida State University,
University of Central Florida, University of Florida, University of North Florida, University of South Florida, and University of West Florida.

University Press of Florida
15 Northwest 15th Street
Gainesville, FL 32611

for Lois Oppenheim

contents

. . . . foreword

The Crosscurrents series is designed to foreground comparative studies in European art and thought, particularly the intersections of literature and philosophy, aesthetics and culture. Without abandoning traditional comparative methodology, the series is receptive to the latest currents in critical, comparative, and performative theory, especially that generated by the renewed intellectual energy in post-Marxist Europe. It will as well take full cognizance of the cultural and political realignments of what for the better part of the twentieth century have been two separated and isolated Europes. While Western Europe is moving aggressively toward unification in the European community, with the breakup of the twentieth century's last colonial empire, the Soviet Union, Eastern Europe is dividing into nationalistic and religious enclaves. The intellectual, cultural, and literary significance of such profound restructuring, how history will finally rewrite itself, is difficult to anticipate. Having had a fertile period of modernism snuffed out in an ideological coup not long after the 1917 revolution, the nations of the former Soviet Union have, for instance, been denied (or spared) the age of Freud, most modernist experiments, and postmodern fragmentation. While Western Europe continues reaching beyond Modernism, Eastern Europe may be struggling to reclaim it. Whether a new art can emerge in the absence—or from the absence—of such forces as shaped Modernism is one of the intriguing questions of post–Cold War aesthetics.

To begin this Crosscurrents series with Michel Butor's intellectual autobiography is itself something of an aesthetic and philosophical coup. One of the central figures of the *nouveau roman* in post–World War II France,

Butor produced four "post-humanist" novels before he moved beyond narrative to other forms of *écriture*. If, as Lois Oppenheim suggests in her cogent introduction, most of Butor's prodigious output has been "a dialogue with his and other's work," then this current volume is a dialogue with that dialogue, Butor on Butor on Butor. And if in much of Butor's critical work he is writing of others as self, *Transformation of Writing* allows him to critique self as other, and to examine not only his writing but the idea of writing, the writerly itself. It is his fourth volume in his series of *Transformations,* whereby Butor situates himself with Rimbaud, Flaubert, and Henri Michaux.

The series henceforth will continue to critique the developing, often conflicting currents of European thought through the prism of literature, philosophy, and theory.

S. E. Gontarski

butor on butor:
an introduction

In the summer of 1991, Michel Butor retired from the University of Geneva after many years of teaching. The last course he offered there was the first in which he explored his own work. That he waited so long to speak of it in class, while others were doing so worldwide, was not entirely a result of modesty. He had been made by the academy to understand the importance of maintaining the distinction between his different hats—one professorial, the other authorial—from the start.[1]

On the eve of his retirement, however, Butor was invited by his colleagues to trace the development of his writing against the background of that of French post–World War II literature. The course was entitled "L'Écriture en transformation." After so many lectures, both at the University of Geneva and at numerous other universities throughout the world, and so many critical volumes devoted to the work of others, here *enfin* was Butor on Butor. The lectures, like those of previous semesters, were recorded, and it seemed to Elinor Miller and myself that the cloistering of the tapes in the library of the university was nothing short of indecent, for too few would know of their existence and far fewer would have access to them. Hence, from these tapes, this fourth volume of the *Improvisations* series emerged.

. . . . . . **Modern Postmodernist or Postmodern Modernist?**

"The danger is in the neatness of identifications," wrote Samuel Beckett. "The conception of Philosophy and Philology as a pair of nigger minstrels

1

out of the Teatro dei Piccoli is soothing, like the contemplation of a carefully folded ham-sandwich."[2] Michel Butor is certainly a case in point. Among the most celebrated writers of his generation in France, he occupies a disturbing if not utterly ambiguous position with regard to contemporary French literature.

Butor is the author of four novels: *Passage de Milan, L'Emploi du temps, La Modification,* and *Degrés,* each eminently successful. Yet he has not written a novel since 1960, and one can no longer comfortably identify him as a novelist per se. He is the author of numerous essays on literature, music, and painting: the five volumes of *Répertoire,* the book-length essays on Baudelaire and Rimbaud, *Essais sur les modernes, Essais sur les essais,* and *Essais sur le roman* come first to mind. Yet to call him a critic also misses the mark, for more often than not his critical studies elucidate far larger trajectories than those implied by the exegesis of a single artist or work. And while his many collections of poetry (the *Illustrations* series alone has four volumes) bear witness to his remarkable talent as a poet, his identity as author of all the rest remains most troubling: *Mobile,* for example, is a study for a representation of the United States; *Réseau aérien* is a radio text; *Portrait de l'artiste en jeune singe* is an autobiography that is but is not one. Then again there are the series *Génie du lieu* and *Matières de rêves,* to say nothing of the multitude of collaborations Butor has undertaken with composers, painters, and photographers. (His personal bibliography lists over five hundred works, exclusive of prints, posters, postal collages, sculptures, films, original texts in foreign languages, and the like.)

It is perhaps in part due to the extraordinary diversity of this oeuvre, a literary corpus developed over some forty years, that the effort is repeatedly made to situate Butor and his creative activities on the horizon of postmodernism, where a kind of anarchy of high culture would account for a superimposing of identities as bewildering as it is beguiling. Postmodernism, however, despite its model of fragmentation and displacement, proves, in the last analysis, too slippery a notion in and of itself to resolve the crisis of identity and of the aesthetic domain from which it derives.

To begin with, the prefix "post" implies a chronology that is at best unreliable, for postmodernism is a part of modernism and not its afterword. As Jean-François Lyotard has remarked, "A work can become modern only if it is first postmodern. Postmodernism thus understood is not modernism at its end but in the nascent state, and this state is constant."[3] Viewing

Butor as a postmodernist, as many critics of late are wont to do, would therefore appear viable only to the extent that he is seen as working very much in accordance with the unifying and progressive assumptions of modernism, though simultaneously destabilizing these very suppositions.

From his earliest novels and his affiliation with the *nouveau roman* to his more recent (direct and indirect) collaborations with a number of painters, Butor has continually incorporated into his writings objects very much a part of our daily lives. Through this privileging of the banal or common-place (a schematic integration into the text of all kinds of extraliterary material) and a reliance on intertextuality (a dialogue with his own and others' work), he has perpetuated the modernist attack on artistic convention in ways closely allied to those of Marcel Duchamp, the pop artists, and the conceptualist painters. His indifference to the orthodoxy of the notion of beauty, in fact, is remarkable in its similarity to what Duchamp himself termed, with regard to the "ready-made" (that forever indignant hallmark of modernism), "a complete anesthetic."[4] And it is not without significance that he ceased writing novels and gave himself completely to a profoundly conceptualist experimental writing at roughly the same time that the pop movement came to the forefront of modern art: *Degrés*, his last novel, appeared in 1960, the same year that the composer Henri Pousseur, with whom Butor was to undertake a number of collaborations, first invited the writer to work with him; the second volume of *Répertoire* was published in 1964, the year Andy Warhol first exhibited his "Brillo Boxes" at the Stable Gallery in New York; *Mobile* and *Réseau aérien* were published in 1962; and *6 810 000 litres d'eau par seconde* came out in 1965.[5]

Like that of Duchamp, what may be called Butor's anaesthetic vision is also, however, inherently critical of the modernist enterprise, and it is this self-reflexivity, this fundamentally epistemological point of departure, that links Butor to the postmodern. To again cite Lyotard,

> A postmodern artist or writer is in the position of a philosopher: the text he writes, the work he produces are not in principle governed by preestablished rules, and they cannot be judged according to a determining judgment, by applying familiar categories to the text or to the work. Those rules and categories are what the work of art itself is looking for. The artist and writer, then, are working without rules in order to formulate the rules of what *will have been done*. Hence the

fact that work and text have the characters of an *event;* hence also, they always come too late for their author, or what amounts to the same thing, their being put into work, their realization [*mise en oeuvre*] always begins too soon. *Post modern* would have to be understood according to the paradox of the future [*post*] anterior [*modo*]. (46)

It is in terms of this temporal paradox, the future anterior, and not as an a posteriori oppositional force (postmodernism as successor to the modernist impulse) that Butor's postmodernism is thus best regarded. While it is clear that Butor writes against himself, in the Sartrean sense, and herein lies the origin of the identity crisis referred to above, he does not oppose any distinct literary tradition, that which would presuppose an aesthetic point of view, something to which he would never subscribe. (*L'Emploi du temps* and *La Modification,* for instance, were not written to revolutionize nineteenth-century European narrative practice, as is so often thought to have been the aim of the early nouveau roman. As Butor has claimed, the French new novels of the 1950s and 1960s did not seek to diminish the function of characterization,[6] for one, but to reflect new rapports between literary characters and the world, rapports indicative of transformations in the relation of the novel genre and reality.[7]) Rather, relativity and contextualization—evident both in the hyperrealistic animation of the fictive (as in the recent *L'Embarquement de la Reine de Saba*) and the fictionalization of the real (as in the appearances of the author himself or members of his family in several of the narratives, or in the character-like functioning of places in the *Génie du lieu* series and elsewhere)—obfuscate any elements that might be deemed intrinsic or peculiar to the work of art. And it is precisely this tabula rasa of the literary as such, of any concept of the purity or fixity of art qua art, and its replacement with a kind of allegorical depiction of its own productive force, that evokes the postmodern epithet.

If the "post" of postmodernism confuses rather than assists us in determining the appropriate horizon on which to situate the work of Michel Butor (for Butor is at once postmodernist and not), it is that the crisis of identity derives at once from a turning away from any traditional delimitation of genres, from the dialogic relation of each of his texts with those of the past, and from the insufficiency of the modernist/postmodernist dichotomy itself to account for the relativism that impels all his writing. With regard to the last, the human being is first and foremost for Butor a cultural creature, and this universal feature of humankind is what renders relativity so integral a part of his work. Culture predominates as a determinant of perception in his texts, and both the interdependence of cultures—on the most primary level of human experience—and their otherness are the talismans of his creativity.

Critical discourse is infused with two kinds of markers: those that position the work of art, literary or not, aesthetically and those that position it sociohistorically. Most recently, anxiety over the persistent reinforcement of the first by the second, specifically, the valorization and consequent privileging of art in accordance with assumptions of Western patriarchal culture, has led to an increasing awareness of the incompatibility of the rhetorics of modernism and postmodernism with the development of a truly humanistic, and hence global, understanding.

The close examination by Butor—a writer for whom the constant interplay of cultural paradigms is the sine qua non of creative expression—of the evolution of his own literary output, and this within the context of the progression of Western European postwar thought, bears witness to the insufficiency of the modernist/postmodernist dichotomy to account for either cultural difference or relativity. For in tracing the transformation of his narrative, poetic, and critical production, Butor reveals the problematic nature of any analytic framework constructed on the categorical denial of otherness. Hence the present volume explodes the myth of homogeneity perpetuated by our critical tradition while serving as a most timely example of the new ethic of literary study that recently raised questions on the relation between aesthetics and culture imply.

. . . . Improvisations IV

Butor aims in *Transformation of Writing* to present a literary life and corpus as a succession of phases that reveal not only something of the writer considered, and of his sociopolitical milieu, but of the complex relation between the (exceedingly rapid) transformation of our world and that of writing. This is to say that—more explicitly than the preceding volumes of the *Improvisations* series (*Improvisations sur Flaubert* [1984], *Improvisations sur Henri Michaux* [1985], and *Improvisations sur Rimbaud* [1989])—this work recapitulates a particular experience of writing (*écriture*) as a trans-cultural activity, thereby representing the universal in the particular, and that it does so outside any semantically charged use of the term that Butor takes care to distinguish from literature.

Three chronologies, which remain at the same time separate and interdependent, form the structural basis of the work. Those problems—aesthetic, personal, ideological—that the author himself has confronted over the course of a long and rich career, and the ways in which they were progressively dealt with within his various texts, are continually juxtaposed to and entwined with those, both national and international, that confronted the world at large. Butor, France, the universe—an awesome triple alliance.

One should resist the temptation to go further, however, in describing the formal construction of the reflections that follow, for, in typical Butor fashion, a web of thematic, intertextual, cultural, philosophical, and cosmic concerns constitute an order as deceptively monolithic as it is antihierarchical and indeterminate. Seeking to uncover a rigorous architectural design of the mathematically playful sort discernible—while all too often overemphasized by critics—in all Butor's writings can only falsify the author's primary motivation, the articulation of experience unencumbered by theory, and his extraordinarily perspectival or relational vision.

Of far greater import are the impressive erudition, which combines with a passion for totalization (Butor has remarked, "je porte un globe dans ma tête" [I carry a globe in my head]),[8] and the optimistic determination of the therapeutic value of writing operative throughout.[9] Indeed, Butor's brilliance here as elsewhere resides not simply in the exceptional lucidity and breadth of knowledge that his readers know to inform each of his texts, but in the ambitious and highly energetic synthesizing of his cognitive and creative minds. And it is this, in the end, that renders the structure of the work fundamentally mutable, and thus not entirely accessible to the dictates of formalism, and its content both liberating and transformative.

Butor begins the volume with a consideration of the prewar and two post–world war eras. Political upheaval, childhood, and Jean-Paul Sartre are interwoven kaleidoscopically on the horizon of uncertainty ("There are a certain number of values we believe to be certain, which perpetuate themselves and are perpetuated by institutions until a shock occurs") and nostalgia (for the struggle of modernity, the avant-garde in art and literature, as a source of strength). Striking in the early chapters are the insistence on the importance of political discourse as a literary genre and on the (conscious or unconscious) political commitment at work in every text. So too the discussion of his first attempts at writing poetry, "resistance" poems that covered hundreds of pages, long since disappeared.

The influence of philosophy (in particular that of the German phenomenologists Martin Heidegger and Edmund Husserl, transported to France by way of Sartre) was decisive for Butor's entry into fiction. He reminds us of the narrative component of the writing of these and, in truth, all philosophers and defines as a reconciliation the working through in narrative form of the problems he encountered writing poetry and those he confronted as a student of philosophy. Though previously described in the first volume of *Répertoire,* this reconciliation is explored here in combination with brief excerpts from the early works, poetry and prose, thereby offering greater insight into his early experimentation with the novel genre. The political anecdotes, memories of and reasons for the French theatrical and literary successes of the time, and philosophical reflections on language and the universe that highlight Butor's writing on Butor also reveal more profoundly than anywhere else the origin and development of those preoccupations that have come to be so closely associated with the ensemble of his writings.

Butor has traveled extensively, and the volume continues with meditations on the influence these voyages (to Egypt, the United States, Japan, Australia, and elsewhere) have had on his writings. What were often prolonged stays in various parts of the world have allowed him to appreciate what he deems the collective sensibility of a great number of cities and other landscapes, a sensibility central to much of his work.

Like so many of his texts, this analysis of the progression of his writing is also an exploration of the cultural climate of societies worldwide insofar as it investigates the generative power of places. We learn, for instance, how instrumental for his resolution of the philosophico-literary dilemma was the stay in Egypt. The longer he remained in that country, whose exoticism he had so steadfastly distrusted (to protect himself against it, he convinced himself of the resemblance of the little town where he resided to one of southern France), the more significant appeared its differences with his own.

To cite but a single disparity, writing for any length of time seated on the floor like his Egyptian colleagues proved a most uncomfortable experience. Procuring a table no less so! As reading about the Arabic language, Muslim art, and the ancient Egyptians took precedence over the completion of a doctoral thesis in philosophy ("It is lost in the sands of the Nile"), another project, a novel, took form precisely because "the story of the table, and many other things, confirmed my idea that it was absolutely essential to make precise descriptions, that the objects one believed to be the most evident, the most simple, were not, that all objects were cultural and founded on complicated histories." The celebrated descriptions of *La Modification* followed not long thereafter.

First, however, *Passage de Milan* would reveal the preoccupation with the relations of space and time that had become so central for the self-exile in Egypt. Butor's displacement in space was accompanied by an exceedingly forceful awareness of the displacement in time to which teaching in the Nile River Valley—where the millennial tradition of Egypt was forced to function in a Western European–type school—gave rise. And, while it is true that the two years passed at the University of Manchester in England soon after intensified the meditation on spatiotemporal structures and their expression in the creative use of language, it was the experience of this first major stay outside France that set in motion what would remain the primary impulse behind all of Butor's writing from that point on. The notion that collective cultural sensibilities are at the origin of Butor's work is in keeping with the author's own idea of the collective origin of all creative expression. For the analysis of any art for Butor is necessarily a kind of "literary criticism of geography"—and therein lies his most central idea of *Le Génie du lieu*[10]—a coming to terms with the artist as master of a conglomerate of disparate powers. A text is no more the work of one individual than a painting or a symphony. Just as the city is a collaboration—a mixing of people, sites, and things drawn and colored to communicate a certain specificity of place—an architect is not responsible for the laying of every stone of a building of his or her design, and an author depends on a certain network for the production and dissemination of a book.

The collaborations with visual artists and composers followed naturally from Butor's initial efforts to rethink geography in collective terms. It followed as well from his early existential concerns: As one is perceptually always at a distance from oneself, as evidenced in the contemplation of objects so pronounced in the novels, and always at more than one place at a time, as seen in Butor's nostalgic focus on one or more places while writing in another (hence the canceled accent of the second title, *Où,* of the *Génie du lieu* series), one is creative by virtue of a multiplicity of stimuli, principal among which are the imaginative realizations of others.

It is not insignificant that so many books by Butor, an extraordinarily prolific writer, are grouped by series. The serial procedure suggests at once both continuity and fragmentation and invites contemplation outside the temporal and spatial limits imposed by the single work. Mary Lydon has written of the "ever widening circle"[11] as characteristic of the *Illustrations* series and noted that, "as in the case of the suite of novels, each ensuing book is written to resolve problems posed by its predecessor and each work, although it may represent an integration of what has gone before, is yet capable of being itself integrated into an even greater system" (244).

It is interesting, however, that the serial technique appears operative within the individual volume by Butor as well, and this no doubt combines with the successive reworking of problems previously identified in other books to enhance what Lydon has called "the organic nature of Butor's *oeuvre*" (24). *Transformation of Writing* is very much a case in point, for, despite its didactic framework, it explores a number of questions that are posed, set aside, and resolved, only to be reiterated again and again on other levels and within broader contexts.

The relation of fiction to reality provides a stunning example. Initially examined against the political background of nationalist, patriotic, and colonialist illusion, later explored in the contexts of poetic and novelistic production, historical reproduction, and numeric and other symbolic construction, to name but a few, this most persistent of Butor's preoccupations reemerges near the end of the book as a reminder that "reality is in great part made up of fictions" and that "we partly see the world as we want it, as we fear it." This of course throws into question all that the preceding evaluation of the transformation of the world has put forth and brings to the forefront once again the role of subjectivity as the primary force in the apprehension of the real. Thus we return—through the unconscious, repression, and (the individual or collective) dream—to the underside of language, the insufficiency of political literary genres, and, ultimately, to the role of *literature* in the preservation of society, whose evolution, along with that of *writing*, was the subject of the very first page.

Butor's meditations in *Transformation of Writing* on the reorganization of space and time, which is the most significant effect of rapid advances in technology, on his anachronistic experiencing of history during many of his voyages, and on the paradigm shifts we are only now beginning to recognize in the creation and reconstitution of cultures, fulfill, in a sense, the Mallarméan dream of "the Book," in which a final victory over chance would be won. From the singularity of the Earth's geometry to the plurality of linguistic and pictorial representation, apprehension of knowledge in Butor depends on an awareness of the relativity of Time to the Place of its perception.

Rather, therefore, than in the supposed revolutionary tradition of the nouveau roman, in the ambiguous practice of the postmodern, or within some other sphere of critical invention, it is in the lineage of Rabelais and Montaigne, Pound and Joyce, that Michel Butor must be situated. For, like that of his literary predecessors, it is a profound love of language, a vast erudition that delights in play with meaning and translation, and a keen vision of the universal within the particular that impel his thought and infuse his work with originality.

A word about the volume. The French edition of *Improvisations sur Michel Butor: L'Écriture en transformation* appeared in 1993. The manuscript was sent to us by Butor prior to its publication in France, however, and it was primarily from this that we worked. Hence any subtle differences that may be noted in the two editions are not to be construed as inaccuracies, though it must be said that certain editorial corrections of the French volume would, in fact, make this the definitive edition.

Also, it should be noted that, in translating Butor's lectures (which she was fortunate enough to attend), Elinor Miller was particularly attentive to their oral character. For it was precisely in order to preserve this aspect of them that Butor, as he himself commented on the back cover of the French edition, avoided unifying "the details too much" when he was obliged to replace, with transcriptions of lectures on the same subjects offered elsewhere, passages left incomplete by a malfunctioning recorder. As a result, Butor remarks, "One will . . . from time to time see passing among the colors of Geneva those of Tokyo." Miller also strove to preserve the "written style" of other passages derived from Butor's having put "the finishing touches on pieces destined for various prefaces." And it is primarily to this sensitivity to Butor's expressive sensibilities that the excellence of her translation (the extracts included) is due.

Elinor Miller and I are extremely grateful to Michel Butor for having worked with us on a number of questions of translation and annotation. This, of course, is not meant to imply that we do not take full responsibility for our efforts, but simply that we wish to thank him for the generous amount of time he devoted to corresponding and meeting with us.

Additionally, Butor has seen fit to dedicate the English-language volume to me, and I am honored by the gesture. Hence I thank him for this as well.

Finally, I wish to express my gratitude to both Montclair State University and the Services Culturels of the French Embassy in New York for their much-appreciated support of this volume.

i

the cold night

1 Transformations

The world we are in is being transformed at such an immense speed that it is very difficult for us to understand what is happening. Inside this world that is being transformed, our writing is also being transformed. I use the word *writing* and not the word *literature* because I can give it a more general sense. When we talk about literature in a Faculty of Letters, we are obliged to talk about the noblest literature, while if I talk about writing, it is possible for me to talk about the very general fact of writing, because it is the case that in our society everyone does some writing, even if it is not literature.

This is a point I will need to come back to several times. These two terms, *writing* and *literature,* have multiple meanings. Writing has been discussed in the criticism of the last twenty years in a completely abstract sense. That is not the sense I intend. I mean the word *writing* in a much simpler sense: the fact of writing. You have a piece of paper, you have a writing implement, and you put signs on the paper. This activity is widespread to an extent we do not perceive when we talk only about great literature. We miss the point that everyone in our society writes sometimes in the noble sense, but writes most of the time in this completely general sense.

In our society, anyone who does not know how to write, the one who

13

does not know how to sign his name, for example, is a veritable pariah, and as a result is everyone's slave. I intend to try to understand these transformations, and the relations between the transformations of our world and those of this fundamental activity, the relations between these two orders of phenomena.

I intend to try to talk to you about problems I have encountered myself in writing. These problems are not specific to me alone. These are problems I have responded to as best I could. They are very general problems, linked to those everyone has, more or less, at one time or another, encountered, and to the problems we still encounter today. This will lead to another question: How can we intervene in this world in transformation?

The fact that our world is in transformation does not automatically mean it is a transformation for the good. Progress is not so automatic as some of our ancestors in the nineteenth century believed. We are faced with great dangers, and at this time we can see that clearly. We cannot say that the twentieth century is ending so joyously as we might have hoped. We must do all we can to assure that the twenty-first century goes by better than the twentieth has. All sorts of thrilling things have occurred in the twentieth, but there have also been all sorts of failures.

Can writing intervene inside this transformation? Can writing be transformed in such a way that the transformation of the world that we are undergoing can be a transformation for the better, or at least for the less bad? We need only read the newspapers to understand that this is absolutely and totally necessary.

I am going to start with the last war to try to show you what questions I have encountered in the course of my career as itinerant writer and professor, how I have tried to reply to these questions within some of my texts, which I shall take as examples of responses to these problems, which are still urgent in the extreme.

I can say that it was during the last war that I was born and became conscious of the problems of writing, and this is true for all people my age. People younger than we do not necessarily understand what happened in this last war, nor, therefore, why people felt about things the way they did. France before 1939 was a great colonial power, one of the most important, richest, and most populous countries in the world. It was a country full of pride. I remember expressions of this pride very well, the great ceremonies I saw in my childhood and participated in a little: the World's Fairs. They represent a very important means of communication.

· · · · · · 2 The World's Fairs

It would be very interesting to review the whole history of these fairs, from the first, which took place in Paris under Louis-Philippe, all the way to the one to be held next year in Seville.[1] Each was a way for members of the international community to question each other, to meet each other, and, naturally, for the host country to gain considerable commercial advancement. This kind of event plays a very important economic role, and, since we are crushed beneath economic considerations, when we are told about the fair in Seville next year, our ears are talked off about the economic advantages Spain will draw from this fair. In reality these economic advantages can be understood and can occur only because of the ideological advantages. Each of these fairs is a way for one country to invite others.

Next year in Spain there are two big international events: the Olympic Games in Barcelona and the fair in Seville. We can consider them to be complementary. They will celebrate the return of Spain to the company of nations after years of tyranny and therefore of lagging behind. We can readily understand why the Spanish are willing to invest so much in the two events. Of course, they must arrange for bankers to lend money. And they must do everything, therefore, to make these bankers believe that the events will bring it in. In reality the Olympic Games or World's Fairs never directly reimburse their costs. Reasonable bankers ought not to lend money for that purpose. But these activities further the region in which they take place and thus, through all sorts of relays and delays, the economic fallout has ideological and mythological results.

In prewar France there were two very important fairs that were phenomena, displays of consciousness, of French ideology. First, the Colonial Fair.[2] Today, when we think of it again, the very name, Colonial Fair, hits right between the eyes. I was six or seven years old then, and thus my memories are very vague. Yet it was a moment that had great significance. Then there was the big World's Fair of 1937. That I remember very well. It was the display of an uneasy France, before the onset of the quakes which would shake all Europe in '39. If we went into detail, we would see that this fair of 1937 had many problems; there were strikes. That fair was held on a tightrope. It was an expression, within Paris, of the dramatic situation of all Europe.

The center was across from the Eiffel Tower—a monument that remains with us from the World's Fair of 1889, the first centennial of the

French Revolution—at the Trocadero Palace, which dated from the World's Fair of 1900 and was replaced by the Palace of Chaillot, which still exists. On the terrace of the center were gardens and fountains, which are still there, and on each side the pavilions of foreign countries—in particular, facing each other along the Seine, the pavilion of the Soviet Union and that of Nazi Germany, like two lions crouched ready to attack each other.

The fair of 1937 represents for me the essence of the prewar period. I was born in September 1926; the war began in September 1939. I was just thirteen. Before the war was my childhood, fairly happy but shadowed by much anxiety. One of the clearest memories for me of the prewar period was a moment when I was still in primary school, the day the German troops crossed the Rhine to enter the Rhineland, which was theoretically demilitarized. From that moment on I expected the war. When it finally broke out it was a kind of relief. Obviously we did not suspect it would be so horrible.

During the war was my adolescence. It was then that I began to do adult reading, have adult conversation, look at adult painting, ask myself adult questions. But everything was filtered: books were in large part forbidden, films were forbidden, painting was hidden in basements, conversations were observed. During the whole German Occupation I found myself in a strange state where knowledge had been confiscated. Knowledge was something that had existed before and that would perhaps exist again someday, but during those years it was night and lies. In 1945 there was the Liberation, and all sorts of things came back or came about for the first time. An insidious and dramatic separation between the generations occurred then. It is very difficult for succeeding generations to understand it.

· · · · · · 3 The Two Postwar Periods

The war of 1939 was experienced by the French and by a certain number of other European countries in a very passive way. In 1940 the French were crushed. For awhile there was a "free" zone, and then that too was taken over. After long years of blackout, liberation came from the outside. Certainly there was the Resistance, but it was quite evident that it alone could not have produced the Liberation. Some conducted themselves heroically, but they were there to bring as large a component of French as possible into this Liberation, which had come from outside. So the French experienced this war in a very painful way. The moment the war was over, those who had truly been involved, those who had been soldiers in 1939 and 1940, especially if they had been prisoners, deported, had only one wish, which was to forget those years, to act as if a horrible parenthesis was finally closed and that they were back in 1939, or, even better, in 1937. They did all they could to put an end to this evil chapter and act as if they were back in prewar days.

It is very telling to compare the two postwars of the twentieth century in France. After the war of 1914, we had a nihilist avant-garde in the dada and then surrealist movement; these were people who wanted to smash everything to pieces. After the war of 1939 to 1945, we also had a nihilist avant-garde, what has been called existentialism, the people around Sartre, who would also have liked to smash everything to pieces. But the mood was not at all the same. The avant-garde after the war of 1914 was joyful. It was destruction in gaiety. The one after the war of 1939 was morose. It was destruction in sad lucidity.

The war of 1914 was experienced in a positive way. France just grazed catastrophe, but it was she herself who chased the enemy away. The French had the feeling of having won something. Let us not forget that—while war today seems to us something horrible, while we believe it is always bad, which is the reason all armament manufacture ought today to be rigorously forbidden, and let us hope that in the next millennium it will be so—our ancestors nevertheless considered war the preeminently noble activity. A nobleman was first a warrior. He who killed and risked death had the most important place in our society. In our language and our literature, in our arts, we have the cult of the knight, that is to say, the warrior. Children, still today, are educated in the ideology of the knight. Watch your brothers and sisters, your children, your grandchildren, in front of the television, absorbed in *Knights of the Zodiac* and other films of its kind. You see to what extent the warrior ideology is still at work.

France was rejuvenated in its warlike and chivalrous ideology by the Napoleonic Wars, and the war of 1914 gave sustenance to this ideology. The ordinary soldiers—"poilus," as they were called—came back home to France as triumphant heroes.

After the war of 1914, some of the most advanced young people perceived that not everything was improving in the kingdom of France, but they were working within an atmosphere of conquest. They cried out to the others, "Don't gloat too much!" But they participated in the general gladness, and for that reason the books of the dadaist and surrealist writers, just after the war of 1914, have titles that surprise us by their cheerfulness.

Aragon published books of poems called *Feux de Joie* (Fires of Joy) or *La Grande Gaieté* (The Great Gaiety), Benjamin Peret *Le Grand Jeu* (The Great Game). But what happiness! Those people wanted to destroy, but they destroyed with a laugh which we envied them.

It is easy to destroy a few old, outdated monuments inside cities where things are going along fairly well, where splendid skyscrapers are being built. No one worries about what concerns the entire city. After the war of 1939, however, everything was different. While it is still possible today to find old people who willingly recount their memories of the war of 1914, it is very difficult to find any for the war of 1939. They prefer not to stir up memories of this war. There is in this a repression; they want to forget.

This temptation to forget, this effort to forget, is such that a cleavage between the generations has occurred. The first wants to forget, to be able to live again in the state of things before the war, which they still know very well. They say, "From 1939 to 1945 there was a nightmare, we will forget all that, we will start again where we left off." People of a certain age, those who participated in the war in the most painful way, have a very precise memory of what France was in 1937. They recognize everything, all the more because during those years of passive war they nourished these memories. The children of those people have of the prewar period only childhood memories, which are not the same kind. In some ways they are more precise, but they do not function as adult memories. One has the impression that if one saw that, felt like that, it was because one was still a child. These children, of whom I was one, found themselves faced with a spectacle that did not correspond to the description their parents gave them.

Parents in 1945 said, "That's it, it's over, we have found our Paris again, our Versailles, our cathedrals, our castles of the Loire, our colonial empire, our steelworks in Lorraine." Children saw that Paris was not exactly what they were told; Versailles was too dusty; the colonial empire was moldy; the steelworks of Lorraine had problems. For the parents that was all temporary because they had a clear memory of what it had been before. We had no such memories; thus we questioned each other. The image in the talk of our parents, of our professors, and naturally of the newspapers and literature did not correspond to what we had before our eyes. We had the feeling they were deceiving us. We were accustomed to being deceived, because we had been deceived during the whole Occupation. Our parents told us: "During the Occupation you were deceived, but now it's over, we are back to French frankness," but we had the impression they were deceiving us differently, but just as much.

That is why the most sensitive writers in this period tried to break free from this atmosphere of lies, but they could not do it in so cheerful a way as their predecessors of the twenties. At that time everything was still standing. There were just some cracks in old buildings here and there, and it is very invigorating to give big kicks to old buildings to watch them crumble in the midst of a superb cloud of dust. In 1945 entire cities were destroyed; it was the entire landscape of French culture or civilization that had been thrown into confusion. There were no more cracked buildings to kick. They had already fallen into dust.

What remained? Traces of old streets that our parents were rebuilding in their memories. We saw perfectly well that they no longer existed. We did not know how to talk about it, to explain it to ourselves, but it was out of the question for us to give happy, hard kicks to old buildings that were barely still standing, because almost nothing remained. The tonality was thus totally different. What we looked for then was writers capable of telling us the truth, of showing us the world just as black or as gray as it appeared; if they showed it to us more black or more gray, at least it was no longer pink. Everyone—parents, professors, politicians—painted the world for us in pink; we could not tolerate it.

When you are in a bombed city and only a few buildings are touched, that makes room for squares; when you are in a razed city, you walk in the midst of the rubbish and look for something possibly worth saving. Then the humblest faucet acquires value. You begin to collect pieces of window-panes, old bathtubs. All these objects, which seemed so ordinary, become precious. After the war people my age began this inventory. We struggled to cast out nationalist, patriotic, colonial illusions, and to see how in the midst of these ruins we could pitch a camp that would not be too uncomfortable, where we could give our parents a few of the comforts they imagined to be their due, and which they believed from one day to the next they would find again just as they were before, which could only lead them, lead us, to everlasting sorrow.

· · · · · · 4 Sartre

For us Sartre was the preeminently lucid writer; at least he did not try to sugarcoat the pill, to represent reality to us as pinker than it was. Perhaps he represented it as blacker, but I am not sure. It was differently black, but it was black. When we reread Sartre today, we perceive that he too was the victim of all sorts of illusions. We still are victims of illusions, but not altogether the same ones. But at least his texts were sad, which was for us curiously reassuring. We had the impression that we could have confidence in him. He had written *La Nausée* (Nausea) before the war; we were filled with nausea. He had written *Le Mur* (The Wall) before the war; we were perpetually bumping into walls, collapsed walls, but which just the same kept us from advancing, all the more because they had so often collapsed right in the middle of the street, which made the paths of former times no longer possible.

I remember having been present just after the end of the war at a lecture by Sartre near the Sorbonne, entitled "A Social Technique for the Novel." It was there that, for the first time, I heard of certain British and American novelists: Virginia Woolf, Dos Passos, Faulkner, writers it was impossible to read during the Occupation. After his lecture Sartre asked the audience who among us had read Dos Passos? No one. And he said, "That is the result of the war. If I had asked that question in 1939, all the students would have read these books." For him the problem was to manage to describe society through the intermediary of the novel, exactly what Balzac wanted to do, and he was seeking narrative techniques that would allow him to go beyond the habitual theme of the French novel, that is to say, what he humorously called "the loves of Babylas and Ernestine"—instead of always fixating on a couple, how to inscribe History. He found useful examples in the Anglo-Saxon writers.

He was working on his great postwar novel published under the general title *Les Chemins de la liberté* (Roads to Freedom). The first volume has a characteristic title that particularly touched us: *L'Age de raison* (The Age of Reason), that is, the moment one becomes an adult. People used to think that the age of reason was seven, the moment one passed from childhood to early adolescence, and this moment was very important in education and religious practice, because it was beginning at the age of seven that one was considered responsible for one's acts and it became important to make confession to a priest and participate in the ceremonies of the Catholic Church.

For Sartre, the age of reason was the moment when one left childhood and adolescent illusions and reached the cold vision of the adult. We were seeking not to let ourselves be imposed upon any longer by the retrospective illusions of the preceding generation. For us Sartre was an essential model. He was then a professor, and it can be said that he became the professor of all French youth. We had a great deal of confidence in him.

Later he dragged us into adventures of a nature that prevented our continuing to have confidence in him any longer in the same way. But for all that, his influence did not diminish; it became deeper. From 1945 to 1950 we believed in the answers Sartre had found.

After 1950, and especially beginning with the Hungarian affair, we ceased adopting his answers, but he remained a master at posing the questions to which we felt we had to find our own answers.

. . . . **5 Cultural Nostalgia**

Political upheavals, wars in particular, bring upheavals of the whole cultural horizon. There are a certain number of values we believe to be certain, which perpetuate themselves and are perpetuated by institutions until a shock occurs. Then it is like a kaleidoscope; when you tap on the device, little pieces of colored glass on the inside are reorganized in a different way. Other figures come to the front. Many of those believed classic grow dim, to be almost forgotten, sometimes to come back years later at the time of other reorganizations.

It cannot be said of the war of 1939 to 1945 that there was a formation of a literature or a culture of war as had happened for the war of 1914 to 1918, because of the passive character of the defeat and Occupation. During the Occupation France was partly cut off from its own culture because of shortages and censorship. Many things that were known before the war—foreign authors, for example—disappeared little by little because one could no longer find them in the bookstores; painters disappeared because there were no more exhibitions. This prevented others from succeeding, because everything that appeared in those times was stained with suspicion.

It was a state of cultural nostalgia. We thought of the former epoch as having been one of culture, and we hoped that one day we would again find what had been lost. At the end of the war the generations of my parents and grandparents believed they had found their prewar culture again. They tried at least to act as if they had. For the others, for the people of my generation, an enormous upheaval had taken place, an enormous revision of values.

The great success of Paris theater during the war was a play that once again is delighting theatergoers and, especially, moviegoers: *Cyrano de*

Bergerac by Edmond Rostand, a work from the very beginning of the century. It is easy to understand the appeal it had for the French during the Occupation, and we may also guess why suddenly this play has recovered its popularity. It is a matter of a certain image of France that was born at the time of Louis XIII and the beginning of the reign of Louis XIV, which corresponds in classic children's literature to the *Trois Mousquetaires* (The Three Musketeers) of Alexandre Dumas with its sequels. It is an image of France that makes one think of the one still found today in comic strips like *Astérix*.

Cyrano de Bergerac, the Gascon, incarnates the nostalgia for a lost France. We hope as we applaud that it is not lost forever. The popularity of the play today corresponds to a new questioning of itself by France. We cling to an image that proved itself. The popularity of the play in no way corresponds to a critical rehabilitation of the author. Professors and reviewers do not even mention Edmond Rostand at all, and he is still considered contemptible, a judgment that is certainly not entirely valid, since his whole output holds up just as well.

At the end of the war there was a reorganization of the landscape, which caused Sartre—who had already published before the war, who had been in Paris during part of the war, and who had had the courage to have plays staged in the middle of the Occupation, *Les Mouches* (The Flies) and *Huis clos* (No Exit), plays of great force and great daring—to arrive. He had also published during the Occupation his great philosophical treatise, *L'Être et le néant* (Being and Nothingness), which at that time remained the reading of a few specialists. At the Liberation everyone began to read this book, which is not, however, easy reading. Certain people gathered around him, and that formed existentialism. Students of that time were profoundly marked by it, even if some judged from the beginning that it was appropriate to keep a certain distance.

He represents an aspect of the situation: rational moroseness, the lucidity of ruins. He pleased us because he was a philosopher. He made us philosophers. We needed to rethink; we needed people who made us think. After that, I was myself a philosophy student, not in order to follow Sartre's teachings but rather to become capable of keeping my distance from him, which amounts to the same thing: it was because of him that I took this path. Studying philosophy helped me a great deal at that time. Then there was a conflict between the teaching of the discipline and what I was seeking. So for years I distanced myself from philosophy, which does not at all mean that I condemn philosophical studies; indeed, I believe that precisely what we are lacking is philosophers.

We have brilliant professors, but they do not bring us what we need, specifically, a new reflection on politics. Today we lack recommendations to change a little the reality that surrounds us. At that time there were some. There was most notably the considerable importance of the French Communist Party. One of the big problems in those years was that of the relationship between Sartre and this party, which never adopted him, whereas he dreamed it would. Sartre, as of a given point, was a sort of beggar at the door of the party, which appeared to him to be a kind of forbidden paradise.

. . . . . . **6 Gray Literature**

Literature is always committed, but it can be well or badly committed, and that is the whole question. The commitment of the work can be very different from the conscious political commitment of the writer. Some works of writers who proclaim leftist ideas are in reality completely reactionary. On the other hand, writers who say they are reactionary may write works with a wide progressionist scope; some of the Marxist critics have demonstrated this very clearly. One must distinguish everyday politics and the commitments emerging from it—for example, joining a particular party—from profound politics, which evolves much more slowly.

Today the word *politics* usually designates discussions that occur in the inner circle of a representative government, whose very essence is election. In numerous countries there was none of that; representation was first of all the nobility. The noble was not elected; he was noble by heredity. The origin of this nobility was "distinction" on the battlefield, "lofty deeds." The word "politics" comes from the Greek "polis," meaning "the city"; therefore its original sense is discussion about public affairs within a city on the public square, the agora. Some societies have few cities. Affairs are not discussed there in the same way. Besides, today our affairs are not really discussed on the public square but decided inside enormous unwieldy and secret administrations, protected by all sorts of censorship.

The word "literature" is not so simple either. It can be defined today as a collection of texts studied in certain university departments. But these texts are not the only ones. What we call literary texts, those given the label "literature," are only a small part of what is printed, and especially of what is said. In our society we have a gigantic production of texts, and politics is an enormous purveyor of texts. Several years ago a very meaningful term appeared for designating texts that are not considered "literary" but play a very important role for all of us: the collection of texts produced inside administrations, whether of private enterprises, national or multinational, or of governments. They are called "gray literature."

If one studies "gray literature," one observes that governmental and nongovernmental administrations are very close to each other, and that the difference between state and business is very difficult to maintain today, whereas it was evident in the nineteenth century. This shows what an enormous task of reflecting on our society we have to do.

Inside no matter what administration, numerous texts are produced, to be distributed within this administration and never to leave it, which are published only within a very limited area of society. Most of the time, indeed, these texts would be of no importance for people on the outside; but when they would be important, their communication is impeded by the multiplying of bans, the covering of them with labels—"secret," "confidential," "top secret."

All these marvelous machines we now have at our disposal to handle texts, with which we will be able to create a truly contemporary literature, were not conceived of for writing novels, or plays for the theater, or poems, but uniquely for gray literature, which is very quickly produced and so quickly dated. Even the invention of machines to destroy texts was obligatory, as much for their nuisance value, their being in the way, as for their use for some kind of espionage.

We have thus an enormous collection of texts that we call "literature" in the university sense, which exists inside a still larger production of texts. We must try to grasp literature in its totality, literature "in color" inside the gray literature, which is very difficult because of the enormity of the mass.

All politics is made with texts, more or less public, more or less "gray." The most specifically political texts are campaign speeches, those trying to attract our votes. When we study other epochs, the political speech clearly appears as literature in the university sense. The political speech, in having qualities that transcend the situation for which it was delivered, becomes thereby literature; it can be studied differently. For those schooled in Greek and Latin literature, it is evident that Demosthenes and Cicero are great masters of prose. Certain orators of the French Revolution can still interest us today, standing out before a crowd of other texts justly forgotten, no longer of interest to anyone but a few historians.

The political speech is a very important literary genre. In the same way that there are mediocre novels and novels of genius, there are, among the thousands of mediocre political speeches, some that achieve the status of literature. I know few in the twentieth century, but in the nineteenth one thinks immediately of the great declarations of [Alphonse de] Lamartine, [Victor] Hugo, or [Émile] Zola, which superbly show the relationship between the efficacy of political speech and the quality of the work that nourished it.

The usual political speech is designed to obtain a result rapidly in an assembly. A proposed law is under discussion, for example, and the speeches try to gain approval for one project over another. Outside the assembly the campaign speech has a very similar aim: at issue is the speaker's getting himself voted in at the next election. Once the election is over, the speech is usually completely forgotten. Indeed, the activity of the elected candidate has often very few points in common with his earlier promises. In French politics we have an eminent example of this amnesia: General de Gaulle held a plebiscite for Algeria to remain French. Once the plebiscite was obtained, he found out the plan was impossible and immediately decided for independence. All the previous speeches fell into a deep oblivion, from which they are fished out by historians.

This question of purpose should be examined closely. The political speech is a literary genre. To generalize on this notion, "gray" literature is a literary genre within which can be distinguished all sorts of subgenres— the report, the memo, and so on—all designed to be texts for publicity. Each of these genres is characterized by rules that assure its functioning inside the enterprise, government, or society in general. These rules can be explicit, and when they are it is easier to break them. It is those rules that we are not yet aware of that are extremely difficult to change. If the speech is to serve the politician's election, he cannot use language that is too complex, too refined; he must at such a time take up a certain number of themes. He must use certain key words. Not only must he announce his program, even if that program is hollow, but he must also criticize the program of the opposition, even if he has no other program to propose and even if the opposition program is also hollow. He must act as if the others have a program in order to be able to criticize it.

Equally important is campaign journalism, whose rules are linked to periodicity. The daily newspaper is conceived so that the day's news wipes out that of the previous day. A piece of front-page news must always be found. Farther back in the paper we can allow some continuity, but it is necessary at least to claim something new each day so that one wants to buy the paper. The rules are different for the weeklies and monthlies.

Some of these rules are well known, others are only endured. There are certain constraining rules for the novel; if we wish it to be distributed in a certain way, if we want to have a literary prize, we must follow certain rules. In the most popular subgenres, the rules are even more confining.

ii

uncertain dawn

7 Resistances

During the war we were cut off from a good part of foreign literature, and even from a good part of French literature. Thus there was nostalgia for the French culture of yesteryear and for the power to which it was linked, and also a nostalgia for the avant-garde, for the peak of this culture as it had appeared between the wars. After the war, this new avant-garde, which we had in the existentialism around Sartre, did not cause the preceding one to be forgotten. Indeed, during the Occupation the memory of that avant-garde was a very important means of sustenance. We were prisoners, and through the bars of our jail we made out signals from time to time; a ray of sunlight reached us to give us energy. In particular, these signals were memories of the modern art and modern poetry of the first half of the twentieth century, which were forbidden during the Occupation, were even considered a disease. This forbidden art was an art of conflict that gave us courage.

For our parents there was nostalgia for traditional French culture in the figure of Rostand's Cyrano de Bergerac; for us there was nostalgia for the avant-garde movements, thanks to the images we could see in the bookstores of the Latin Quarter, for example. I remember, on the sidewalk of the Boulevard Saint-Michel, leafing as I pleased through issues of the *Minautore* review, and everything I saw greatly intrigued me. Through the bars I made out something.

At the end of the war we thus very much looked forward to the restarting of the joyful fires of the prewar days. In that period of perpetual shivers we longed to find them, with a new consciousness, with many more precautions. I have the impression of having always been cold during the war years. It seems to me that even the summers were cold. It took time of course for books to be republished, for paintings to reappear, for galleries to be reopened.

One of the advantages of Sartre for us was that he was there during the war. As for André Breton, magistral figure of surrealism, who appeared to us as the preeminent manifestation of modern art—for we were evidently incapable then of making fine distinctions—he was in the United States, where he had gathered a certain number of personalities, particularly painters, some of whom had never been a part of the surrealist group, properly speaking. Breton was representing France on the other side of the Atlantic.

Today I have the feeling that there was a certain resemblance between the figure of Victor Hugo at Guernsey during the Second Empire and that of Breton in New York during the Occupation. One made him out through the bars from a distance as on a kind of rock. During the Occupation an anthology of his poems translated into English appeared in the United States for which Marcel Duchamp—who had been in the United States for a long time, that personality who formed an essential link between the French and American avant-garde during the first half of the century—had made the cover: it showed the Statue of Liberty, to which he had given the head of André Breton.

At the end of the war we waited for Breton's return, which was a little slow in coming; then the surrealist group started up again, on somewhat new bases, but with the same sorts of quarrels. We were enthusiastic over all that, but there, too, with the desire to keep a distance. Breton helped us, me especially, to keep a distance from Sartre. Sartre helped us a great deal to keep a distance from André Breton. Both helped some of us a great deal to keep a distance from a whole French culture of that period, within which we tried to introduce something that could take into account both these two sources but that would be more solid than either.

I met the people of the surrealist group in rather roundabout ways. During the war I was in the philosophy class at the Louis-le-Grand high school. In my family I had a distant great-uncle who had been professor of philosophy at the Collège de France, Edouard Leroy, student and friend of

[Henri] Bergson, whose successor he had been after having been professor of mathematics. One day I went to see him in his office filled with dusty books. He had a long beard all stained with nicotine and the air of deep goodness that aged professors of philosophy have.

I asked him if he could lend me one of his books. He did not have many anymore, but just the same he found me something. Then he gave me the program of a series of lectures, telling me he was going to speak on the problem of God in a little group that met somewhat secretly at a corner of the Place de la Sorbonne. I made the acquaintance of a few of those present. Some of these lectures were rather stormy because my old Bergsonian uncle said some things that scandalized young Thomist students, reactionary in a way unimaginable today; they considered him a blasphemer.

In the midst of this tumult I surprised myself by speaking up in spite of my timidity, wanting to defend my great-uncle against the attacks of students who were not so much older than I. In this way I began to talk with people I saw again at other sessions and, one thing leading to another, I reached the woman who organized the lectures, Marie-Magdelaine Davy. Thus there were during the Occupation a few centers of semiclandestine intellectual unrest, with connections that kept them in touch with one another; it was a sort of scholarly or university resistance beneath the surface of Paris life. I saw exactly this kind of phenomenon years later in the countries of the East. A sort of tissue of nerves with nuclei and neurons.

Marie-Magdelaine Davy also organized colloquia in an abandoned castle on the outskirts of Paris. In the middle of the Occupation she succeeded in renting buses that, in front of the stairs of the Sorbonne, took on board the professors of that institution or of the Collège de France and some young students, among whom I had the good fortune to be. When we were leaving, everyone was a little anxious because there were German soldiers everywhere, and then we reached that deserted castle with its park taken over by weeds, and we slept on pallets in rooms with no other furniture.

For me it was an enchanted castle. Suddenly I found myself in the center of the philosophico-literary temple. While still young, at the end of the Occupation, I thus met all sorts of people who later became famous. Within this atmosphere many ideas fermented within me. I discovered a thousand things, and in the midst of this philosophical meditation there was also an aesthetic meditation, with the presence of that modern art and that surrealism that appeared to us through the bars. From time to time eminent old professors had conclusive words to say against this decadent art. I tried to find confederates to reestablish what seemed to me to be the truth.

· · · · · · 8 The Enchanted Castle

I wrote a little about these end-of-the-Occupation meetings in a semi-autobiographical book called *Portrait de l'artiste en jeune singe* (Portrait of the Artist as a Young Monkey). Here is the way the clandestine philosophical congress that I have evoked is described in this much later *Portrait*. This text was written about halfway between what it recounts and this moment when I read it here. There are within it things I no longer remember except in reading it; yet there are many elements that I can now interpret quite differently than at those two periods:

"Under the Occupation, when I was in the class at the Louis-le-Grand high school of Monsieur C., author of a philosophy textbook that was very popular at the time, one of my great-uncles, an old man with a long white beard stained brown with tobacco, to whom we as a family went regularly to wish a happy New Year during the first days of January (from the little salon where we were ushered in, we could see his office through the half-open door, walls plastered with books, an enormous table filling it almost entirely, covered with papers, all blurry with cold smoke), a former professor at the Polytechnique, then at the Collège de France, Bergsonian, one of the stars of the 'modernist' quarrel and intimate friend of Father Teilhard de Chardin, gave, on the Place de la Sorbonne, a series of lectures on the problem of God, who certainly had not finished tormenting me; an excellent chance to get information.

"A certain number of young Thomists came to make a disturbance (yes, one would think these discussions took place centuries ago); with beating heart I entered into the controversies that followed, straining my ears, sometimes daring a remark, with the result that I ended up making the acquaintance of the woman who organized these lectures, who invited me to participate in colloquia going on in a castle on the outskirts of Paris, famous for its Flaubertian memories.

"We met at the Balzac restaurant on the Rue des Ecoles. We left in a bus. She succeeded in finding buses, whereas the streets were no longer used by anything but bicycles, and the passing of a truck, even German military, was an event. I did not dare to buy something to drink while waiting. I hung around on the sidewalk, giving a discreet little wave to the people I recognized. We got in. We took off. Jolts. Suburbs. Conversations began.

"That lasted several years, before and after the Liberation. I can no longer tell the different sessions apart, nor at which time I saw this or that person.

"There were students, even high school students like me at the beginning, writers, doctors, clergy of all colors and sects, and especially professors of all ages and specialties.

"Many of them are famous today; others have been forgotten by everyone, even by me; there are some whose names, faces, faiths I confuse; first names or titles may have shifted from one to another. I drank in their words.

"It seemed to me I had discovered the password, a sesame, a secret entrance permitting me to find my way, almost fraudulently, into a cavern of intellectual treasures, of discussions to be consigned in golden writing to purple leaves, or rather engraved, with the greatest skill, with an iron needle, in beautiful and very clear colored Latin letters, on bark unwound from tender bushes, the open entrance to the closed palace of the king.

"Certainly not everything that reached my ears seemed to me of the same quality, and I recognized very clearly the ignorance and insensitivity of some of the great authorities in some field that captivated me, but they were for me no less 'their magnificences,' with their threadbare clothing, their undernourishment, their worries, their wartime appearance, great dignitaries of a court without a caliph, of a fabulous academy of Baghdad or Laputa.

"I followed them at a respectful distance on their walks, ears alert, vigilant. There were only a few whom I dared approach and to whom I dared sometimes address a word, novice at an intermittent monastery. All the air they disturbed with their wise speeches or even with their most banal civilities seemed to me charged with keys and formulae that strove to collect and confront.

"It was spring, famine, the age of lead. It was in general very cold. The castle was scarcely furnished; in each bedroom a camp bed with a pallet and military covers, a folding garden chair. There was heat in the guard-house, a little more comfort for the old couples. We gathered for lunches no more frugal than those I had been accustomed to for years; and the lawns all around were transformed into superb meadows, grass as tall as I was, with a few alleys cut through with a scythe, as for explorers in a fierce savannah.

"It was the reign of the beautiful speech and the wise question, of the slow approach and of meditation, it was all the splendor of knowledge, all the abysses of inquiry, finally dislodged from the rags of attendance at school. There the masters were accessible; it was a seminary of daring full of drafts and sweet austerity, the Thélème of poverty, in the middle of sumptuous trees, with the whispers of war, the reign of Saturn changed into the Age of Gold.

"And all those who were there, even the youngest, by the fact that they were there, by the fact that they had been chosen to enter that bus, which had the air of such an ordinary bus (even though at that time a simple bus that was not German military, and then that was not French or Allied military, in the streets of Paris was already something extraordinary), that bus about which none of my schoolmates at Louis-le-Grand, then at the Sorbonne, if they had passed by at that moment, could have imagined what it contained, what it was the antechamber to, all, by the fact that they came into this cold, to these beds, all, in spite of the barbarity, the coarseness or the prejudice that they could show in some respects, must be, in one field at least, 'masters.'

"I was the only one there who was nothing, who knew nothing, could teach nothing to anyone whatsoever, who benefited from a remarkable grace that I certainly did not wish to let go by, I and perhaps some of the others of my age, but as far as they were concerned I was in no way sure; they seemed to me so eloquent; they were masters at least in a versatility, a rapidity of response. In their eyes, through their youth, I read years, years, a whole lifetime of studies, solitude, and complicity with other brilliant young old men, other young hermits in the middle of the city, in the middle of the high school, in the middle of the Ecole Normale Supérieur, in the middle of the Sorbonne, too, but in other classes, with other young virtuosi, prodigies, laureates of I knew not what contest, the wonder, the hope, almost the envy of their professors.

"They talked, they laughed, and I mingled with them, which was normal, since for the others it was to that group that I should belong, and they accepted me, they tolerated me; certainly I was not one of them, but I did not bother them; and often I did not understand the reason for their laughter, often their words were completely unintelligible to me, and some of their words plunged me into hours of reflection and perplexity.

"I was a lay brother, I was a monkey."

Thus there were little groups of resistance within that resistance, and thus I made friends in modern art. In particular, I met one who had published numerous books after the war, Michel Carrouges, who initiated me into surrealism, who put his library at my disposal. It is especially thanks to him that I met a certain number of members of the group and, after his return, André Breton.

All that gave me a bizarre personality, which posed problems for me. In a way my head was cut in two. It was very difficult for me. My philosophy studies at first went very well, but then I ran into a sort of wall because I had to find solutions no one could help me with. I had in my head a Sartre hemisphere and a Breton hemisphere. The first did his philosophy studies and immediately after the war began to write some essays, in which I tried to be as clear as possible, essays on various writers. The other wrote poetry that in many respects resembled the surrealists'.

This poetry, born under the Occupation, was a means for me to set up a resistance. There is an entire architecture of resistances, with resistances inside one another. There were the real resistance networks in the mountains, and from one day to the next one was always more or less in touch with them; there were these networks of intellectual resistance.

. . . . **9 Interrupted Poetry**

When I was in high school in Paris during the Occupation I expected a great deal of my professors, and some disappointed me, for example, because they had political positions that did not correspond to my family's image of patriotism; others I mistrusted because of their taste. Some taught me something; they acquainted me with poetry; there were others who prevented me from understanding. I would feel there was something in a text, but the false explanations they gave me would cause a kind of curtain to come down.

When I felt a professor was dangerous for me I set myself up at the back of the classroom, making a rampart of my books; I built a citadel of books, behind which I wrote poems. When I entered my junior year at the Louis-le-Grand high school, a professor of English had the fine idea of having us read Shelley's "Ode to the West Wind." I found it extraordinary; therefore, with the other professors, when things were not working, I wrote odes to all sorts of things, odes that have of course disappeared. I covered thus hundreds of pages with poems of "resistance."

The model for these poems passed gradually from Shelley to the surrealists. But it was a heterodox surrealist poetry. It had surrealist prosody. The production technique corresponded approximately to what I understood of surrealist automatic writing. In that back of the classroom where I had installed myself, I opened in a way a faucet inside my head, and I tried to catch the flow. And it certainly did flow; I could write that way for hours. But I always wanted to pick it up again, correct it, go back over it. And the images that came were much more somber and certainly more deliberately tame than those found in the poetry of [Paul] Eluard, [Benjamin] Péret, [Robert] Desnos, the "classic" surrealist poetry.

Beginning with a certain period there is in surrealist poetry a very strong vein of anguish, in particular with the writers who separated themselves from the surrealist group properly speaking: [Antonin] Artaud, [Michel] Leiris, [Georges] Bataille. With them one can hear coming closer a tolling knell. Little by little it would be heard in all of them.

In this schoolboy or student poetry, one was in the presence of the war, in ruins where I made a sort of language in ruins flow, with a general tonality very close to the existentialist gray. In the midst of the existentialist gray I produced, I tried to insert surrealist irisations. I was trying to open the door between the hemispheres in my head.

At the end of a certain time I found myself confronting an almost schizophrenic product. My head was really divided in two. I felt a profound discord between these two aspects, both of my production and of my personality. As of a certain point I had to find a way to put things together better.

Here is a sample of a poem from that period. There has already been a certain evolution relative to earlier texts, which were, from the point of view of form, much more down-to-earth. This text is part of a whole that I published subsequently under the title *Hespérides et harengs* (Hesperides and Herrings). These two words evoke two poles: on the one hand the Hesperides, the isles of the West, the whole dream of the discovery of America; on the other hand the herrings, dried fish, taken out of their water. It is the feeling of exile. Years later I was asked if I had ever written poems; I said yes; I showed a few that had been kept by friends. Now they are there without my being able to judge them well.

The poetry I wrote at that time was a kind of recording of the beatings of a lost heart. A collection of earlier poems, it, too, published much later, is called *Mouvement brownien* (Brownian Movement). This is the movement that perturbs the molecules of some liquids; it is one of the examples one can give of completely random movement. In the text I am going to read, one can already see a figure appearing. There is already the search for a completely different form, which will be directed gradually toward the novel.

There is a character in this text: a rat, the animal living in our cities, where there are always at least as many rats as people. As soon as there is a human civilization it is matched by a population of rats. They are generally down below. They walk around in our sewers and come out at night. They have a whole teeming life below ours. This is the animal at once both detested above all others because we know it transmits all sorts of diseases, in particular the plague, and at the same time it is the animal studied, the laboratory rat, the animal put in labyrinths to be taught certain routes. The rat is a metaphor of humanity from several especially interesting aspects. Here is one of these down-to-earth texts:

My hairs are all sticky
with the sweat of the pavement
my horizon narrowed
like the inside of a fish's stomach
the rain my only companion
which has remained faithful begins again
and muzzle on the tracks of shoe soles
I sniff the low wind

The lights change from red to green
but they are not for me
the cars turn blithely
and do not see me
a quarter of sun
at the crack in a house
and the rustling of water
on the fading posters

I have no fixed residence
I wander from fence to fence
my rat's heart fills
with all the rain of the street
when I see the remains of a demolished house
because that is a dwelling for me
those vestiges
and that wreck
the only possible dwelling
the only armor for that repose
which will not let itself be persuaded

I have tried to attract it with a thousand tricks
I have decorated the corner where I lived
with dead leaves
gleaned in danger
and with debris chosen from newspapers and books
with beautiful flakes of paint
and beautiful abandoned flowers
that I had to drag in at night
in terror of the speeding vehicles

So I stay hidden
like an observer in wartime
contemplating the wall opposite
where human rooms now disappeared
have left their traces of color
my look climbs upward
with all the fatigue of continued attention
the lower panels of this alphabet
and the rest is lost in the heights
forbidden to rats
who cannot hold up their head

For they are condemned to the ground of cities
and to exploration of the dust
and all the exhortations
to lead a better life

cannot reach us
because we know our task
is at gutter level
and in ditches
hunters of tracks and odors
cursed workers
for the destruction of things.

What strikes me now is the steady shift between the first and third person, the kind of grammatical hesitation that gives a feeling of depersonalization. Also the insistence on urban reality. I truly am a child of the city. As Verlaine said,

Né l'enfant des grandes villes
Et des révoltes serviles,
J'ai là tout cherché, trouvé,
De tout appétit rêvé . . .

[Born the child of the big city
And of servile revolts,
I have there sought and found everything
Dreamed by any appetite . . .]

I was born in a suburb of Lille and came to Paris at the age of three. I developed, like most Parisians, a passion for this city, a love that after several years reversed itself and became tinted with hatred before reaching a richer equilibrium. In all that I did up to a certain period, there is an essential urban component. The rat is for me the expression of that.

This rat condemned to the ground of the city despairs of finding anything other than the city, and he has the impression that the city is the best there can be for him. This is one of the reasons why the presence of the desert, when I went to Egypt, was an extraordinary opening. I began gradually to question the very fact of the city, which leads us to a whole group of meditations that will go on developing for years.

iii

the road of the novel

10 The Novel and Prosody

In the midst of these difficulties, I told myself that one way to bring back some unity to my life could be to write a novel. In the philosophy of that period, German phenomenology, which Sartre in particular had brought into France, was exerting a great influence.

The founder, [Edmund] Husserl, starting with problems in the philosophy of mathematics, sought to bring new solutions to problems by studying the way the problems were posed. One describes the way problems are posed before solving them. This approach gave rise to another that was very important in those years, Martin Heidegger's. The title of Sartre's *L'Être et le néant* (Being and Nothingness) is a reprise of Heidegger's *Sein und Zeit* (Being and Time). The latter attempted to adapt Husserl's method to problems of the human condition. Like all student philosophers of the time, I was bathed in these influences. I was certainly far from accepting all their theses totally, and it was this lack of adhesion that in actual practice separated me from philosophy then. I have never written philosophical texts since.

This philosophy taught me at least that literature was of great importance for philosophy, and that one of the best ways to solve difficult problems was to describe the way in which they were posed. It can be said that, within the philosophical work of Sartre and those philosophers (and,

38

to tell the truth, all philosophers), there are, even when the language is extremely abstruse, moments that are actually moments of narrative or novel-like.

To make something understood, one tells a story and one describes the way a problem arises. Whenever one achieves a better setting of the problem, some difficulties disappear by themselves. One sees that some problems that have been under discussion for years are in reality false problems. They do not have solutions because they are badly set. Instead of persisting in trying to solve them one must go deeply into the very way they are set, which can only be done by giving examples from within human reality, which is already to be making a novel. I can give an example by saying "somebody does this," but rapidly I am led to give a name to this character.

The philosophy of the time led in an almost inevitable way to the novel. To find a solution for our uneasiness, changing the setting of the problems was indispensable, and thus working on language. The best means was to describe. There would certainly be reactions, currents striving to render philosophy as theoretical as possible and, by giving it a quasi-mathematical appearance, to try to make it rival science.

The solution to my poetic problems was also found in an approach of this sort. Since the issue for me was to manage to describe the reality in which I found myself, and to describe it if possible in a complete way, that is, not only the day's reality but also the night's, not only clear consciousness but also dreams, everything that I tried to put into my poetry could appear in novelistic forms. I could describe not only the way people behaved during the day, how they perceived this or that, but also follow them into their reveries and their sleep. Thus all my own fantasies could be worked in.

I emphasize here the word *form.* One of the problems I encountered in the poetry I was producing in a rather surrealist way was that it lacked form. It did not resist me enough. I produced it with a certain ease, but as I was never really satisfied, I felt the need to come back to it. This process of revision could have continued indefinitely. I needed a certain number of determinants. The novel's determinants permitted much better control of the product. I wanted to find in them the equivalent of what prosody used to be.

When one studies classic French or other poetry, one is immediately confronted with problems of versification and its rules. What use are they?

First, to make the poetry easier to learn. They have musical value, which permits not only incantation in the practice of sorcery or religion, but also much easier learning of a text.

It is easy to learn a text by Racine, because we know that each of the lines must have twelve syllables and rhyme in couplets, and that after two masculine rhymes there must be two feminine. That means if I forget a word, I know something is missing. If the line no longer rhymes, I know I have made a mistake. There is an internal control in the text itself. It is made in such a way that I can know if it has been properly constructed. It is a little like a banknote on which are printed details that permit the tracking of counterfeits.

This internal control is also a means for invention. The poet's need to satisfy a certain form obliges him to find ideas he would not have thought of on the first try. He will no longer always keep the first word that comes to him. In many cases he will search for another and then another, until all the rules are respected. One can adopt traditional rules from one's predecessors, but the great poets have invented new rules.

In French poetry of the twentieth century, classic prosody has been completely exploded. People today can still write rhyming alexandrines. They can write stanzas similar to those of ancient songs, which is what happens in popular forms. Today, in poetry that is not sung, respect of classic rules always has an archaistic side, often with a touch of the ironic and sarcastic. The most daring poetry will generally explore other directions.

Many twentieth-century poets have sought other means of organizing texts. Surrealist poetry in particular brought another type of prosody, what poets of that bent have called the "image," consisting in the unexpected encounter of terms belonging to different fields. One thus has shocks in meaning, from which sparks fly. A surrealist text is a succession of images. Words are linked one to another, no longer by rhymes, as in classic poetry, or by the rhythm of twelve or eight syllables at all, but by a series of contrasts. What the texts called "automatic writing" have to offer is a succession of images contrasted with one another, sometimes giving us extraordinary poetic landscapes.

For me this surrealist type of prosody had the defect of remaining purely linear. The second term must contrast with the first. For example, let us take the title of a collection of Breton's poems, *Le Revolver à cheveux blancs* (The Revolver with White Hair), two realities that ordinarily are not spoken of at the same time. We have never seen a revolver with white hair. If we want, we can make one; it then becomes a surreal object. In a title it remains isolated, but in a text this first contrast must be succeeded by another contrast, and so on.

In studying such a text, one can discover a certain number of themes; that is, from time to time spheres of meaning will reappear that will be illuminated by the presence of other spheres. This permits the formation of texts of great structural richness. But the principle itself is of a sort of chaplet, a chain formed by links, each hooked to the previous one. I needed to see things in a vaster way. I could no longer stay with poetry in which one instant followed another.

It seemed to me that forms of the novel would allow me constraints, modes of regulation through which I could invent better than I ever had up to that time. There was another interconnected influence: a part of modern music. Just as French prosody at the beginning of the twentieth century deteriorated completely, having no longer anything but sentimental, archaistic, and ironic value (one can, by the way, do wonders in this vein: I very much like in particular to write eight-syllable lines, and I have amused myself recently by varying the rhythms of my songs, using lines of five and seven syllables), in the same way at about the same time the rules of classical music deteriorated.

With the work of Wagner especially, the rules of classical music underwent a great upheaval, so much so that musicians tried harder and harder to disobey the old rules. They were thus at a point where they no longer knew exactly how to organize a musical work. A Viennese musician, Arnold Schoenberg, had the idea of proposing a new kind of organization of musical material, organization by a series of twelve tones.

One begins by running counter to certain fundamental rules of earlier music. On the piano keyboard, between one C and the next C there are twelve halftones. In classical music you are forbidden to use one part of the keyboard: if you select the scale of C, you may use only the white keys. Sometimes you can use black keys because that produces emotions, because one is risking something, one is brushing up against the forbidden. To raise the ban against the black keys for a longer time, you have to take a trip into the kingdom of modulation, to switch to another scale, which is possible only according to certain rules.

In dodecaphonic music, on the contrary, you are forbidden to use the same note a second time until you have used all the others. You are obliged to use the twelve notes of an octave, and even to use them in a certain order, which is called a series.

I tried to find something of the same sort to organize my poetry. I was not the only one in this field. I am only one example among many others. I had the feeling that by using sufficiently controlled structures of the novel, I would have the equivalent of classic prosody or of these musical structures, which have the same advantage as the structures of classic prosody, that is, they give a means of verifying if a score has been properly done. In this organization by cells of twelve notes, which can moreover be superimposed on one another, if one of the twelve is lacking, one knows there is an error.

. . . . 11 The Egyptian Table

In describing a certain number of aspects of the human condition in precise circumstances, it was possible for me to have the same kind of control and the same possibilities for invention. Thus at a certain period I turned toward the writing of novels. This took form in rather curious circumstances.

Through the intermediary of the meetings in the enchanted castle during the Occupation, I had met a Hungarian refugee doctor linked to the surrealist group who was a specialist in Paracelsus[1] and alchemical texts. He permitted me to read some rather rare and very beautiful ones. One day he suggested that I spend a vacation in a German castle at the home of a refugee count from the Sudetenland region, one of his uncles. I spent six or seven weeks there, I no longer remember exactly. In the book that recounts this adventure, *Portrait de l'artiste en jeune singe*, I arranged for it to be seven weeks exactly because the number seven plays an important role in this book.

I had the feeling of being suddenly plunged into another epoch. I took a trip in time. I found myself in full German romanticism, which was very pleasant. When I returned, I had a greater and greater desire to leave France. I had plunged into a kind of elsewhere that had caused me to think all kinds of thoughts.

I had already taken some little trips, but they were not enough to de-Parisianize me at all. This trip had already been a little more serious. I needed distance. I needed to go a little way on the other side of the scenery to be able to begin really to work.

I went to the Ministry of Foreign Affairs and asked about positions for teachers abroad. They first proposed some that failed to tempt me. Then they called to tell me there was a post that would require my leaving for Egypt, an extraordinarily attractive country for me: first, it was far away and I needed distance; second, there was all the prestige of the pyramids, the pharoahs, the Valley of the Kings, the Colossi of Memnon, and so on; and finally, it was the classic land of meditation, the Thébaïde,[2] the land of hermits. I needed to reflect on my philosophico-literary problems; the Thébaïde was a sort of irresistible celestial sign.

This was in the time of King Farouk. Before the deluge. Egypt was still—not officially, but practically—a British protectorate. The notion of a protectorate is already very difficult to understand today. In what was called the French Empire, or the British Empire, there were differences between the colonies proper and other categories of territories. Thus the French Empire distinguished between the colonies that France purely and simply exploited: there was Algeria, which had recently become three French departments, but of a totally special kind; there were the protectorates, countries in which the old administration theoretically was still in place. In Morocco the sultan was still there, as he still is; but he was "assisted" in his government by a representative of the French government. There were, finally, territories under mandate, the former German colonies, taken from Germany after the war of 1914, or the former provinces of the Ottoman Empire, distributed to the conquering Allies. Lebanon and Syria were under French mandate, as was Togo.

Morocco and Tunisia were still then, for a few more years, official French protectorates. Egypt was an official British protectorate. But it was seeking liberation. One of the means had been the transformation of education.

The Minister of National Education under King Farouk that year was a talented writer, Taha Hussein, a blind man married to a French woman. The French cultural influence in all the countries of the Middle East was considerable at that period. This very Francophile writer tried to put French on an equal basis with English in secondary Egyptian education. This led to a cultural agreement under the terms of which some professors were sent to Egyptian high schools. I was sent off in the group. A difficult adventure, but fascinating.

I was very drawn to Egypt, but very mistrustful of exoticism. I would not have been moved by the kind of poster seen nowadays in travel agencies. I tried to barricade myself against these illusions. I said to myself:

I am going to disembark in a little Egyptian city that will resemble a little city in the south of France, like two drops of water. The greatest danger will be boredom; therefore I will take work with me. First, a project for a philosophy thesis that I never finished. And a project for a novel.

When I actually arrived in the little city, Minieh, two hundred kilometers south of Cairo—aside from the fact that all the signs were in Arabic and that everyone spoke Arabic, and that, therefore, I understood nothing or almost nothing—at first sight it was like a little city in the south of France. The longer I stayed, the more deeply the differences were incised in the littlest things in life.

In the first volume of the series *Le Génie du lieu* (The Spirit of Mediterranean Places), I broached the problem of objects as it was posed for me in Egypt. As a young French professor I was accustomed to working with a table and a chair at my disposal. The high schools had desks and benches. My Egyptian colleagues had no need for tables or chairs, because they were perfectly well able to write on the ground or on little writing boards. When I tried to sit on the ground, it was fine for five minutes. After a quarter of an hour I began to suffer; at the end of half an hour it was intolerable, and, as a result, work was out of the question. It was thus an absolute necessity for me to find a table and chair.

The chairs were not very difficult [to find]. There were British there, because the city is located at the cultivation center of the best Egyptian cotton, and there were British factories and therefore villas with lawns, and a sporting club that a few weeks earlier had just ordered some garden chairs that arrived in too great a number, which suited my needs perfectly. Fortunately, the hospital had needed beds, which permitted me to get one. After that it was necessary to make a mattress. I learned a lot there. I did practical phenomenology. I revised the setting of the problems.

As for tables, neither the hospital nor the sporting club nor anyone in the city of Minieh had needed one recently. I could not worry about that! I shared an apartment with an Egyptian accountant, who spoke French very well. We went to the carpenter to have a table made for me. I drew a design with all the dimensions. The carpenter said "next week." We went back. "Oh, we have had a lot of work lately. Next week."

At the end of six weeks, a miracle: a little boy came to tell us the table was ready. It was much too high for me. It seems that the carpenter had been very surprised that I asked for so high a table, because he knew that tables inside houses are always low. He told himself that I was a foreigner and that as a result I had made a mistake. But to please me, since I wanted such a high table, he made me a really high one. No problem; all we needed to do was trim the legs of this table. I thus marked with my pencil the exact place where they should be cut. "Next week."

Six weeks passed. Obviously it would have been easier to buy a saw, but where would I find one in Minieh? And I could not imagine it would be so difficult. Finally the table was ready. Now it was much too low. I told myself that I would have to make do with it. I thus took the books I had brought for my thesis and put them under the legs of the table until it was at a height that would permit me to write and read the few books remaining. This is how I succeeded at least in doing my work in the high school where I was teaching.

I also worked a great deal at learning the indispensables for daily life. I was led to read many books about the Arabic language, from which I learned a few words to enable me to do my shopping, words that I have now forgotten, and many on Muslim art, on the ancient Egyptians. I learned many things, but my thesis advanced not a single line. It is lost in the sands of the Nile. The novel, though, gained strength because the story of the table, and many other things, confirmed my idea that it was absolutely essential to make minute descriptions, that the objects one believed to be the most evident, the most simple, were not, that all objects were cultural and founded on complicated histories.

A few years later I published a book titled *La Modification* (Change of Heart), which takes place in a railroad car. When it was translated into English a critic said, What is the use of describing a railroad car? Everyone has taken a train and everyone knows what a railroad car is. But today trains are not at all the way they were at the time, and as a consequence nothing would be comprehensible in the book if the description had not been so precise. Thus, from the sunlit exile in Egypt I tried to reconstitute the city of Paris by means of a sort of reduced model of an apartment situated in the quarter called Europe.

· · · · · · 12 Marvel and Boredom

Here is a more precise version of the story of the table, which I wrote now more than thirty years ago, in the first volume of *Le Génie du lieu*, thus only a few years after the events. You will see many other details in it, but, as I improvised, my memory has brought me others.

"The day after my arrival at Minieh I went to see a cotton merchant whose address had been given me, a rather old Alexandrian Jew who advised me to rent part of an apartment in order to get settled.

"As it happened, one of his accountants, who spoke French very well, had just found one he would be glad to share with me.

"It was thus that I made the acquaintance of Hassan (who in a way served as my guide during my whole stay), who led me into an empty, high-ceilinged, tiled room with cement walls painted a soft green, which were soon punctuated with little spots of blood up to a certain level, because it was autumn and the Nile was just beginning to subside and there were, as a consequence, many extremely annoying mosquitoes that I squashed before going to sleep.

"We hired a man with a cart to move my locker trunk and then left in search of a bed, which was not difficult to find because the hospital had sent for some, I believe the previous year, a few more than they could use, a metal bed with a mesh of metal wires stretched on noisy springs.

"At a fabric merchant's we chose canvas for the mattress, thick and silky with gray stripes, like those that the peasants used for their robes; we got samples of cotton-wool at the warehouse, and we confided the whole to a man to be sewn.

"Then we bought a pair of sheets and a blanket so that as of the next day I was able to settle down in the apartment, which had for its only other furniture Hassan's big double bed and, in the corner that served as kitchen, on the ground, a Primus oil-stove (a jug, a water bottle, some earthenware plates with pink flowers, some glasses and some tableware, two pots with their covers).

"I had no difficulty in finding chairs either, because the 'sporting club' had acquired a quantity for its garden; but I still needed other objects in this room; I considered it impossible to live without a table, needing one to read and to write, to carry out my work as a teacher, however elementary that work might be, needing one even to eat comfortably.

"Now, if the richest Egyptians of Minieh had in their homes many pieces of furniture, heavy, stupidly sumptuous, thickly gilded in an over-loaded Louis XV style, upholstered in cretonne with big flowers, they generally ordered them from Cairo, or else directly from department stores in Paris or London, and there was not at that time in the whole city a table for sale.

"As I had very little money at the beginning of my stay because of the slowness of the royal administration, the only solution was to have a table made by one of those very skillful carpenters who took the greatest pride in very slowly realizing complicated contours for sideboards they hoped would be able to rival with those sometimes unloaded from the train; to buy the wood; to make a diagram marked to show exactly what I wanted; then to go every day to the workshop, for three weeks, to learn patience and the fact that it is totally impossible to find in Arabic an equivalent of the French 'too late,' to see how it was coming, until the moment when finally I saw this longed-for table, varnished, with a drawer as I had specially asked, but much too high, so that it was necessary to have the legs sawed off, and sawed off again, before being able to use it.

"Next we undertook the making of another similar table for the dining room, of which we celebrated the installation with a banquet, and then, encouraged by these outstanding successes, I went so far as to order, with a precise drawing, a little cupboard, and I do not know if it was finished before or after Christmas, the dimensions I had given having been respected but in reverse, in which I was finally able to arrange, sheltered from the dust, my linen and my books, which I had not, so to speak, been able to take out of my locker trunk since my departure from Paris."

Within this setting, I wrote a poem that I considered for a long time to be my last poem, and which I have since published under the title *Poème écrit en Egypte* (Poem Written in Egypt). I tried to express the feeling I had at that time, of both wonder and of boredom. In Paris I was bored, with moments of intense emotion; at Minieh there was, in a way, a permanence of the marvelous.

I discovered beautiful weather in that place, the variety of beautiful weather. In Upper Egypt where I was, as it is an oasis in a desert, it rains very rarely. The water comes from the ground, comes from the Nile. At Minieh they estimate it rains an average of two hours per year, which makes rain a completely extraordinary event. People go out in the street when it rains, to absorb as much as possible. And as the old houses—most of them at that time were exactly the same as those of five thousand years ago—were made of unbaked brick, which had excellent qualities of thermal protection, when it rained a little too hard, they melted. It was then necessary to rebuild the houses, which was not very dramatic. It was not at all like the cement rubble after bombings, which I had known in Europe. At Luxor, much farther south in the valley, people, the young French archaeologists, for example, amused themselves by saying that the last time it had rained was during Bonaparte's expedition.

Parisian as I was, I adored clouds, "the marvelous clouds," and I love them still more since I also love other climates, other states of the sky. I had thought that a sky without clouds would risk being monotonous. But each morning, when I came out of my den to go to the Egyptian high school or elsewhere and walked along the Nile, I was stupefied by the newness of the cliff on the other side. The sun each day, at the hour I passed, was at a slightly different point in the sky. Since the atmosphere was extremely clear, all the relief was differently lit and produced different shadows. I was led to pay attention to things I had never paid attention to before. I had in that Egyptian year a sort of astronomical experience. It is a country in which one experiences the world according to the stars, which led me to reflect on the civilization of the ancient Egyptians, the pyramids, and so on, which made me look at the world around me in a different way.

There was a feeling of permanent wonder. I very much mistrusted exoticism when I arrived in this country, which was my first big plunge into a foreign land. But little by little I managed to insert myself through all sorts of cracks, to glide under the surface with a very special feeling of happiness, and at the same time a very strong feeling of exile. I had the feeling that objects that looked like those I was accustomed to were perpetually escaping from me. Everything slipped under my hands and under my eyes. After having gone to so much trouble to get that famous table, I imagined that I could work, carry through the projects I had brought from Paris.

In fact, the work I had to do in the Egyptian school was very tiring, and, beyond that, daily life was very demanding, with the need to learn at least a little everyday Arabic, and about the daily life of those people. For either I would live on the surface of this reality, and then it would be absolute boredom, I would not even have the feeling of wonder; or I could try to enter into the world of my Egyptian colleagues a little, and especially the world of my students. That was work, a great effort. As I absolutely had to situate it all in a historical fashion, with the means on hand, I gave myself up to serious study, which kept me from pursuing the projects I had had before.

Feelings of wonder and at the same time of powerlessness. There were things that did not go well in Egypt at that time, and we were far from seeing an end to the upheavals of the former Ottoman Empire; we still are experiencing these upheavals, which will endure for years, but at that time this was not an issue for me. I had no "political" intentions in Egypt. I felt powerless vis-à-vis myself. I was in a hurry to find a place where I could work, where I could sew my new existence together with the one I had left behind.

That is what I tried to put into this text, the only or almost the only one written on that table, with the particular feeling of time that I discovered in Egypt, notably because I was, in that valley of the Nile, in an educational establishment organized on the European model, with, consequently, an hourly schedule in which the ringing of bells, three minutes of lateness, were supposedly givens of great importance. But the thousand-year-old tradition of Egypt had great difficulty functioning in that framework. I was thoroughly used to it, but my colleagues did not manage to get used to it, with the result that everything worked very poorly. And my students did not get used to it. Time functioned differently, and so did space.

When I was in Western Europe, space for me spread out in all directions of the horizon; it was obvious. And, especially when one is a little Parisian, one considers Paris not only as a center but as *the* center, as Rome was formerly. And the centrality of Paris is expressed like the Roman centrality by the fact that these cities are the departure point of roads, roads of earth or of iron, which go in all directions: the star of the Roman roads around Rome, those of the railroads around Paris.

When I was in the valley of the Nile I found myself in a space that in many ways had only one dimension. One could travel from north to south almost indefinitely, but from east to west one ran very quickly into a wall. Certainly one could climb up on the wall to see what there was on the other side, but, for a European, on the other side there was nothing. It was an absolute desert in which, once a year perhaps, a troop of Bedouins could be made out. They were thus two completely different parts of a world. Here is then a sample of this Egyptian "color":

> Don't let me die
> gods who make fun of me
> here no pond nothing
> but glory and patience
> scorpions and fish

fallen in the midst of briars
life that unfolds waiting
in the symbiosis of extremes

The little boat turns
in the dry and lasting brightness
in the sun that becomes a wall
and hail of glass scales
that terrorize the serpents

The sail is set
but it will never reach the horn
of the one in the sky
that climbs up the wave of the day
from the blood washed by sand
to the gates of plumes and metal
that navigates
from one landscape of death to the other
and terrible even on the valley
because what it brings is indeed splendor
but not life even at night
the inevitable window of the moon
that bursts on the fields of wheat

In this landscape, in the nostalgia for Paris and the wonder of this other
world on which I slid along as if there were a windowpane separating me
from it and into which I tried to infiltrate myself, to insert myself a little
bit, which was immense work, I felt in an acutely strong way the need to
fix some landmarks. It was thus that it became clear to me that this novel,
which I had already planned before leaving, ought to concern the city of
Paris.

I was in the Thébaïde, the land of meditation, and the subject of this
meditation could only be Paris, the land I had left. I had to profit by the
distance at which I found myself to understand a little, to see a little more
clearly, how the country from which I had come and to which I would
return functioned. When I was in Paris itself I was too close, I could not
see. I needed to back away. Egypt gave that to me, but in such a way that I
could not set to work immediately.

...... 13 Unity of Abode

I was thus haunted by this project for a book. It was by no means to be a geography book. I needed to make a sort of model to study this region of reality, just as to study a bridge or any monument or even any city. It was not a matter of taking the city as a whole. I needed to concentrate on a significant sample, as one does in any scientific study. This significant sample, that was evidently for me the housing unit of the city of Paris for the last several centuries: the apartment building, usually rental.

The city of Paris (this is not the case for all other cities) is made up of islets of brick, stone, or cement, inside of which are wells that are the courtyards. These islets are themselves formed of apartments attached to each other, in which families live one above the other. I had spent my whole childhood in one of these apartments, rue de Sèvres, across from the rue Vaneau, in the Sixth District, and there was outside my windows a fountain that made me dream a lot, one of the rare monuments remaining in Paris from the period of the return from Egypt after Bonaparte's adventure, the Fountain of the Fellah, which represents an Egyptian peasant as he would have been represented at the very beginning of the nineteenth century.

I invented a street in Paris and I made a series of plans and cross-sections. I worked especially on the cross-sections, on the way the elements could be separated out in relation to their surroundings. I had been very struck by the rules of classical tragedy. I said to myself that within a novel one could use rules of the same sort as those of the three unities. One could use the unity of place—that was the apartment building; a unity of time—not twenty-four hours, but twelve, the twelve hours of one night.

Little by little my book defined itself: a book of twelve chapters, each corresponding to one hour, to be marked by the bell of the convent of the neighboring sisters, that which already gives a musical organization. The apartment has basements, a ground floor with shops that are closed at night, and a certain number of floors inside inhabited by very different people, who virtually do not know each other, although they meet every day on the staircase. This apartment might make one think of the one Émile Zola described in one of the volumes of the *Rougon-Macquart: Pot-Bouille* (Pot-Boiler). Above these different apartments, there are the servants' rooms.

iv

obsession

14 Stratification

The novel project had germinated in Egypt, but it was only after I left that this text was realized. The following year, instead of going back to Egypt, I had the opportunity to go to England, as lecturer at the University of Manchester, where I stayed two years. In Egypt I was nostalgic for France but in bored wonderment at the beautiful weather, whereas in the north of England I was in the fog that prevailed at that time.

Manchester was one of the darkest cities in the British Isles, the preeminent city of smog. There was a great deal of smoke, which produced a thick fog. There were days when, in the street, you could not see your own hand. There was something poetic about it nevertheless. It was a great climatic shock for me. On the nostalgia for France that I had had in Egypt and kept in England was superimposed almost as strong a nostalgia for Egypt. This went into the novel I wrote during those two years, a book written very slowly, therefore, compared to the way I wrote the succeeding ones. I gradually acquired a certain facility.

Into the model of a Paris apartment I had to weave this nostalgia for Egypt. During the twelve hours of a night an accident happens; a young girl dies without anyone's having sought her death, which causes a great commotion. This apartment building, seen from seven o'clock in the evening to seven o'clock in the morning, is divided into seven floors. Given the French way of counting, that makes five principal floors plus the ground floor, plus the floor for the servants' rooms under the roof. Below there is a basement where no one lives, but where they store old and generally useless objects, and where the boilers for the collective central heating are. Lower still, definitely lower, there is a metro tunnel, whose shaking is felt throughout the building. One hears the hours striking from the bell of the sisters on the other side of the street, and from time to time the rumbling of the underground trains.

On the ground floor are shops, closed at night, and a married couple of concierges. On the second floor two clergymen, Roman Catholic priests, live with their mother. The problems of my relations with the Catholic religion of my fathers led inevitably to their presence. They also have a cook, of German extraction, who enjoys the benefits of painting in her kitchen. She has painted bouquets of flowers on the cupboards, which give a very special air to this place.

One of the clergymen is chaplain in a neighborhood high school. The problem of teaching is already there. The other is an Egyptologist. During the night there will be moments when almost all the inhabitants of the building will be sleeping. Some will dream. The Egyptologist priest will have an Egyptological dream. That is one of the ways Egypt is present in this Parisian apartment building.

On the floor above, the third, lives a large family. I am a child of a large family. We were seven brothers and sisters, and we lived in an apartment together with one of my grandmothers. To give scope to the thing, I have put in my book not only a grandmother but also the other grandfather. This evening we are present at dinner when some other family members arrive as well. We therefore have a very crowded table, with all the problems that are posed within a closely packed family, where people are constantly bumping into each other. These apartments are occupied by very different numbers of people, and their inhabitants represent very different levels of society, though they are normally found in a building of this kind.

On the fourth floor there is an old collector, Samuel Leonard, who is particularly interested in Egyptian objects. From his travels in the East he has brought back a young Egyptian houseboy, for whom he feels a certain tenderness. Rich, the old collector has a cook as well.

These apartments communicate with each other by way of the stairs, where the people meet almost every day but generally do not address a word to each other, almost not knowing each other at all. There is a principal staircase where there is an elevator, and a secondary staircase called the service stairs. Today these arrangements are largely out of date, but they explain the original appointments of the buildings. This model corresponds to Paris in the forties. In Zola's *Pot-Bouille* the opposition between the two staircases also plays a very important role.

This evening Samuel Leonard is receiving some friends in his apartment because he is president of a sort of science-fiction club. All his guests write futuristic novels and are talking about their work or their writing projects.

On the fifth floor is a well-off bourgeois family with an only daughter. This night is her twentieth birthday, and for a "surprise party," as they said then (but there was no longer the original element of surprise, which was that friends got together at the home of one of them who was not forewarned), she has invited some young people, among whom are those who live in the apartment on the third floor. It is the first time they will enter this apartment so near theirs, which they have so often passed. It is there the accident will take place.

On the sixth floor is a family of painters, who use the apartment as a studio. The husband is an abstract painter with a whole complicated intellectual story. In the middle of the room that serves as his studio is a painting that he is in the process of working on, which is itself, without his knowledge, a representation of the whole apartment. Almost everything that happens in the course of the night is expressed in one way or another in this painting, constructed on the basis of a pack of cards. The young men and women become knights and queens. The grown men become kings.

At the very top are rooms, formerly those of servants, some of which have become permanent, complete lodgings, miniature apartments, called studios today, and others that still function as servants' quarters. On this floor the cooks and also Samuel Leonard's young Egyptian boy will encounter each other.

For these twelve chapters, each covering one hour, I have assembled quite a troop. This apartment building is swarming inside. Apparently very many things and at the same time very few things happen to the occupants. This was the first book I worked on. I had already written poems and essays. I had already published essays in journals, but this was a question of a book. When you work on your first book you are never sure that it will be published, and especially you are never sure there will be another. As a result, a young writer has a tendency to try to put as many things as possible in that first book, so he will have done more or less what he had to do. First books are thus often stuffed, and that is the case with this one, which makes reading it rather difficult.

Relationships in space are particularly important in it. If one wants to understand it, one must pay attention to all the clues that allow us to see where the scenes take place, although the narration passes perpetually from one floor to another, and on the same floor from one room to another. The narrator's camera perpetually changes its place, its lens, its speed, its filter. There is perpetual mobility. This is the cause of the greatest difficulty in reading. If I compare this book with poems I wrote before, I see in it a definite connection. For example, personal pronouns wander about all the time, a means of capturing in the best way possible both people and objects. The latter will play an essential role for reference.

The moment at which this book appeared was the very one when people were beginning to talk a little about the "new novel." That journalistic notion, which would spread over the next few years, brought together works that in fact were very different but that had very important points, aspects of the contemporary. These books did not resemble those one was used to, in particular those that regularly win the literary prizes. What was so surprising about them?

First of all they were difficult to read. They demanded a great deal of attention on the part of the reader, and the journalists or critics felt this attention was not clearly justified. There were other difficult books, for example Sartre's novels, but they obviously treated important questions: war, strikes, problems of the working class. In these books, especially those published at the Editions de Minuit, to all appearances neither war nor strikes were discussed. There were no descriptions of events of this type. If problems of contemporary society appeared in them, it was through the intermediary of all sorts of signs and mirrors. They appeared through details in the behavior of the characters and through what one could call the adventure of objects, something that should have seemed very classic for the French novel, since the preeminent novelist of the adventure of objects is Balzac. These new novels led to the rereading of Balzac in a very different way.

These new novels, which claimed to compel our reading in spite of their difficulty, led to all sorts of discussions, which scarcely clarified things. Gradually the light came.

. . . . . . **15 Objects**

Why such importance accorded to objects? In this model it was indispensable, in order not always to be saying "on the fourth floor or on the fifth," to have a system of signals, and that required precise attention to material elements. From this came the importance of the sound signals: the rumbling of the metro, the hours striking from the bell tower, the noise of the elevator, which pass through all the walls. When one turns on the faucet in a room one hears the water run not only in that room but in the one on the other side of the wall or of the floor, particularly if it is at night. A noise that during the day would not be noticed will catch the ear of a person who is still awake, even of one who is asleep.

In a Paris apartment building, the floor plan of the apartments is the same from one floor to the next. The walls continue through floors and ceilings. The kitchen is in the same place, as is the living room, and so on. Indicating where such a character or such an object is on one floor, I can deduce the place of another on another floor. When I know, for example, where a certain light fixture is in the apartment of Samuel Leonard I can use it as a reference point, a geodesic point, in my cartography. These objects, which have such an important function in the book, must be described minutely, which requires us to look at them in a different way from the one we are accustomed to. This goes back to my Egyptian experience of objects.

I had learned in the Nile Valley that I had never really looked at the objects that were the most familiar to me. I had always taken them for granted, as evident, necessary, without asking any questions. Beginning with that experience, all objects began questioning me. The height of a table began to imply a whole civilization that could be contrasted with others, a whole history, a whole collection of relations between people.

While I was working on this book I gave it a different title from the one it has now. I called it "l'Entrepôt," (The Warehouse), which indicated the mobile nature of the objects inside, and of the people, who are always linked to a certain habitat, but much less so than before. It used to be that the peasant was in his village; he was settled in a house that had been his family's for generations and which he felt would continue to be his family's for a long time to come.

None of that is there any more in a rental building. The feeling is that you are there for awhile. If you can remain, you are fortunate. But very often all sorts of considerations, of finances or of overcrowding, of changing jobs or of assignment within the job, cause you to move from one of these lodgings to another. For however long you are there, you are there temporarily. You are there between two moves. It is generalized nomadism. The immobility of the city is a surface hiding a mobility that is very difficult to verify, to perceive. This entire building can therefore appear as a warehouse, a place where objects or people are put temporarily. In the collector's apartment there are rooms overcrowded with souvenirs from Egypt; in the large family there are rooms overcrowded with people. When people are squeezed one against the other, their relations become the relations of objects.

Objects permit us to circulate within this very complicated mechanism, which is the least building in the least of our cities. What is presented in terms of a Paris building could be done for a building in Geneva or Milan; what is presented in terms of a building constructed at the beginning of the century, as it is inhabited halfway through that century, could be for other types of buildings constructed in recent years and inhabited today, those "machines to live in," as Le Corbusier said, where men themselves become cogs of the wheel.

At the time of publication I changed the title to *Passage de Milan*. It was first of all an indication of the neighborhood in which the building is situated, the neighborhood called Europe, on the right bank of Paris, near the Saint Lazare train station, where all the streets are named after European cities. Most cities have onomastic neighborhoods, where the street names are taken from a particular vocabulary. This happens especially when construction is very rapid. One is faced all at once with the problem of naming. The new neighborhood calls for a new section from the dictionary: for example, the names of trees; then we have Elm Street, Plantain Street, Poplar Street, even if none of those trees grow there, even if it is a neighborhood with no trees. The real-estate promoter tries to find names as quickly as possible. In other neighborhoods one is with writers.

In the neighborhood called Europe, we thus have streets named Rome, Amsterdam, Lisbon. If, among these names of cities, I chose Milan for my Passage, when there is no question of this city, when it is not even mentioned, I believe it was because of the plays on words that could be made with this title.

. . . . . . 16 Titles

Titles of books are much larger words than the words in the text. A book is the linking of at least two texts. In the same way it can be said that a painting in a museum is a work composed of two parts—the painting itself and its title, which is on the frame or on the wall beside it, or quite simply in the catalog, often with numerous appendices, the name of the painter, his dates, and so on—a novel is what is called the body of the text, what one begins to read on plunging in, and the title, another text, the words of which have a great importance relative to all those inside the body.

This is often expressed by the addition, at the top of the page of the body of the text, of a reminder of the title, what is called the "running title." I no longer pay attention to it, and yet I know it is there. A statistics on style would have to show that the words of the title are in some way perpetually repeated in the course of the book. In some books we have a whole architecture of titles.

Let us take, for example, Victor Hugo's *Les Misérables:* the body of the text is divided into parts, themselves divided into books divided into chapters, which are sometimes divided into subchapters. There are titles and subtitles on each level, thus a whole scale between the general title and the body of the text properly speaking. It is a pyramid, or a tree. The words of the title, perpetually repeated, a ground bass, will serve as reflectors or as resonators. When I find a word from the title in the text, a kind of launching takes place.

Let us take a title in appearance completely simple. In the nineteenth century a novel was frequently named after the principal character, for example, *Madame Bovary.* As soon as we start reading the book we anticipate the arrival of this person. Now the very clever Flaubert does not at the beginning of the novel use the name "Madame Bovary" for the character to whom this name will ultimately apply and who will keep it for us after our reading. She is the third character bearing this name. First there is the mother of Charles Bovary, then his first wife. It is only after those two that Emma Rouhaud will finally become Madame Bovary. The title on the cover or at the top of the page gives great importance to these successive characters, whom we await from the beginning.

Words found in a title, on all its levels and on different steps of the pyramid, are organized with a different grammar from those in the body of the text. The words of the title are under a magnifying glass, and they are presented with all their potentialities. When we read the same words as the text unrolls, they are taken in context. When we see Madame Bovary within the novel, we know what character these words designate. In the title the words are still open. We do not know yet what they mean. They display their ambiguities and will function as those ambiguities are developed. Also, titles very often contain popular expressions that, in a particular presentation, pass through a sort of fountain of youth, everyday expressions that we pay no attention to anymore but which in a title leave us feeling there is something suspicious going on.

For example, "he has lost his illusions." From that Balzac took his title, *Les Illusions perdues* (Lost Illusions). Or "to lose (waste) one's time," which Proust turned into *À la recherche du temps perdu* (In Search of Lost Time [published in English as *Remembrance of Things Past*]). In this title the wasted or lost time will be, first of all, the reproach made to a child: "You have wasted your time again." As we read the book, each of the words in the title takes on different meanings and all sorts of literary memories come to the surface: "in search of" will evoke Malebranche's title *De la recherche de la vérité* (In Search of Truth) and all the ancient searches and quests, such as that for the Grail. As for the "lost time," it will become the equivalent of *Paradise Lost,* and thus the lost paradise of childhood, which one tries to find again by means of a work of art. On reading the title of the last part, *Le Temps retrouvé* (Time Regained), anyone familiar with English literature immediately makes the connection with Milton.

In the twentieth century many titles are commonplaces borrowed from popular language or literature. This is particularly evident with the surrealist writers. Almost all the surrealist works have titles with dual meanings: first an appearance of banality, which is then metamorphosed by the content of the book. Since I have played about here a bit with the adjective *lost,* I come to the collection of Breton's essays called *Les Pas perdus* (Lost [Wasted] Footsteps). This is a popular expression. In railway stations or in many public buildings there used to be rooms of lost or wasted footsteps [*salles des pas perdus*], places where one could pace up and down while waiting for the departure or arrival of a train, or the end of a trial in court. The word *footstep* gradually takes on a very different meaning: not only setting one's foot down while walking, but also the negation, "not" [*pas*]. In Breton's title, the wandering that is so characteristic of his behavior in the middle of a city is shown as not having been lost or wasted. As with Proust, this "lost time which is never found again" according to the proverb, is indeed found again at the end.

Thus we can study the special behavior of words in titles. In *Passage de*

Milan the first word evokes, first of all, a city and, by its intermediary, a neighborhood in Paris, but the word *milan* also designates a bird of prey, the kite, which in the first pages one of the characters will see hovering over the city. Numerous birds pass through these lines, real or represented. The kite interests me particularly because one of the principal sun gods of the Egyptians, Horus, is represented in the monuments by a hawk or kite. We pass from the passage de Milan, the street, to the fact that a bird, a hieroglyphic sign, is passing somewhere. My name is the name of a bird, and each time I encounter a name of a bird something is set off within me. It is the passage of the bird-narrator across this whole urban structure. When we delve into the book, with all its references to Egypt on the one hand, to the future on the other, we recognize a more and more obsessive play on words: a thousand years [mille ans], in this night, where one has the impression that almost nothing happens; yet, thousands of years can pass from one character to another, from one moment to another.

V
glimmers in the fog

17 Northern England

A young Frenchman went to spend twelve months in a city in the north-west of England, Bleston, which is a transformation of the city of Manchester where I myself spent two years. Arriving in the month of October, he begins to write his adventures in the month of May. There are five months remaining until the compulsory end of his stay at the end of September.

The book is in five parts. The first is the writing done during the month of May. The time of writing is within the time of the events. But also, there are either events or there is writing: either the character is in his office, in the export-import business called Matthews and Sons, hurrying through the streets, meeting people, and so on, or he is in his room at his writing table composing his text, little by little, like a caterpillar spinning a cocoon for his metamorphosis.

In the first part, in the month of May, he writes about what happened to him in the month of October. In the second part, in the month of June, he continues and recounts what happened to him in November; but, at the same time, as a very important event for him has just occurred, which disturbs him greatly, he notes what happened that very day or week. He thus interlaces the account of the November weeks with that of the June weeks. Two temporal sequences are apprehended at once. The narrative moves regularly from one month to the other.

61

In the third part, in the month of July, my scriptor continues and recounts, after the events of October and November, those of December and, after the events of June, also those of July. But that event that occurred at the beginning of June continues to disturb him so much that, to try to understand it better, he makes himself go back further. He tries to remember what happened on the eve of that first of June, and then, as one thing leads to another, he methodically goes back in time. Thus in this third part we have three voices. The third voice recounts the month of May backwards. In music this is called a retrograde voice. The distance grows greater and greater.

Time reverses itself within his narrative, as it does very often in ours, without our realizing it. As Balzac remarked, when we meet someone it is always in the middle of his existence. It is later that we will learn what he was before. If we know him well we will sometimes know all the way back to his childhood, and even his birth. As in the history of humanity, archaeological research digs more and more, and still more deeply. After having encountered recent layers it digs into more and more ancient layers. The archeologist makes History in retrograde movement.

Musicians recognize this figure in three voices, one of which is retrograde, two of which have the same movement, but with one starting after the other. It is an imitative structure and, if it is very strict, a canon. One of the fundamental structures of polyphony is the canon, with reversals, mirrors. Musicians have composed pieces in which a second voice imitates the first, and where sometimes a third moves backward from the last to the first note. These are fundamental structures of our perception of time and of History. Thus music can give us narrative models. Musicians have worked a great deal with texts, assigning them to different voices; they have brought forth from well-known texts—liturgical texts, for example—totally new meanings and emotions.

In the fourth part, written during the month of August, the earlier movements continue. The narrator, after having recounted the events of October, November, and December, will tell us those of January. After having noted the events of June and July, he continues to note from day to day or each week those of the month of August. After having gone back from the end to the beginning of May, he continues his retrograde movement from the end of April to its beginning. By the end of July he already has on his table a fairly large mass of pages.

The written text becomes more and more cumbersome. The narrator-scriptor has difficulty in finding his way not only among his memories, not only in the complicated city in which he is searching, but also in the text that he has written and which is a part of the reality that surrounds him. He has difficulty remembering not only what he did seven months earlier, or a few days earlier, or at a distance growing larger and larger between the two, but also what he has written. He is thus led to reread his text.

Now at the beginning of August, he rereads what he wrote about the event that happened at the beginning of June and which provoked all this distress. Naturally, the events that have occurred since then, and all the research he has done, will lead him to see quite differently what he recounted the first time. Within this ensemble of writing a moment of reading intervenes. He then annotates and corrects a certain number of things.

In the fifth part, the month of September, a fifth voice is added. The first continues: after the events of October, November, December, and January, he recounts those of February. The second also: after what happened in June, July, and August, he notes what is happening in September. The third also: after the months of May and April, he goes backward through the month of March. The fourth: after what he had written in June, he reads what he was writing in July. Then certain events cause him to reread, in addition, what he wrote during the month of August, but this time in retrograde movement, from the end to the beginning.

We have thus a musical structure with five voices, two of which are retrograde. In this way two remarkable points are obtained. As there are retrograde movements, certain narratives approach others. At the end of February voices two and three meet; at the end of July, voices four and five. These succeed in coming together: there is in the text an event on the last day of July and the first day of August. For voices two and three there is a gap. At the end of February the calendar offers a marvelous possibility: there is a day that does not exist three years out of four—the twenty-ninth—because of leap year. One feels more and more that something very important happened that day, which would probably be the key to everything, but the narrator leaves the city on the train before he can tell us. He leaves the city and his text. Thus we will never know what happened on February 29 that year.

This is a detective story that remains open. There is something there that prevents one from knowing the solution. The structure controls the events. At those two remarkable points of the structure there had to be important events. When I wrote, I managed to foresee the events in such a way that they could be narrated in this fashion. It was not that the events were there first of all and then a question of how to recount them. First there were the possibilities for telling and then the question of what could be told in this fashion.

This said, I did not begin by making a grid of this sort. I was fascinated by the possibilities of contrapuntal temporal structures, but it took me a great deal of time and work to reach this definitive grid. In the same way, the events control the characters. A writer usually does not have characters first of all and then narrative structures. He gradually brings the narrative structures into focus, and it is their evolution that controls the appearance of the characters.

Specifically, a character in a novel is composed of his ways of speaking. The great novelist is the one capable of giving a voice to his characters, capable of making their tone, their way of speaking, recognizable. In conversation flowing around him, he identifies forms of discourse that keep their intonation when written down. There are forms of discourse that are neutral in this respect but to which an actor can restore intonation. This is what happens in the theater. The playwright is much more free in this respect. But the novelist who gives voices to his characters—Balzac, Proust, or others—is necessarily an analyst of the conversation surrounding him. He is capable of distinguishing what will preserve a color, a tone, and it is on that basis that characters like Charlus, Françoise, Rastignac, and Vautrin are composed. An ensemble of characters in a novel is a linguistic analysis and an analysis of the whole of society. The relations between form and content are often the reverse of what one thought in the traditional criticism of the nineteenth or the beginning of the twentieth century.

. . . . . . **18 Long Sentences**

In order to link all these different points in time, I had to use very precise grammatical structures. I had difficulty because, when I published my first book, *Passage de Milan,* as a result of the complexity of the relationships between the elements, a certain number of pages were written in relatively long sentences, which, however, did not exceed about ten lines. When I showed the book to some people, they were shocked by their length because, in the traditional French teaching of my childhood, long sentences were hunted down. They said, French is a clear language, and therefore sentences must be short.

I did a first version of *L'Emploi du temps* (Time Schedule) trying to use sentences that would not be too long. Each time one of my sentences started to exceed five lines, I told myself that people would be after me again, and I tried to put a period and add what was needed to make a second sentence. But that version did not satisfy me. I found it wordy. What was natural for me, given my venture, was to use long sentences. I had to destroy part of what I was producing to make my text fit the measurements of the short sentences demanded by traditional criticism. After awhile I said to myself, I must write this text in long sentences. Either it will be written in long sentences, or I shall never succeed in doing it: it will not be.

As a result I sought out assistants, and I studied French literature to see if our great writers always wrote in short sentences. All I needed to do was to ask the question to see that this affair of short sentences was an illusion kept up for ideological reasons worth the trouble of studying, but that in reality the great writers always used long sentences when they needed them. The French writer given as the preeminent example of the short sentence, Voltaire, in his long books, is also a virtuoso of the long sentence. I thus found innumerable accomplices who were builders of very long sentences. French has the advantage of having a range of verb forms making it possible to modulate very precisely the succession of events relative to each other.

In teaching French to foreigners I had had occasion to reflect on all these structures proper to our language. With all my temporal superpositions I needed the French tenses. There they were at my disposal. It depended only on me to issue a pardon to this arsenal of beautiful, good, and long sentences. I also sought accomplices in English. So when I was working on the last version of this book, I systematically read the novels of Henry James.

The use of long sentences led me to audacity in typography. In *Passage de Milan* there were already sentences cut up into sorts of free verse. That was a recognizable structure. In *L'Emploi du temps,* as soon as one of my sentences exceeded a full page, to make the structure more evident, I divided it into paragraphs. Ordinarily a paragraph is divided into sentences. I reversed that: inside a sentence I put several paragraphs, a system that brings this prose close to poetic structure, which I accentuated by putting repetitions of terms at the beginnings of the paragraphs. In this way I succeeded in writing this text almost exactly the way I wanted.

These provocative long sentences drew cries from critics and some professors. I remember that after the awarding of literary prizes that year, at a reception, I ran into a very fine man who took part in the Goncourt Prize, André Billy (who had known Apollinaire), an amiable and noble old man, who said to me: "We were interested in your work; you should continue, but there is one point you ought to pay attention to: you let yourself write long sentences; now you know very well, they have told you in class, in French you must write short sentences." I answered him: "One doesn't always write short sentences in French; think of Proust." "Oh, yes, but Proust was Proust." By which he meant someone fairly interesting, but a little bizarre in some ways, and whom it would be better not to imitate too closely. "There was not only Proust; there was, for example, Saint-Simon." For a writer or a French professor, Saint-Simon is an irreproachable stylistic authority. "Yes, but Saint-Simon was . . . Saint-Simon." I answered him, "Perhaps someday they will say I was Butor." This helped me to write as I wanted, which is the most difficult thing in the world.

Doing what one wants is what takes the most courage, even in details of this nature. Printers, when they print textbooks, are very accustomed to typographical fantasies. If you look through a political economy or accounting textbook, you see extraordinary pages with tables, all kinds of paragraphs. But printers of novels thought a paragraph must invariably end with a period. Thus they had great difficulty printing this book. I had to correct a great deal and to explain several times that it was very important to begin certain paragraphs with a small letter. Gradually we managed it, which has facilitated the task for other writers.

· · · · · · 19 Overflowings

Work on temporal and spatial structures emphasizes the fact that space and time are constantly overflowing. If we stay with fairly loose structures, they work approximately. If I do not pay much attention to the sequence of events, I can believe that I am telling a story in chronological order. But, if I look at things very precisely, I perceive that there are always returns to the past, that the sentence itself brings about returns. In the same way, if I try to outline a narrative in time or space, I perceive that it is in communication with something else. If I try to describe what is in a room, I perceive that I am obliged to bring in elements that are outside. If I want to describe events that took place on one day, I perceive that I refer constantly to earlier events or projects. Within the year of this book, the events narrated will little by little stretch so much toward other regions of the year that we end up with a structure that is rather complex, but in reality much simpler than our most ordinary daily experience.

Events not only do not remain within the hours of writing, but they cannot remain within the unit one has chosen to narrate, either. Trying to narrate the events of one week requires making allusions to those of another; narrating those of a month overflows onto another. By controlling time very firmly, resonances across temporal networks are emphasized. This schema can be considered a network, a grid. What occurs in one region awakens echoes in other regions. Within this year, with its secondary units—month, week, day, even the hours of writing—within this city, with its secondary units of localities—neighborhood, house, room, interior of the room, the space, even, of the piece of paper—there will be an inevitable throwback or recourse to the exterior, locally and historically.

Since it is impossible to go outside directly, the exterior is manifested within the city itself as a compensation. In the city we will find representations of other cities in all sorts of forms—in particular, the shows. Our Frenchman is bored in England. His writing work is a means of fighting the boredom, which is becoming more and more weighty and polluting. He goes to the movies; he likes to see Westerns, which allow him to emerge on a completely different landscape from that of the streets of Bleston.

He particularly likes the "News Theater," a little cinema that shows newsreels, pre-television short subjects, travelogues on different, particularly famous places. He gradually attends all the programs presented there, part of which one can very well imagine is repeated fairly regularly from one year to the next, as the fair moves from one neighborhood to another, that which allows him to see images of Rome, Greece, and Crete in particular, which will have great importance for him because he considers the city of Bleston a labyrinth. The places he sees in this "theater" are in some way complementary to the one in which he finds himself. Since he is in the fog, the crowd, and the soot, he sees sunlit deserts, places of luminous life. He has a sort of generalized nostalgia for places where one can see. From those places the city begins to appear in the midst of a whole collection of other cities, of other landscapes.

The time period that he is in (the leap year is not identified, but everyone is free to look for it as close as possible to the date of publication) is, likewise, situated in relation to other periods and moments that will permit understanding it. The presence of exterior places is accomplished by the documentary films but also by restaurants. The cuisine of the northwest of England has a poor reputation in France. Our young Frenchman in his British year has difficulty with the food, which seems to him to be a sort of concentration of fog and boredom. He is thus drawn to restaurants offering exotic food, in particular the Chinese and Hindu restaurants that have an oriental word in their name.

The presence of earlier periods is accomplished by the historical monuments, ancient or recent. There is a museum in this city, in which are seen tapestries made in France in the eighteenth century, which represent as if by chance the story of Theseus, which connect us to Crete and its labyrinth. There are also two cathedrals: an old, genuinely Gothic Anglican cathedral, and a new, neo-Gothic Catholic one, not at all to be scorned, as the architect who built it was extraordinarily imaginative, a kind of British Gaudi.[1] It has thus all sorts of virtues and mysteries. The false Gothic reflects the true in the same way that the neoclassic reflects Greek and Latin monuments, which themselves reflect earlier periods.

Within the ancient cathedral there is a celebrated stained-glass window, also made in France, but in the sixteenth century, which represents the history of Cain, three of whose descendants are described in the Bible as the first city builder, the first industrialist, and the first inventor of musical instruments. From a historical point of view, each monument develops gradually a spectrum, as is said of a chemical element, a spectrum of resonances from century to century more or less complementary to that of the other monuments. Studying them together, one ends up with a model of general history, certainly incomplete and therefore deceptive, but decisive. That is why it is always so difficult to know what is happening in this book, since there are so many historical layers and swells implied within.

vi

La Modification
presented to the Chinese

. . . . . . 20 The Problems of the West

As this lecture was not recorded, I replace it here with an essay asked of me
some time ago by a Chinese. It was before the events of Tiananmen Square;
the book may have appeared over there in two different translations. This
will give us an opportunity for some recapitulations:

"I want first of all to say what an immense joy this first publication of
one of my books in Peking is for me. If it were given to me to start my life
over, while preserving a little of the experience I have amassed, one of the
first things I would want to do is to learn Chinese.

"But *La Modification* is such a Western book, being a meditation on the
problems of the West, that it should be useful to furnish its new readers
with some indications and references to help them find their way in it.

"The last war was a great trial, not only physical, but moral, for the
French population. The position of our country in the world was profoundly changed, and it has been difficult for most of my compatriots to
realize it. Still today, a minority, all the more important because it controls
a large part of the economic and cultural power, refuses to admit certain
facts.

"Once peace returned, most people in my parents' generation tried to
erase, insofar as possible, the memory of those years of trials. They covered

some combatants and victims with medals, but they wanted to be as they were before, in the same France as before.

"This naturally produced innumerable misunderstandings, in particular between parents and their children. Words, especially the most noble, were used by the two groups with meanings that grew more and more different. It is impossible to summarize here a history of French literature in the years following 1945. Let it suffice to recall that in the fifties a certain number of works appeared that were characterized specifically by meticulous descriptions of familiar objects; these works were given the collective name of 'new novel.' As profound as the differences among the authors were, they nevertheless had in common a quasi-scientific approach to literature and a willingness to cure words of the maladies that were eating away at them more and more."

• • • • • • 21 The Roman Empire

"The whole history of the West is organized around a fundamental reference, the Roman Empire. It has so profoundly impregnated our languages and our institutions that, even if we are only rarely conscious of it, even if some of us have only the most vague ideas about this period of our history, it is still our constant point of reference.

"The Roman Empire was the political and cultural unification of all the peoples surrounding the Mediterranean about two thousand years ago, under the direction of the city of Rome, which was located approximately at its center. The essential is that this organization embraced practically all the regions known to these peoples, the other regions appearing to them only through the intermediary of uncertain tales often qualified as fabulous. It was thus easy to identify the empire as the whole world.

"This empire was remarkably centralized. All the great communication routes passed through Rome. It can be said that it was divided into two parts of nearly equal importance: the city on the one hand, the provinces and frontiers on the other hand. Still today, the pope, head of the Roman Catholic Church, which has been called the 'phantom of the empire' after the progressive splitting up of the latter under the pressure of barbarian, especially Germanic, invasions, gives his solemn benediction 'urbi et orbi,' which is to say, 'to the city and to the rest of the world.'

"But the Roman Catholic Church, by directing the attention of the faithful toward another world after death, only underlined the state of war in which this world found itself. That is why Westerners have perpetually tried to reconstitute the lost Roman peace, to organize a new empire around a central city, which would be the heir of Rome.

"The first great attempt was the empire of Charlemagne, which survived throughout all the Middle Ages in the German Holy Roman Empire. The attempt was revived with great vigor at the beginning of the nineteenth century by Napoleon Bonaparte, who gave to his son the title of 'King of Rome' and had the pope abducted from Rome to come crown him emperor in Paris.

"All the background and the vocabulary of this daring venture came from ancient Rome.

"It was with Napoleon that a tendency, already very strong in France, was considerably accentuated: centralization, the division of France into two halves: the capital city and the 'province.'

"But France was not alone in trying to reconstitute the Roman Empire to its profit around its capital, and in considering itself as the center of the world, with distant regions appearing only as simple lands to be colonized for the exploitation of riches. The city of London in the nineteenth century wanted to be the center of the empire of the world, like Vienna, Berlin, and later even New York City, with its 'Empire State Building,' or Washington.

"The imperial vocation is manifested in particular by a certain number of characteristic Roman monuments, more or less adapted: triumphal arches, temples with columns, amphitheaters; or borrowed from an earlier civilization, which the Romans themselves sometimes took as a model, the Egypt of the pharaohs, with its pyramids and obelisks.

"This permits measuring the essential political role that certain works of art, the Museum, and in particular the Museum of Ancient Art, being an instrument of essential prestige, have played.

"The principal character of *La Modification,* traveling from Paris to Rome, gradually realizes that the relations he has with two women, his legitimate wife and his mistress, are closely dependent on the relations between these two cities in his mind and in the minds of his compatriots."

. . . . . . **22 Baroque Art**

"During his promenades in Rome, alone or accompanied, Léon Delmont takes an interest not only in the monuments of antiquity but in those of another, much more recent, period, extending from the end of the six-teenth century to the end of the eighteenth, which art historians today call the age of the baroque.

"Throughout the Middle Ages, Westerners thought the Roman Catho-lic Church was the legitimate heir of the imperial culture. Now, at the end of the fifteenth century, that belief would be questioned. There was first the Turkish threat, which ended in the taking of Constantinople, the last vestige of the 'Empire of the East,' and then the discovery of America, the unexpected continent, which greatly transformed the image that people had of the World. They then questioned the ancient texts with new eyes and began to think that the Church had not managed either to preserve or to interpret them very well. This period of intense intellectual and artistic ferment is called the Renaissance, meaning, first, the rebirth of the arts and sciences of Greek and Roman antiquity. The questioning of ecclesiastical tradition with regard to the texts of pagan classic writers was soon ex-tended to the sacred texts themselves, which were considered the founda-tion of the Christian religion.

"They then said, not only has the Roman Catholic Church been unable to transmit to us correctly the science of Aristotle or the poetry of Virgil, but, that which is much more grave, it is also incorrect as far as the reading of the Gospels or the prophets is concerned. This movement is called Protestantism, the origin of innumerable wars that would render the West more divided than ever.

"To address this situation, the [Roman Catholic] Church launched a great campaign, often designated by the name of Counter Reformation, Reformation being another name for Protestantism.

"The people of the Renaissance wanted to go back to antiquity, those of the Reformation to the first Christians; the Counter Reformers, abandon-ing to their critics the exterior forms of the Middle Ages, the Romanesque or Gothic, recovered their essential positions and felt that ancient culture had been only a preparation for Christian culture. The baroque accepted from the hands of the Renaissance the rediscovered vocabulary of Greco-Roman art, but drew from it quite different effects in conformity with the enormous changes occurring in the image of the World.

"In the twentieth century the image of the World has changed as greatly as in the sixteenth. Issues involved are not only discoveries in physics, astronomy, and archeology, but also a completely new consciousness of the contemporary world, made possible by the new means of information and communication, whose implications are only beginning to become clear to us.

"There are great affinities between a whole part of our contemporary art and the art of that period. But as baroque art was still controlled by the Roman Catholic Church, which owed to it a great renewal of brilliance, everything was organized toward a recentering around that city and that religion, and baroque art only sketched out a certain number of the traits of the modern art through which at least some Westerners have begun to realize the fact that the Earth has no center and that Europe is not more central than any other continent.

"Baroque art is, in a way, ancient art set in movement. The city of Paris is full of monuments, either Roman or trying to compete with them; those of the Napoleonic era tried to be as ancient as possible, but those of the previous two centuries took as their point of departure the Roman baroque, which they tried to modify in such a way that the recentering would no longer occur around Rome but around its heir, which would be Paris."

. . . . **23 Conjunctions**

"New astronomy had rendered the sky immense; recent navigation showed that the Earth really was round; the issue was to master all these distances, all this vertigo. Baroque art excelled in trompe l'oeil, in the play of perspectives and mirrors; its characteristic form is the spiral.

"One of the aspects that struck the first readers of *La Modification* the most, and scandalized some readers the most, was the length of its sentences. It is easy to see that to relate the minute details of an anecdote, which had been chosen to be as banal as possible, to the principal events of the history of the West, fairly complex grammatical structures were necessary, in order to be able in some way to capture certain themes in big loops, as with a lasso, accomplishing thus a literary equivalent of the spirals of the great baroque architects.

"Today in France these long sentences no longer surprise anyone, and it is easy to show how they use fully some of the riches of French grammar, in particular its marvelous arsenal of verbal tenses, which makes its translation particularly arduous in certain languages. But what is the most difficult to translate is the most interesting to translate, because it is in this way that one really opens a door in the great walls that separate nations, that one builds bridges over the abysses of borders.

"In the education of my youth short sentences were obligatory. If a sentence exceeded two lines, one was absolutely required to cut it to pieces, which prevented saying certain things with enough precision, which bit by bit condemned certain forms, atrophied certain organs of our language.

"Finding myself constrained to lengthen my sentences, I sought in earlier French literature whether other writers had not faced the same problem, and I discovered that, contrary to what my professors had told me, our great classics did not hesitate a minute to make admirably long sentences when they needed them, and that the French language was remarkably well suited to them. I was thus led to question the reason for this strange contradiction.

"In so doing, I realized the contradiction was linked to other prohibitions, that it was a matter of preventing the establishment of certain relationships, of preventing questioning, and in particular questioning the Roman model, that is, the absolute and definitive primacy of the West.

"I emphasize this issue, because I have no idea how it can be resolved in Chinese, where the articulations of speech function in a completely different way. Certainly pruning, transposing, distributing differently will have been necessary. On the other hand, certain things are very easy to say in Chinese that would demand innumerable explanations in French. I hope many happy meetings will occur."

. . . . **24 The Second Person**

"Having traveled a great deal, striving to understand the people among whom I lived as well as possible, I have used, more or less, a number of languages, although there are very few in which I could express myself even roughly today. This has led me to consider that a language always exists among others and thus always to examine mine in comparison with others. Since I write in French I must use the resources proper to French, must show what French can be used for. I always hope that my texts will someday be translated. Not only do I want readers, but readers in other languages. I want translators who will succeed in saying in their language what was impossible to say in it before without the aid of a French text. It is impossible to render the task of translators easier, because the difficulties are different according to the languages, but it is possible to render the task still more fruitful by striving to know better the roundabout ways and secrets of one's own, and everything to which they are linked.

"The long sentences of *La Modification* thus use certain resources of French grammar, and all the ingenuity of a good translator is needed to succeed in transposing into another idiom whatever has seemed most interesting in what he has read. Another aspect characteristic of French, which has posed many problems for these ferryboatmen of languages, is the systematic usage of the second person plural, the 'vous' of courtesy.

"Most narrations are made in the third person when one recounts the adventures of someone else, or in the first when a character recounts his own. For me these two traditional forms had both advantages and disadvantages. The first person permitted me to distinguish clearly the principal character from all the others, to allow the reader to enter, in a way, the interior of his mind, but prevented my using, at a critical moment, the pronoun 'I,' and permitting this character to 'take the floor.' That I insisted on absolutely. After having mulled the problem over a long time and made several fruitless efforts, I thought of the existence of this second person, and from the moment I used it, my text, even though it continued to pose for me innumerable problems of detail, took form without difficulty.

"I do not wish to dwell on the properties of this second person, much more mobile than the other two, but in the same way that I had needed to seek godfathers for my long sentences, I explored French literature in search of guarantors who could enlighten me, not only in noble literature, but also in popular literature. I found all sorts of examples, especially in what I could call active literatures, texts that are written to tell how to do something, whether in daily life, recipes in cookbooks, do-it-yourself manuals, gardening handbooks, or in spiritual life, meditation techniques. A particularly interesting example is that of the examining magistrate or detective in a mystery novel, who tells a story to the principal character in order to obtain from him a confession of the truth.

"In French we use the second person plural to keep a certain distance from the person with whom we are speaking, distance often compelled by respect. The passage from second person plural to second singular, when a friendship becomes more intimate, is often difficult, its occurrence requiring special circumstances, celebrations, or events. Such a distinction has its parallels in other Western languages but never its exact correspondent. In

English, for example, the second person plural is used today in all cases, and the old second person singular is strictly reserved for religious texts or their parodies. Other languages use forms of the third person, with sometimes richer ranges than the French.

"This form, used from one end to the other of my text (with examples of all the others within it), certainly imposes on it a great unity, and it is tempting for the translator to maintain that by using a single form, to which one gives an approximately equivalent function. But this is obviously not the only solution, and in some cases perhaps not the best. Changing from one solution to another at a strategic moment can be imagined. The translation of a text that adequately exploits the properties characteristic of its language is never achieved. Languages shift in relation to each other, and we will never have accomplished the translation of Shakespeare into French, and much less the Chinese classics."

25 The Book

· · · · · ·

"[*La Modification* is a] meditation on the West, and especially on the Western book. My principal character is a businessman, but at the same time a well-read one. He reads a great deal, and not things currently in vogue. Thus we know that he has read the *Letters* of Julien the Apostate with much attention. [Julien] was proclaimed emperor at Lutèce, the Roman name of the city of Paris, for which he bore all his life a particular attachment. He was the nephew of Constantine, the emperor who had converted to Christianity and made it the official religion of the empire while moving its center to Byzantium, renamed by him New Rome, or Constantinople. Julien strove to reestablish the cult of the ancient gods, accomplishing thereby a first "renaissance." This figure, disgraced by the Church, intrigued a number of daring French writers, in particular Montaigne and Voltaire. He is in some way the emblem of the death agony of Roman antiquity, which lives on still under all our trappings of modernity.

"Léon Delmont would like to be a sort of new Julien, combining a Christian childhood with a return to the ancient gods. He knows very well that today he can be only a miniscule caricature of the emperor, but he takes Julien as a kind of guide to get out of his hell. For him Julien is the last veritable emperor, one who discerns on the horizon, after the long

Middle Ages, the emergence of a postimperial era where the dream of the Roman Empire would be once and for all transcended and replaced by a better organization of peace.

"During almost all this decisive voyage from Paris to Rome, Léon Delmont holds in his hands a book, the essential instrument of Western culture, as of many others, a book whose title one does not know, but which could be, ought to be, the letters that some new Emperor Julien addresses to him as to his true heir. Gradually he understands that such a book would be the most help to him, and to all those who are like him, in attaining what he seeks; but if he can imagine some aspects of it, taking his adventure as a point of departure, he knows that he is incapable of carrying it through, that therefore someone else will have to write it, that it will have to be read by still someone else, to get him across the frontiers, this book whose material, paper, was invented long ago in China and which comes to China today, where it will be interpreted in the interior of another, much more vast, story, questioning the heirs of another empire in the construction of another peace."

This is the way I tried to present *La Modification* to the Chinese.

vii

railway consciousness

. . . . **26 Plans**

The point of departure of *La Modification* was to relate two cities, which would serve as characters. In *L'Emploi du temps* the principal character was a city. These two cities [in *La Modification*] were necessarily specified as Paris, the city of my youth, and Rome, because it still haunts the city of Paris today, as it does many others.

This was the period when people were talking about the new novel and when questions of narrative technique came to the forefront of the critical scene. In *L'Emploi du temps* I had used a certain number of temporal unities—day, week, month—and I had superimposed a certain number of these units to obtain a sort of grand counterpoint in which I respected the conventional normal units: time such as clocks give it to us, the day organized by work, the week as we live it, the month of the calendar. I tried to have something a little more supple in *La Modification*. For this I used very precise durations, but a little different from those of the clock or the calendar.

In *L'Emploi du temps* I had used five narrative voices, which entered progressively. One followed five series of events, with an opposition between the present of the journal, which intervened beginning with the second part, and a certain number of leaps into more or less distant parts of the chronicle. In *La Modification* I wanted to add another consider-

78

ation, which naturally existed already, though not by design, in *L'Emploi du temps,* and which I wanted to make more precise: that of the future, of plans.

For this character going from Paris to Rome, it was essential to accomplish a certain plan, which is modified, destroyed in the course of its very realization, this plan for a different existence with another woman. But his existence is so determined by a certain number of conditions that it is impossible really to change it. To do so it would be necessary to change a good part of the society around him. If I have written books, it is because I tried to transform the society around me, which was the only way to change my own existence a little bit. This character wants to change only his own existence, and as a result his project is doomed to failure.

The notion of a plan is fundamental here. Among the narrative voices I had to have not only a present, and memories superimposing themselves on it, but also projects. Memories imply a narration that can be corrected little by little, but in principle do not transform what the narration tells; the narration only tells it better and better. Little by little a historical version of the events is fixed in an asymptotic[1] way. On the other hand, as far as the future is concerned, one can very well pass from a first vision to another that is profoundly modified or which will be accomplished to the detriment of the other. We already had considerations of the future appearing in the science-fiction club of *Passage de Milan.* To follow these different layers, I needed very strict premises of time and space. Hence the railroad.

. . . . . . 27 The Railroad

I was born into the railroad world. Not only am I Parisian, but I am also a railroad child. My father was in the railway administration. During my whole youth it was the only reasonable means of transportation for me, for my family. We had reductions and sometimes even could travel free. The automobiles that some uncles had therefore appeared to us as a phenomenal luxury.

The railroad is an admirable example of a precise link between time and space. At that time in France it was run well. The timetables could be trusted. There are regions in the world where that is not the case, where it is usual for a train to be four hours late. Airplane schedules can hardly be trusted either; they, however, present us with very interesting structures, which I used a few years later in a text written for the French radio, *Réseau aérien*.

Here I had the railroad schedule, which gave me the precise link. From the narrative point of view, it was priceless because at the end of a certain time, once this link was well established, I would have a considerable economy of means. Indeed, I needed only to give the time where one was for the place where one was to be deduced, and vice versa. During a trip on the railroad, if I know where I am, I know what time it is. It gives a very strict narrative line. From Paris to Rome there is one railway line and one only.

Of course you can act on a whim. You can take a week to go from Paris to Rome if you wish, or still longer by taking a roundabout way. But a businessman always takes the fastest train, much faster today than at that time. He always passes through the same stops, which he finds in reverse order on his return. At each station memories of preceding voyages can catch hold of him. In the course of the trip, the train passes others going in the opposite direction. The continuation of his trip will quite naturally open onto junctions or switchings leading to earlier trips in one direction or the other, or to later, planned ones. Each stop can be considered an intersection.

The life of the character, since he is a Paris representative of a Roman typewriter company, is measured by his comings and goings, in the course of which the train is the preeminent place of memory and of projects.

A train presents the landscape to us in a particular way. The vision we have from the train is entirely lateral, unless one is the engineer, in which case one sees the roadway straight ahead. But those inside the car, the travelers or customers, see the landscape file by on each side. The windows look like movie screens. One slides alongside the landscape, whereas when one drives a car one dives in, one penetrates its interior.

The driver of an automobile looks at the road, while the traveler on the train contemplates a sliding panorama, which can serve as a metaphor by which to consider history. The landscape of the automobile driver is a metaphor of the present, of the way we dive into the future with the past behind us. We slide alongside the railway landscape, and we feel relative to it a much greater freedom.

Inside his compartment, the character going from Paris to Rome is led to encounter a certain number of stations and of trains going in the opposite direction, which lead him to try to recall the reasons causing him to be on the train that day, which is not the usual day for his business trip. It is an exceptional trip. When he takes the train for his business he always goes first class, as it is the business that pays. But this time, as it is a private trip, for the first time in years, since he is something of a skinflint, he is traveling third class. The usual train seems different. The characters are different. Whereas ordinarily he travels within the wear and tear of daily life, of routine, this time his attention will be intensified, and that is what leads him to recapitulate what could have made him travel in such novel conditions.

On this narrative voice, which is in the present, will soon be superimposed one in the past, in which he will remember what happened to him just before the departure of the train, on the platform at the train station, then what happened in the morning, the night, the day before in the evening, a retrograde voice that will take us to his preceding return trip. The first voice is the railway track of the present, which will lead us from the departure from Paris to the arrival in Rome. The second soon plays with it, leading us from the departure from Paris to the preceding arrival in this city. A third permits us to imagine what is supposed to take place between his arrival in Rome and his next departure to return to Paris. [This is a] play between the trips and the between-trip regions.

. . . . **28 Transitions**

This linking of time and space allows for much suppleness, but to facilitate the reader's circulating within this network, I added a fundamental signaling of what one could call the railway conception of reality, a signaling in some way mimetic within the text itself. I can give to each of these regions of the narration numbers or names or letters. I wanted to introduce into the text signaling switches that would permit the reader to pass quite naturally from one region to another. Between these regions, which I called A, B, C, D, . . . (there are seven) in my preparatory work, I introduced transitional texts, which I called *t,* made with little formulae that are linked to the view of the compartment or through its windows, and which gradually associate themselves with such and such a region of the text or of the life of the character.

The book is in three parts, each composed of three chapters. Within these chapters the structures become more and more asymmetrical. I have always tried in my books to move from the simpler to the more complicated. One reaches the fairly complicated rather quickly, which means that if I were to try to walk around again inside, if I were to try to find the scaffolding again, I would have to do a great deal of work. I would have to consult my sketches or manuscripts, but I no longer have any idea where the ones for those books have been dispersed. Those for later books are in large part at the Municipal Library in Nice. In the first part of the book things remain very simple, and that is why I will take my examples from that part.

I call the first voice A, the narrative present, the trip from Paris to Rome on this occasion. I call the second voice B, the recent past, the retrograde voice, which goes back over what has just happened before the departure from Paris. The first chapter has the form ABA. In the second chapter I introduce a third voice, C, the project. It has the form ABCBA. The third chapter has the form ABCDCBA. These texts are sorts of parentheses, the ones within the others. Then the structures become more and more asymmetrical before reaching a structure ABACAD, and so on, in the last chapter.

As the passage from one region to another is always marked by a little transitional text, in reality the first chapter is AtBtA. The second is AtBtCtBtA, and so on. The transitional texts, which I called t, are constructed in the following way: everything that will cause a leaving or returning to the first region or voice A, all that evokes the passing of a station. Here is the first appearance of this formula:

"The Fontainebleau-Avon station passes."

Little by little, even without being clearly conscious of it, when one finds a formula of this sort, one knows that something is going on inside the text.

The B region is evoked by the formula "on the other side of the corridor." This gives us the following paragraph:

"The Fontainebleau-Avon station passes. On the other side of the corridor a black 11-HP^2 stops in front of the city hall."

I have a little hinge of two elements. To close the parenthesis I reverse them:

"On the other side of the corridor a black 11-HP[2] starts up in front of a church, follows a road that runs along the railway, rivals with you in speed, comes closer, distances itself, disappears behind a woods, reappears, crosses a little river with its willows and an abandoned boat, allows itself to be passed, makes up the lost distance, then stops at a crossroad, turns and goes away toward a village whose steeple is soon effaced behind a fold in the terrain. The Montereau station passes."

We then come back inside the compartment. In the second chapter I will pass from A to B in the same way that you already know, to the extent that I can embellish this hinge with a little vignette:

"The Saint-Julien-du Sault station passes with its lampposts and their signs, the inscription in big letters on the side of the building, the steeple, the roads, the fields, the woods."

Vignette:

"The young married couple is conversing about a detail that they point to on the map."

Formula of voice B:

"On the other side of the corridor, wild rabbits are scattered, foothills, with a road in front where a truck is driving which draws away, comes back, disappears behind a house, is pursued by a motorcyclist who passes it in a beautiful curve in the form of a slack bow, lets itself be outpaced by him, by your train, leaves the scene."

Voice C will be brought in by the formula "on the other side of the pane, between the priest and the young woman." Here, in the second chapter, is the passage from the second to the third voice:

"On the other side of the corridor there is a yellow farm, a sunken road that bends, reappears behind a big comb of furrows, bulging, pecked by crows, where a motorcyclist comes out in a helmet with a leather jacket, who comes close to the railway, who dives between the embankments under a bridge, where you see the locomotive that is carrying you start over and the first cars that precede you. You try to see him again on the other side of the pane, between the priest and the young woman, but he must now be far behind you."

The close of this interior parenthesis, the passage from voice C to voice B:

"Beyond the window, between the young woman and the priest, high-voltage pylons succeed each other along the road where an enormous gas truck with a trailer is driving, approaching the railway, which makes a sharp turn across the fields after a bridge under which the truck turns. The man across from you perhaps now sees it from the other side of the corridor, where for your eyes other high-voltage pylons succeed each other on more and more pronounced foothills."

Finally, closing of the big parenthesis, return from voice B to voice A with the vignette between the two formulae:

"On the other side of the corridor, between a barn and a thicket near a pond, a motorcyclist who turns to the right, then is suddenly covered up by a big blue bus with its roof covered with baggage, turns to the left toward the barrier guard's house, which the train passes as does the bus soon while in the distance appears a village with its steeple and its water tower. The young married couple look out the window, the two heads close against each other, trembling together. The Joigny station passes, the whole town reflected in the Yonne."

All through the book one can follow the evolution of these formulae, which are mathematically placed and which are a little like placards on a highway network or signals on a railway network. Thus in the third chapter, passage from A to B, opening of the big parenthesis with a double vignette:

"The Darcey station passes. Fairly far down the corridor, the conductor comes out of a compartment to go into the following one, which must be the last, then a young girl about the same age as Madeleine comes along, followed at some distance by the business representative who was a little while ago in this corner that you had chosen on the departure from Paris and which you have succeeded in taking again. The young married couple are again seated next to each other but their positions are reversed, he being next to the window and she beside the Englishman. On the other side of the corridor passes a long freight train with wooden refrigerator cars painted a dirty white, marked with big black letters."

Passage from B to C, opening of the second parenthesis, with a simple vignette:

"On the other side of the corridor, the clouds do not appear to be about to lift. The Englishman crosses one knee over the other. Beyond the window a slow surge of hills covered with leafless vines vibrates."

Voice D recounts the preceding trip from Paris to Rome. It is announced by the allusion to the iron heating register that was located between the seats on trains of that period:

"Beyond the window, among the vines under the sky, which is becoming heavy and black, the high roof of a church with its lozenges of varnished yellow tiles towers over a closely bunched village. On the iron heating register between the seats the iron stripes intersect like miniscule rails in a sorting depot."

Return of voice D to voice C. Closing of this third parenthesis. The two elements of the hinge are reversed:

"On the iron heating register your two feet scrape. Beyond the window, the rain, whose coming was only too certain ever since the departure, begins very softly, in very fine drops, which trace little lines on the pane, like hundreds of threads."

Return of voice C to voice B, closing of the second parenthesis with a simple vignette:

"Beyond the window, the rain has become more violent, striking the pane with fat drops, which begin to come down slowly, tracing oblique rivulets. The Englishman closes his newspaper again and shoves it back in his pocket. On the other side of the corridor, below the shaking and blurred telegraph wires, you can still vaguely make out the mass of a house or of a tree here and there among the hills covered with leafless vines."

Return of voice B to voice A, closing of the big parenthesis with a double vignette:

"On the other side of the corridor, unrecognizable under the rain that is raging, a long freight train passes, coal cars first, then others, loaded with long beams, with unfinished automobiles, bodies not painted, lined up against each other like the wing cases of dead, pinned insects, then those carrying animals with their barred windows, those containing gas with their little ladders, the flatcars filled with rusty flint to grade other road-ways, and the last, finally, with its little tower and its lantern, not immedi-ately against the window but a little farther. The young married couple is silent, each engrossed in his reading; they have stretched out their legs under your seat. In the corridor now, the professor is leaning against the copper rail, and he is smoking. A station whose name you cannot make out passes."

After having had two cities play, I wanted to try to have more cities play. I wanted to arrive at a more general structure in which I would try to describe our culture and its problems.

· · · · · · 29 The Professor

At the time I was writing *La Modification* I was in Geneva, a professor at the International School, on Chêne Road. In the program of the last years of the French secondary program I had to give classes in philosophy, which I was already accustomed to from France, [and] French classes, which I had already given in various foreign countries and which were very fruitful for me, since with what I was writing I was perpetually plunged into problems of French language and literature. But that did not give me a full schedule. It was thus that I became a professor of history and geography, two disciplines that fascinated me but in which I had never been trained.

During that year I therefore needed to study history and geography a great deal before being able to teach them to my students. As I had international students, in certain cases they knew much more than I about the geography of their countries, which sometimes put me in a delicate situation but was a magnificent stimulus to prepare my classes for the next week. So I spent considerable time studying closely French textbooks on history and geography, and I told myself that I could try to study the whole set of textbooks used in the last classes of secondary education.

The teaching of history and geography made centuries pass admirably under my eyes, through a grid still richer than that of the railway schedules: the grid of the school program.

In *L'Emploi du temps* the typical business schedule allowed one to know from what time until what time on what days my character was obligatorily at what place and therefore that he could only write on certain days and at certain hours. In *La Modification* the timetable permitted me to know where I was if I knew what time it was. Within a teaching program, the hourly grid of a teaching establishment, I know incomparably more elements. I can know at what moment which person is found in which place. If you are a history professor, you go to the seventh-grade class Tuesday at 2:00, and Tuesday at 3:00 you will move to another room, where you meet the eighth-grade class or the pre-baccalaureate class.

Following the professors' trajectories, I traverse cells of an extraordinary richness. The time gives me, at once, the place someone is and also his companions, the society. I know that at a certain hour of the week a certain person is with this or that other person and also what he is talking about. All I need to do to end up with a prodigious economy is to succeed in establishing narratively a program of teaching. Naturally, very quickly a great deal of attention on the part of the reader will be necessary. If he misses certain signals he will be lost, but he will be able to find himself again, and there will be a particular pleasure in finding himself again once he has been lost.

Gradually one has the feeling that with a certain amount of work one could establish exactly the narrative parameters of a given paragraph. In taking no matter which paragraph, one can know where one is, at what moment, with whom and about what the people are thinking—officially, the professor's class, and what one is thinking clandestinely. All those who have some experience in teaching know that the attention of schoolchildren and students fluctuates a great deal. There are moments when they are very attentive, others when one sees by their eyes that they are elsewhere. The good, attentive professor then swoops down like a vulture on the unfortunate student to ask him with a sardonic smile, "Where were we?"

We have in the school schedule a construction in which we live and in which children, especially, live; a very rich and very constricting grid, from which to derive the idea of a text that would try to recount what happens in French teaching and what goes on throughout it.

Teaching is the most sensitive of all areas of our society. It is through the intermediary of teaching that our society is perpetuated. And it is also in large part through its intermediary that society is transformed. Nothing is more important than reforms in teaching. That is why they are so difficult to make. What is going on in teaching is indeed very difficult to understand. The reality is too complex for our ordinary means of description or narration. We do not yet have the means for this immense task. That is what I wanted to hook up to, as best I could, in *Degrés* (Degrees).

La Modification, with its story of adultery, having had the luck to win a prize, I had a little respite in daily life, but at the same time some problems arose because I had awakened jealousies where things had been relatively simple before. I told myself that it was the moment, now or never, to do a really daring book. I wondered if after that I would not be obliged to become reasonable. I had to take advantage of the right moment to go as far as possible.

. . . . . . **30 Polysemy**

The word *degrees* is remarkably polysemous. It is therefore particularly suitable for a title, its ambiguity to develop, unfold in the course of reading. Almost all the terms of our languages are ambiguous, and that is why literary translation is so difficult. Ambiguities not being the same from one language to another, one never translates but a part of a word. In daily life we are in general constrained to use a single sense and to eliminate the others. In a title the writer assembles the different senses of the word, which he presents like an enigma that the reading will resolve, little by little, in general justifying the ambiguity of the term, showing us that the union of these meanings, which we separate in daily life, in reality is justified. The study of the title thus allows us to pass to the other side of a barrier, of a horizon, or of a stage set. The title is a key to the book and, thanks to the book, a key to language and to society.

Frequent use of the dictionary permits us to encounter terms that have many more diverse meanings than others. In French *degrees* is particularly interesting because all its different meanings have the advantage of being linked to precision. Etymologically, it is simply a footstep; from the horizontal step one passes to that on a staircase, from the step to the steps.

This term also serves to indicate measures in all sorts of scientific domains—the measure of the arc of a circle, of temperature—and serves also in daily life to designate regions of French education where we speak of three "degrees," and also in the fundamental mathematics of kinship. We speak of different degrees of cousinship. The book is a sort of development in the photographic sense and of justification of this semantic richness. I tried, in the body of the book, to give to this title all the meanings distinguished in the dictionary. With my sentences I was able to give examples of grammatical degrees, as with my anecdotes, examples of degrees of kinship.

• • • • • • 31 Entropy and Recurrence

The essential theme of the book is teaching, the transmission of our knowledge, of our ignorance, of our wisdom or folly, of our way of life. As soon as one finds ways to describe it one perceives that it works badly. Everyone has complained about it for the last fifty years, in all the countries of the world. It is a general lamentation and powerlessness.

Teaching such as ours produces an enormous entropy of knowledge. Transmission takes place badly. There are masses of things that we ought to know, which we consider it would be indispensable to know in order to live properly, and which we do not succeed in transmitting. We ought to know a mass of things, and in reality we do not know them. When we see the program to which children are submitted we are overcome with dizziness for the effort we ask of them, and for our ignorance, that is, the vanity of that effort. The mode of narration will aid in reproducing this vertigo.

In the aging, which we feel so strongly, of our world, hopes arise for a new world in which there would be new teaching. This opposition between old world and new world leads to the essential theme of the discovery of America. The whole book centers on one hour in a French eleventh-grade class. In the second week of the school year, Tuesday, October 12, 1954, a teacher tells his students, aged fifteen or sixteen, about Christopher Columbus's first crossing. Around this fundamental class will cluster the preceding, following, and concurrent classes. The whole system will thus appear, little by little, playing on the resonances existing in this network.

The teaching program of a class in a high school or college is recurrent. Each week reproduces the spatiotemporal and cultural schema of the preceding week and will be taken up again the following week. There is the rhythm of the school hour, of the day, of the week, of the trimester with the vacations that punctuate them, and of the year. The history program that you have taught to a given class, you will teach again the following year to students who will then be the age of the students to whom you are teaching it this year.

The sentences will twist their way from echo to echo. To the hour will be added the preceding hour and then the same hour the day before, the preceding hour of the preceding day, and then the same hour of the same day the preceding week, and so on, and even the following hour, the following day, week, trimester, and following year. There was thus the risk of having an interminable construction. At the end of a certain time I had to find a way to batter through the wall in this Tower of Babel so that my text could remain not only in my book but in my life. It was necessary to make holes in order to breathe, and to make cuts.

At that time I had never been to the United States. After writing such a book, it was urgent for me to discover America.

viii

transatlantic

. . . . . . 32 The Discovery of America

After the war one country became a powerful magnetic attraction for all European intellectuals: the United States of America. Every young man the least bit adventurous or curious wanted terribly to cross the Atlantic and see what was happening on the other side, because with the last war the United States had acquired not only economic importance, which it already had, but considerable cultural importance. Before the war of 1939, Europe and, of course, especially the British thought of the U.S. as still being a cultural colony.

People in the U.S. thought of themselves that way, too. It was indispensable for the young U.S. citizen to make his trip to Mother Europe one day or another. It was a necessary complement to his studies. It was best to do it at the beginning of one's life, but often it did not become possible until much later. It was a sort of crowning of one's career, the mark of success. For the U.S., cultural inventions—literary, pictorial, musical—came above all from Western Europe. There were interesting things in the U.S., but the center was Western Europe and, in particular, Paris.

The great American literature of the first half of the twentieth century was thus to a great extent formed in Paris. The most innovative minds—Ezra Pound, Faulkner, Hemingway, and so on—had their Parisian season in the twenties in Gertrude Stein's circle.

91

With World War II, with the German Occupation, a sort of wet blanket was laid over Europe. Many intellectuals and artists were led to cross the Atlantic. In this way there was established on the other side a kind of European intellectual colony that considerably vitalized American culture, in particular that of New York. The result of this was that French intellectuals were avid for news from America. We had the impression that a quantity of interesting things happened over there that we did not yet know about. For a certain number of years after the war, someone coming back from the U.S. had an immense advantage over the others. He was in advance. He already knew things that would come only little by little for the others.

The U.S. had always had this role of prefiguration of the future, a role both positive and negative in European culture of the nineteenth century and the first half of the twentieth: on the one hand, what one could do, and on the other, what one risked having happen. Some minds would dare to confront these new possibilities the world across the Atlantic offered. But what had remained vague would become considerably more clear after the end of the war.

Young French intellectuals dreamed of going to the U.S. a little as in the sixteenth or seventeenth century they dreamed of going to Italy, especially to Rome. It was from there that certain ideas came whose fecundity we recognized. Like the others, I dreamed of crossing the Atlantic. I was waiting only for a chance, especially after having written that novel that revolved around an hour of class devoted to the discovery of America by Christopher Columbus.

I had the good luck to have the opportunity to go as the sabbatical replacement for a professor friend at Bryn Mawr College in a well-to-do suburb of Philadelphia. He proposed it and I jumped at it in spite of the practical problems it presented for me. I had just become the father of a daughter, and my wife and I were expecting another child. I left just after having published *Degrés* and the first volume of *Répertoire* (Repertory). At that time people still traveled on ships. I had the good luck to cross the Atlantic on the *United States,* "the biggest ship in the world," and to arrive in the port of New York in the early morning with numerous emigrants, who had a variety of feelings, on the deck. It was a little like Elia Kazan's film *America, America.* I too wondered what was waiting for me on this other side.

It was not original of me to want to go to the U.S. at that time. We were all haunted by this desire. And that is why I knew very well that all my friends and colleagues would be questioning me, and all the more because I had already published the book entitled *Le Génie du lieu.* They would ask me if it was all right, if one could live over there, and if Coca-Cola, a rather mysterious commodity still rare in France, was truly drinkable.

From my arrival on, I asked myself what I was going to do to tell about what I saw and felt. Since *Le Génie du lieu* had been published, I imagined I could use the same form for this purpose. At the beginning of my stay I was asked to give to the alumnae bulletin of Bryn Mawr College a little text in which I told of my first visit to the city of Philadelphia, a text that I have never republished elsewhere and which, for that matter, I have been unable to find again.[1]

. . . . . . **33 The Spirit of the Place**

This idea of the spirit of the place is that of a kind of literary review of geography. Studies can be published on texts, which analyze, for example, the relationships between these texts and the life of the person who wrote them. Studies can be made of the way these texts function, why they touch us, interest us, what they bring us. The same thing can be done for paintings, sculpture, or music. It can also be done for architectural monuments. It is considered perfectly normal to publish books on certain great architects.

In the greatest part of this criticism there is a presupposition that I shall call "romantic": the idea that a work of art is the expression of an individual. Literary works can often be studied in this light. One studies the life of the author and sees how this existence is expressed in his works. One can do individualist criticism of painting. With architecture it is already a little more difficult, because it is too easily seen that the architect is not the only one producing his work, that he needs numerous helpers. He is not the one who puts the stones one on the other or who pours the concrete.

If one looks at things more closely, it is not Rubens who painted his pictures, either. He was at the head of an enormous painting enterprise that covered meters and square meters of a church or palace. He made the sketches and organized his work in such a way that he could use all sorts of specialists, some for the flesh, for the famous Rubens complexions, for the fabrics, for the landscapes, for the animals. Some of the specialists are well known and themselves have works bearing their signatures admired in museums. Rubens himself might add at the end some details, put a little more moisture in the eye of the martyr, or red on the shoulder of the bacchante. But these are in reality collective works.

Pictorial works are always more or less collective works like architectural works, and literary works themselves, for in order to write one needs a certain number of tools, paper, which the writer has not fabricated. If I can write things, it is because I have machines. In many respects, alas, I do not communicate my text directly to my readers. I need the heavy and constrictive machinery in the gears of which one is obliged to twist one's way, a machinery of editors, printers, distributors, bookstores, critics, and so on, people who are all involved with books but who only like some, most often those that do not upset them too much. The individuality of the writer cannot manifest itself except to the extent that he can succeed in negotiating all sorts of pacts with the powers.

From the moment one understands that a work of art is fundamentally collective, with a master of the work who will detach himself from it more or less, then certain other works present themselves to criticism, in particular cities. A city brings us something. There are some where one lives differently from the way one does in others; one thinks differently. To walk in some cities is like listening to magnificent music, or playing it. It is like reading a book or a score. But it is the ultimate in rare for a city to have "one" architect. Certainly it cannot have a single builder. Further, a city is not only its stones, it is the people who live within structures built of them, conditioned by these stones, these bricks, or this cement. In some cities there may be very important architects who have left their mark. Their names are known or not. There may also be other artists who have given them color. If we travel it is to go question certain places we know have something to say to us.

Some Italian cities leap immediately to mind as works of art having a certain number of principal "masters"—Siena, Florence, or Venice. There we have quantities of architects who worked together or successively and who realized these marvels of stone and bricks within which marvelous images wait for us. Venice for us is not only churches or houses on the edge of canals; it is a whole way of seeing that was born there; it is also a whole school of painting that lasted for centuries; it is also a literature, a music, and so on. It is possible to write not only books on Tintoretto or Titian but also books on Venice, to try to analyze the reasons for the effect Venice has on us. Why did they make the city like this, and why does it appear to us with such power of dream and revelation?

That is what I call the spirit of the place. A certain number of cities I have visited have spoken to me sufficiently for me to try to understand this spirit better. I have tried to analyze their spirit. I began with three cities that had especially impressed me: Cordova, Salonika, Istanbul. Each particularly interested me because of its historical stratification: at Cordova the Spanish partly covering the Arabs, in the big mosque become cathedral since Charles V of Germany, the presence of the tomb of a mixed-blood Inca, the great writer of colonial Peru called the Inca Garcilaso de las Vegas, son of an Inca princess and a Spanish general who was a cousin of the great poet. Similarly at Salonika, the superposition of the Greek and Roman sites, of the Byzantine city, of the Turkish city, and of the Balkan city of the postwar of 1914. To these three cities I added a text on Delphi, a dead city of which only ruins remain.

Then three little texts, two on Italian cities, Mantua and Ferrara, and another on a village in Crete, beside another great archeological site, Mallia, where I had to spend the night by mistake because I had not paid attention to the fact that it was Saint Sylvester's night, during which, on the island of Crete, at that time at least, the buses did not run. When the bus I wanted to take did not come, I found myself in this village, all alone, very small, unable to speak Greek well enough to make myself understood in such circumstances. But the mayor of the village took pity on me and I spent an unforgettable night, during which we played card games that were generally European enough to provoke all sorts of laughter and exclamations.

The last part is about Egypt, with three precise places: the little city of Minieh, where I had been a teacher; the big city of Cairo, which fascinated me; and the ruins of Luxor.

. . . . **34 Sites**

Not only can a city be studied as a human work with a certain number of authors linked to each other in all sorts of ways, but a site can be considered as a work. The choice by some men to settle in such or such a place is something decisive. Geography is thus charged with cultural choice of considerable aesthetic force. This is evident to anyone traveling in Greece. Most Greek ruins are not very impressive in themselves. The greatest Greek ruins are outside Greece, in Sicily or in Asia Minor. There are some very moving ruins in Greece, but they draw a great part of their power from the locale in which they are set. The site of Delphi is truly Apollonian. If one wants to understand what Apollo was for the Greeks, it is indispensable to go to Delphi and to Delos. If we want to understand ancient Greece and its mythology, it is necessary to go and see these sites.

I went back to Salonika recently and from there was taken to the digs in process on the site of Dion, at the foot of Olympus, home of the gods. As its name indicates, the temple of Dion is one of the principal sanctuaries of Jupiter, or Zeus. When Alexander left for his expedition to Asia, he began by going there to offer a sacrifice. I had the good luck to see a superb storm there and could feel forcefully what Zeus was for the Greeks. Greek sites are marked by ruins that are like labels indicating to us, for example, at Cape Sounion, that here there was a Poseidon site, a site of the god of the sea. In the cities the character of human work is particularly evident. But what one calls a "site" is, in general, quite simply a landscape.

There is, therefore, the possibility and the necessity of a geographical criticism different from the usual geography or touristic brochure. About a city like Florence or Venice we can have texts of very varied natures and types. We can have, for example, texts taking into account the writers who passed through and the way they saw these narrow streets, their vision conditioning ours like that of the painters.

· · · · · · 35 The Trip to the United States

I knew I would have to talk about the U.S. on my return, and the literary genre "My Trip to the U.S." or "My Return from the U.S." is one of the most glutted in European literature since the end of the war. Any writer who goes to the U.S. is required to recount his American experiences. Most of these books are, naturally, very bad, even those signed by fairly interesting authors. I was struck during my first stay there by the fact that these books were profoundly deceptive. They appeared to me to be net-works of misunderstanding. For example, in *L'Amérique au jour le jour* (From Day to Day in America), everything that Simone de Beauvoir re-counts is literally exact. She definitely does not try to deceive us. And yet the way she recounts the anecdotes prevents their having the sense she gives them. The meaning is constantly mistaken.

Thus I found myself facing the following problem: how could I succeed in talking about the U.S., recounting my own little adventures in this country, without their becoming false? How could I find a way to restore the mental and geographical American space in such a way that everything I recounted would become conceivable, even for Americans? I very much feared the American critics saying, "Another one of these little Frenchmen who spend a few months in the U.S. and who imagines he can give us lessons, that he has understood everything." So I patiently collected some materials that seemed able to help me talk about the U.S.

To avoid those justified criticisms on the part of American readers, I had above all to do the book on the basis of citations. It would be the Americans painted by themselves. I sought texts I could translate. In any translation there is much interpretation, and some of my translations in this book—I recognize it—are very critical and even very naughty. According to the stage one chooses in the word one is translating, according to the distance one takes between etymology and usage, one reveals completely different things. I thus little by little collected texts by great American men—Franklin, Jefferson, Carnegie—or texts from daily life—catalogs, prospectuses, texts edited by Americans and destined for Americans. Their study should permit me to make a sort of spectral analysis of another kind than that in the first *Génie du lieu,* an analysis of what goes on in the head of an American.

In spite of all the precautions I took, the same thing happened to me with this book, *Mobile,* as with some of the books I had criticized, which brought on a frightful scandal from which I have scarcely recovered.

How would I organize these citations, how would I make a sort of gigantic collage? I had models of literary collage in the U.S. with a certain number of great poets of the twenties. The fact that they had lived in Paris made them ready-made guides for me. Two were particularly important for me: Ezra Pound and William Carlos Williams.

On the other hand, in American popular art on the East Coast there is what is called a "quilt," eiderdowns covered with mosaics of fabric, sometimes of great beauty. I therefore sought to have American textual fabrics that I could cut and sew as the old American women in Vermont or New Hampshire did when they prepared, in their evening gatherings, the trousseau of a young bride.

· · · · · · 36 Returning Names

One of the points that struck me the most during that first stay in the U.S. was the phenomenon of reduplication, of reiteration. It is a phenomenon that existed already in Europe, but is considerably stressed in the U.S. I tried to make a model of American space, starting with the recurrence of certain names. Indeed, when one travels in the U.S., especially in a car, naturally, since that is the normal mode of locomotion over there (the person who does not know how to drive is disabled), one sees a certain number of place-names passing again and again. If you take one of the big highways that extends away from the east toward the west, you cross first, for example, the state of New York, and there you find the city of Springfield and that of Manchester. If you continue, you enter Pennsylvania, and you find again a Springfield and a Manchester. Then you cross Ohio, where you find once again Manchester and Springfield. You arrive in Indiana and, oh surprise! here are Springfield and Manchester.

These names of cities or towns, which return perpetually—I tried to use them like a cello, as the double bass does in jazz. I wanted to manage to make these words, which perpetually return in the landscape, return also in my text. I thus made a systematic study of the names of cities and towns. If I had had at that time a little computer at my disposal it would have spared me a great deal of work. But I had to transform myself into a computer. I tried to make a systematic index. I sought in particular which names were found again in two neighboring states. I hoped thereby to establish regions of vocabulary.

The book is formed of cells hooked to each other, all ordered by the key of a place-name that is echoed by a similar name in a neighboring state. The same name thus designates two places, then three, then twenty different ones. After many tries, I finally decided to arrange the states in the French alphabetical order: I put North Carolina under the letter C, whereas in an American alphabetical atlas it comes under N for North Carolina. I tried to make vocabularies specific to certain regions.

The U.S. can be considered a gigantic text. The country is, like all of ours in Europe, covered with words, which can be divided under three big rubrics:

First, Indian names, which, due to problems of transcription, are generally very long and are almost always unique. The same Indian name of a town is not found again from one state to the next. (Certain names of rivers are Indian and do cross state lines.)

Secondly, nostalgic European names. The Dutch who left the city of Amsterdam founded on the other side a New Amsterdam, occupied some time later by British who came from the city of York, or who, more exactly, were militarily linked to the Duke of York, and it was transformed into New York. Similarly, the French who went to Louisiana made a New Orleans. So we have in the U.S. quantities of Londons or New Londons, Yorks or New Yorks, Bristols or New Bristols, Parises, Berlins, and so on. All the nostalgia of the country left behind, often with deep regret, is expressed in an effort to reconstitute it. But they hoped that the trip had not been in vain, that this disquieting world that had been discovered would present some possibilities of improvement through its very newness.

Thus, thirdly, a nostalgic name is transformed into a utopian name, into a name of aspiration. It is this transformation that is expressed in the word *new*. But there are many other utopian names, in particular the names of great men, which baptize cities, towns, and all the rest. The most frequent name on American maps is "Washington."

Washington is first a little British city, as is Lincoln. Then they are the American statesmen who are felt to be paternal and prophetic symbols. In almost all states there is a Washington town and a Washington county, to which the town does not necessarily belong. There is a state called Washington. Almost everywhere the highest mountain or hill in the state is called Mount Washington. Many rivers bear this name. In the cities and towns we find Washington, Franklin, Lincoln Streets, and so on.

We have even more distinctly utopian names, for example, Eden, Harmony, Paradise.

The study of American topographical vocabulary alone gives us a spectral analysis of the U.S. and of its history.

ix

the squaring

The World Seen from a Plane

I like traveling by plane very much. I went to the U.S. for the first time on a ship, because there were still regular lines that crossed the Atlantic then and they were the cheapest transportation. Now that is over. I had already traveled by plane before going to the U.S.; I no longer know which was my first flight. But during that first stay I traveled around inside the U.S. a great deal by plane, and I found it an irreplaceable way to study the country.

Very often people tell us that you cannot see anything from a plane; even employees of airplane companies, who ought to be promoting their "product," tell you it isn't worthwhile to sit next to the window, because you can see only clouds. They are already an amazing spectacle, but what one sees besides, between the clouds, or when there is clear weather, is a landscape that is completely new, so new that we do not yet have models for it, or terms of comparison, or inventories, or references. Alas, very few painters have given us aerial landscapes. When we look at a landscape on the ground, we know what to compare it to in our culture, our usual museum. We isolate in what we see a Claude Lorrain, for example, or a Ruysdael, and now Claude Monets or Cézannes. There has not yet been a Claude Monet for the airplane.

Only a very few writers have been able to speak to us about what one sees from a plane. When we look through the windows we are astonished for the first few seconds, but then, since we do not know how to talk about what we see, we do not know how to name it, to compare it with what is in the museums, we give up looking. Little by little aerial photography is giving us terms of comparison. I think of the Swissair posters, which have certainly taught a great deal about how to look, not only to customers, but also to pilots and all the employees and managers. I very much like to look out airplane windows, and I have tried to write about views from planes.

Traveling by plane above the U.S., I have noted that regions one would not distinguish from each other very much when one is at ground level are in reality profoundly different. On the ground level there is a sort of unifying covering. One sees the same kind of names, signs, advertisements, fast-food restaurants. When one goes up, one perceives that there are very different organizing structures of the ground. One can distinguish at least three principal regions:

First, in the East, the Appalachians, the traditional landscape of the thirteen former British colonies, thus of the early American Republic, with a European structure. The cities and towns are the centers, with roads going out in a star to meet other centers, winding inside a fairly uneven relief.

Above this fundamentally European landscape there are a certain number of American traits whose specificity was much more evident at the time of my first trips than today. Europe has so much taken the U.S. as a model for the last thirty years that the surprise is definitely less great now for someone disembarking over there. Most Europeans do not suspect that a good part of their present-day landscape is an imitation of the American. It has been a very rapid evolution, which took at the most about ten years.

I think above all of the expressways. In 1960 there was not a single expressway yet in France. This German invention of between the wars came back to France via the U.S. These great straight or almost-straight lines crossing the landscape, with the interchanges adding loops to them, seemed to me extraordinarily new and beautiful.

The book *Mobile* is dedicated to the memory of Jackson Pollock, the American painter of the immediate postwar, who put his immense canvases on the floor and, standing over them, dripped liquid paint on them, which allowed him to materialize great journeys from one end to the other of this territory. He took possession of these rectangles by exploring them from one end to the other with lines to which his hand movements added loops that play in the painting the same role that interchanges do in the real landscape.

Another premonitory aspect of the U.S. of that period was the supermarket. In 1960 there was not a single supermarket in Europe. There was not a one of those little metal carts that we fill with all sorts of products in those wide aisles where we stroll a little as though in a city street, where we see people snatching cans or sacks with movements comparable to the line, to the dripping of paint by Jackson Pollock. Before my first trip to the U.S. I believed he was an "abstract" painter, as they said at the time; I found over there all his "realist" virtues. He taught me a great deal about looking at American daily life and its landscape.

Secondly, on the other side of the mountains, one reaches the Midwest, the country of the right angle, the most extraordinary realization on the face of the earth of one of the fundamental themes of our culture.

. . . . . 38 The Kingdom of the Right Angle

Since the origin of Indo-European cultures, one of the principal distinctions, much stronger than in others, is that between the right and the left, with preeminence given to the right. It is the origin of all sorts of expressions in our daily language. It is why for so long a time the left-handed were discouraged. They were an anomaly; you had to use your right hand, with all the practical and moral meanings linked to this word.

In all the European languages the word *right* develops an immense tree of meanings, most notably its university sense: the faculty of law, of justice, of right. On the right side we have the very clear geometric distinctions; on the left side, on the contrary, the tackings and the obliques. In French we have the technical opposition, used of craftsmen, between the person who is adroit (right) and the one who is gauche (left). We have also a moral meaning: justice, the good, is on the side of the right, the law.

We also have political meanings in which we are still entangled today. It is not because the progressivists were found on the left in an assembly that the word took on its current sense; it was because the word *left* already had considerable weight that those who wanted to overturn what was there naturally placed themselves on the left. It is because the word *right* and all the feeling of rightness is anchored in our language that the conservatives placed themselves on the right.

Passing to the other side of the Appalachians, we arrive at the most remarkable realization of a geometricization of the landscape. When you fly above these immense expanses, you cross a checkerboard with colors varying widely according to the seasons: black and white in winter; all sorts of greens in the spring; browns, fawns, and golds in autumn. The landscape is divided into squares or at least rectangles with great axes corresponding to the regulatory squaring off of occidental geography, the horizontals, which go from east to west, and the verticals, which go from north to south, or the reverse.

On the Atlantic side, the roads go from one city to another. People settled somewhere in a corner of the landscape, and it is from those preexisting settlements that the roads became clear. On the contrary, in the Midwest it is the general squaring off that controls. A city is thus a meeting point between a much used horizontal road and a vertical one, the thickening of a crossroad between a north-south line and an east-west line. Thumbing through American road atlases is particularly telling. Some states have almost perfectly rectangular squarings, with, at the meeting points, cities in which all the streets are at right angles, with obviously rectangular houses, inside which there are rectangular rooms with rectangular furniture.

This idea of the rectangle, which is not exclusive to the West—one should think of the layout of oriental capitals, Kyōto or Xian—has pervaded it at least since Greece. Already in the ancient period there are examples of rectangular networks—like Priene, now Samsoun, in Asia Minor. Rome is not organized this way, but Roman camps were, and a number of medieval cities reproduced this arrangement, because straight streets permitted easier surveillance. It was a preliminary sketch of what would happen in Paris under Napoleon III. [Baron Georges Eugène] Haussmann dug out the great boulevards so the cavalry could charge on the crowd more easily in case of a riot. In the medieval stronghold a single archer could control two entire streets going from one end to the other of the city.

Flying over the Midwest, one has the impression of traveling above certain works of other modern painters who are the great bards of the right angle. If one concentrates on the subtlety of colors of these squares one thinks of Paul Klee. He did not create his works to represent for us landscapes seen from a plane, but happily for us he painted them, which permits us finally to look at these landscapes and enjoy them. The other

champion of the right angle is the Dutch [Piet] Mondrian. Modern painting becomes realistic when one explores the U.S. this way. These painters
gave us eyes to see the New World.

This organization of reality in a geometric network in which one part of
space can be considered as equivalent to any other, in which an individual
place can be characterized by Cartesian coordinates, by numbers along two
rectangular axes, parallel and meridian, was imposed by the political power
of the East Coast. The right angle is linked to power, to the imperial. It is
linked to the reduplicating, the recurrence so characteristic of the language
of the U.S. Any habitation, any individual can be moved according to
certain axes.

Thirdly, when one approaches the Rockies, one reaches the region of
the deserts. Here we have completely straight roads, but they slice into a
completely different nature. These lines show us to what extent nature is
not straight.

Already in the Midwest there is an opposition between a posterior layer
or covering and an anterior layer, which is like the Indian names not
repeated in the language, a layer visible on the map in the capricious routes
of the rivers, which persist in winding inside the squarings, which have not
accepted submission to the right angle. From the plane one can very well
see through the grid the traces of this earlier world that they would like to
eliminate, to hide. The grid becomes that of a prison. This persistence of
what was on this continent before the arrival of the European is incarnated
in the mystery of the autochthon, of the Indian.

Finally, when one crosses into the mountains and deserts, the earlier
structures can no longer be engulfed. On the contrary, they are accented by
the modern trenches that open up on the West Coast, where characteristics
of the three other regions are mixed.

· · · · · · **39 Cells**

The squaring off of the Midwest is what is most characteristic in the U.S.
in relation to Europe. It is this structure that I tried to capture and use for
the organization of my text. It is formed of rooms, or cells, which combine
in different groups. They are made of two elements: a frame in roman
type, straighter, blacker; and inside it, a heart in italics.

The frame is formed first by those repeated place-names. Within a page I have placed, in perspective, cells belonging to neighboring states, cells laid out in rows that become increasingly narrow. Following the very common name of Springfield, I pass from Springfield in Illinois to that which is in Wisconsin, just to the north of Illinois, then to that which is in Minnesota, to the north of Wisconsin, and so forth.

There is a first margin on the left with the name of the city or town, followed by some lines in roman type. That is the opening of a cell. It will be closed by some other lines in roman. Inside this frame there is a heart in italics. The same name, belonging to a neighboring state, shifted relative to the margin, introduces a similar, narrower cell. Still the same name, but belonging this time to the neighboring state of this first neighbor, still farther shifted relative to the margin, introduces a similar, still narrower, cell.

The frame elements make what is in common and what is individual alternate. What is in common is the name and a certain number of signs, slogans, objects. The supermarket was then characteristic of American reality. It is the expression of an industrialized society in which objects are reproduced in a great number of copies considered to be interchangeable. What happened to books with printing is transposed in all that is called today "consumer objects."

Besides the consumer objects of food that we find even in Europe today in the supermarket, there are objects of daily decor. The U.S. is the preeminent country in the sale of objects by mail order. This system was inaugurated in France under the Second Empire by the brilliant inventor of the department store, Aristide Boucicaut, founder in Paris of the Bon Marché department stores, which still exist today, the model at the time of all those that have been disseminated throughout the whole world. Émile Zola showed the importance of this phenomenon very well in *Au bonheur des dames* (At the Ladies' Delight), where he made a masterful analysis of them. The French seed, transplanted to the U.S., took on impressive proportions there.

With mail-order sales, starting at shipping centers spread out over the territory, similar objects reach almost all sides. One can get to know them first in the department stores. When I arrive in a foreign country, one of the first things I go see if I will be staying some time is a department store, because it is the museum of daily life. If one goes to the fine arts or archeological museum, one will see what people do not have in their homes. In a department store, one sees what people have at home or what they would like to have. There are different prices, and the expensive objects shown help in selling the "cheap" objects, because the expensive objects are those people would like to have at home but which they cannot procure for themselves. They are "dear" in both senses of the word. They are dreams.

These museums of daily life have catalogs that are like dictionaries. For this book I took two catalogs of those years, Sears' and Ward's. Studying these catalogs would allow me to invent, to deduce, all sorts of particular points of American reality. In fact, flipping through them, I was certain that in a Clinton or a Springfield I could find one of the objects present on the page. These objects spread over all the surface permitted the creation of thousands or millions of probable American interiors.

In the frame a very widespread object touches the name of a river, an Indian name for example, thus very individual, or a particularly picturesque European name. That permitted me to create an illusion for some American friends, who believed in reading certain pages of *Mobile* that in order to write them I had been in the state where they lived and which they recognized, whereas I was far from having been in all fifty states at the time of that first stay. Today, still, after more than thirty years of trips to the U.S., I have not yet managed to visit more than forty. But in this book it was necessary at least to evoke every one of them.

In each cell were what I called, in my own jargon, in order to find my way inside this work, "coats of arms." Each state is characterized by a coat of arms. For example, all the states on the ocean, whether Atlantic or Pacific, are characterized by a little song or stanza of six lines in two columns, alternatively, which gives a movement of waves or tides, and which begins always with these two words: "the sea." Each time you see that, you know you are under its influence.

All the southern states, the former confederates of the War of Secession, have in their coat of arms the black problem. In some mountain states there is alpine landscape. In others, where the botany is particularly interesting, bunches of flowers appear, and in others, or the same ones sometimes, flights of birds.

Thus was constituted an image of the U.S. that should permit seeing the uniformity as well as the differences. The pages of the text look like grids. One has the tendency to move from one cell to another to follow a certain thread, and thus never to read but a part of the page. At the time of another reading, one will select a different route.

. . . . . . **40 Mammoth Cave**

For example, to bring out the individuality of the state of Kentucky, I took what Chateaubriand called a monument of nature. A little later, in another text, I devoted myself to what was for Chateaubriand the preeminent monument of nature of the New World, that is, Niagara Falls. Here it is a question of a gigantic cavern called Mammoth Cave, not because any remains of those animals have been found there. The term evokes here only its dimensions:

"Mammoth Cave National Park. Indians lived here. Mummies are found here . . . and moccasins. One hundred fifty miles of galleries have already been explored. Water filled with lime and other minerals drips down the walls and arches, forming stalactites and stalagmites, draperies, petrified fountains, phantoms, needles, pendentives, flowers of gypsum. Iron and manganese have added their yellows, reds, and purples."

Inside this cave there are guided tours. Men have felt the need to name what they saw there. Here is a list of the curiosities that have been baptized in this natural monument:

In Mammoth Cave, seven-mile guided tour. You can see there:
the temple of King Solomon,
the drapery room,
the crystal lake,
the saltpeter mines of the War of 1812,
the nuptial altar,
Jenny Lind's armchair,
the onyx colonnade, . . .

The cave acts like a sort of Rorschach test. The imagination projects itself on these forms, which one has difficulty naming at the beginning, like clouds, but which last longer than clouds. These efforts produce a cross-section, a spectrogram of mentality and mythology. The singular trip through Mammoth Cave, which one can only accomplish in that state, in that place, I link to elements that are spread over the whole U.S., such as a decoration for a bathroom that Montgomery Ward could at that time distribute to any town in any state. It is an earthenware covering made of plastic for which a whole rainbow of shades is offered.

We project our imagination into the caves and their details, but also inside the ranges of colors. It was fascinating to consult catalogs destined for ladies for their own beautification. The makers of lipsticks or of nail polish found wonderful terms, which sometimes equal those of our greatest poets. Unfortunately they are only little sparks. In the catalogs of the department stores, the colors are proposed only because it is hoped they will attract clients. They are seductive colors, the same kind as the great couturier's gamut of colors at the time of the presentation of his models.

But it is not only the colors themselves that must be seductive, but also the way they are named. In fashion, the passing from one range of color to another is critical. In the new range, there can be a shade that is exactly the same as one already in the previous collection, but it plays a different role and thus usually merits a different name to underline its newness, its power in fashion.

The catalogs of Montgomery Ward or of others tried to seduce their American clients of the 1950s with elaborate gamuts of colors:

Five new pearly tints:
cloud pink,
turquoise,
lemon ice,
mother of pearl,
apricot.

Note the gustatory character of this seduction.

Twelve marbled shades:
pink ice,
foggy green,
desert sand,
flame,
Dresden blue,
driftwood gray, . . .

I have two projections of the American imagination. I multiply them by each other by placing them in two columns, which I can slide, one in relation to the other. Here is what it looks like:

In Mammoth Cave, seven-mile guided tour:
the temple of King Solomon,
the drapery room,

Montgomery Ward proposes a covering of earthenware tiles of plastic for your bathroom:

Five new pearly shades:
        cloud pink,
        turquoise,
        lemon ice,
Mammoth Cave:
        mother of pearl,
the crystal lake,
        apricot,
twelve marbled shades:
        pink ice;
the saltpeter mines of the War of 1812,
        foggy green,
the nuptial altar,
        desert sand,
Jenny Lind's armchair,
        flames,
the onyx colonnade,
        Dresden blue,
the star room,
        driftwood gray,
the bottomless well,
        burgundy,
the misery of the fat person,
        charcoal,
the ruins of Carnac,
        heather green,
the freezing of Niagara,

caramel,
lemon zest,
turquoise,
solid white or black.

These two ladders multiply each other, because it is possible to slide them in relation to each other like two sliding-gauges. I can have:

the lake of crystal,
foggy green
the saltpeter mines of the War of 1812,
desert sand,
the nuptial altar,
flame, . . .

Or else . . .

And if you look at the text itself you will find there many other stripes.

X

flutterings of the Parisian heart

. . . . . . **41 The Difficult Birth of Europe**

One of the principal problems France has encountered in the second half of this century has been the difference between the space it occupied on the face of the Earth before the last war and then after. We have been present at the reversal of influence produced between Western Europe and the United States. Whereas until the last war the latter was still considered a colony, which had gained independence but remained a colony, after the war the United States achieved recognition as a cultural power and as transmitter of a way of life, which was admitted with difficulty by the former great powers, who saw their situation diminish considerably.

England was formerly at the head of an immense colonial empire that experienced divisions, first with the American Revolution, then with the establishment of the Dominions, which are still linked to the British Crown, but today in a purely nominal fashion. The rest of that colonial empire has been detached, often painfully. Holland reigned over all Indonesia, Belgium over the immense Congo, which has become Zaire plus several lesser states. Italy and Spain had colonial empires. Portugal still has one, more or less. Thanks to its colonial empire, France could pride itself on being the second power in the world from the standpoint of landmass.

All that has collapsed. The French Empire has shed its leaves. The French, like other Europeans, have had great difficulty admitting this transformation. England is very far from having recovered from it, and France has not yet really understood in its depths that the situation it had in the thirties is no longer the one it has today. France no longer has a colonial empire. It has cultural and sometimes economically privileged relations with countries that have developed on the remnants of that former empire. But there are many frictions, rancors, and even hatreds.

The city of Paris—which until the war of 1939 was universally considered the world capital of culture, and especially of painting—no longer plays the same role as before. Parisians, journalists, critics, Parisian administrators, the French government, had great difficulty admitting the decline or degradation. From this arose a sort of Parisian aggressiveness to try to recapture this empire that was ineluctably escaping. From this arose the great difficulty for the French to understand some of the phenomena going on outside their borders.

We are present now at the slow and difficult birth of the European Community. Its realization is an absolute necessity, but in a way it comes from the exterior. Almost all the governments now in place based their electoral propaganda on the fight against European integration. But when they won, they found themselves facing flagrant realities: they have had to forget their electoral proclamations and have been obliged to go toward Europe in spite of the public opinion that they had used, thereby accentuating the prejudices against it.

It is certain that one day Switzerland will be a part of the European Community, but it is also certain that if a referendum on that subject were proposed, the European Community would be rejected by an overwhelming majority, because of the education given in Switzerland. It was the same in France until the last few years. For most of the French it was viscerally impossible to be allied with Germany in a supranational community. It will take a gigantic reform of teaching in all the countries of Western Europe for these prejudices to be abolished.

When one refuses something, one builds walls to prevent that thing from being seen, hence difficulties for travelers. It is just fine to go see, to go do tourism outside one's country, but very dangerous to go there to learn.

Paris found itself wobbly in relation to itself, to its own consciousness, of which writers are an essential element.

The taste for travel puts certain people under suspicion relative to the

Parisian institution, which, feeling itself threatened, becomes aggressive. It seeks more or less to punish those who debate the preeminence it is still trying to claim.

If Paris no longer plays the imperial role it played, notably with regard to painting, for at least a century, it has not, however, been replaced by any other city, which would have become the Paris of the sixties. For a few years there was a strong rivalry between Paris and New York, also a very imperial city, a sort of duel that kept both French and Americans from knowing what the others were doing then. In fact, the French center had been replaced by a whole network of other centers, enclosing little by little the whole planet.

In recent years we have seen efforts, declarations of ministers, to defend French culture against the invasion of American culture, efforts made in vain because they were trying to wipe out symptoms without understanding what was underneath. If they diminished the quota of American films in French theaters, they did not prevent the diffusion of the supermarket system throughout all Europe. They acted only on the effects, without understanding the power of their roots.

The city of Paris held as suspicious those who went somewhere else, but as it still believed in its preeminence, it did nothing to keep them from going there. That provoked a sort of sourness and uneasiness.

Very attracted by foreign countries myself, I felt this suspicion more and more on the part of my publishers, of journalists, of my professor colleagues. I was doing something forbidden. I was putting the images of France and Paris in danger. I was uneasy if I stayed in Paris, but if I left I was condemned. I had to find a solution, a compromise, in order to live a good distance away. This is what more and more writers have encountered.

• • • • • • 42 The Trip around the World

In the first book of *Le Génie du lieu* I had wound around the Mediterranean. In *La Modification* the essential relationship between Rome and Paris was a fundamental theme. I tried to enlarge the circle. I tried to increase my trips outside the classic Roman orbit, to travel in a more vast circle. It is thus that I published a second volume of *Le Génie du lieu*, which winds around the Earth.

This work includes a certain number of accounts linked to the weather of a site. There are thus five "meteorological anecdotes" that wind around the Earth:

The mud at Seoul, in Korea

The rain at Angkor, where I was fortunate enough to go before the misfortunes of Cambodia

The fog at Santa Barbara, a city in California that today everyone knows because of a television serial, but at the time the genre did not yet exist

The snow between Bloomfield and Bernalillo, two tiny villages in Colorado and New Mexico, in which I told of an expedition with my colleagues of the time, at the university of the Mormons, in Provo, Utah

The cold at Zuni, an account of a festival in a pueblo, celebrating the winter solstice, a sort of Indian Christmas

A good part of this work was written while I was in the United States, in Albuquerque, New Mexico, in the Far West, at the edge of the desert. I had a little desk with a window looking out on a magnificent mountain, Mount Sandia, which resembles a little the Salève above Geneva, a very sharp cliff. For months I meditated in front of it and on it, on this world exterior to humanity. I found in it a little of the cliff of Minieh, in the valley of the Nile, of the Thébaïde. It is a site, but a site chosen as a limit. I scanned the entirety of a number of attempts at describing this mountain, in the obviousness of the impossibility of such an enterprise.

I had already written a text on Hokusai, the Japanese artist of the beginning of the nineteenth century, who published two series of engravings in color on Mount Fuji, thirty-six views, to which he later added ten new ones. Later he made a book in black and white, with gray, entitled *Cent vues du Mont Fuji* (One Hundred Views of Mont Fuji), but which I did not consider at that point. I tried to do a little as he had, to learn from him, but I wanted to mark my respect in making only thirty-five and nine views of Mount Sandia. All that is set within parentheses in which I tried to clarify a little my position relative to the city of Paris.

A German tourist magazine, *Merian,* which publishes an issue on a different place every month, asked me at that time for a text on Paris. They had published several issues on the subject. Awhile later I sent them a text titled "Je hais Paris" (I Hate Paris), which surprised them a little, but they read it and understood that to hate Paris in that way one had to be very attached to it. Since I was in Albuquerque I framed this text with a big parenthesis, which ended up surrounding the whole volume, called "J'ai fui Paris" (I Fled Paris).

I gave this second volume the title *Où* (Where/Or). This word can have two principal meanings, which are distinguished by a sign that is not heard, which functions only through sight, through reading. *Ou* can be the conjunction of alternatives: it is this or else it is that. *Où* can be the relative or interrogative pronoun that indicates place: Where are you? To distinguish it from the other one, one puts the grave accent on it. I specifically wanted to insist on the fact that one is never in only one place. One is always in several places at once. I am in Albuquerque, but I am writing about Paris. I am in Geneva, but I am talking about a book that I wrote in large part in Albuquerque and in which I talked about Paris and other places.

The alternative *ou* (or) is superimposed on the local *où* (where). I cannot say I am only in one place or another, [nor] in one place and another. That is why for the cover of this book they made a special printing character in which the grave accent on the word *où* is crossed out. It is present, so it is not only the alternative *ou*, but it is canceled, so it is not only the local *où*. It is *ou* or *où* (or, or where), a sort of cry, of ululating, hooting, which begins to wind around the entire Earth.

The book begins by the distancing from Paris to go all the way to Albuquerque. At the end one will have the return toward Paris. In the middle there is this sort of sarcastic elegy, which is "Je hais Paris." The text, entitled "J'ai fui Paris," gets progressively farther from the capital of France to cross the Atlantic and then the U.S., to arrive at the foot of Mount Sandia.

"I put between Paris and me a whole thickness of countryside: hedges, hollow roads, loops of the Seine, affluents of the Loire, willows, orchards, woods, and villages where the roofs are barely beginning to bristle with television antennae,

"then the ribbon of beaches with their guard of islands, cliffs, rocks, pebbles, dunes, swamps, and ports,

"the Atlantic Ocean, where the big ocean liners, more and more rare, only change their clocks every evening,

"American couples leaving to free themselves once and for all from all their obsessions with the country of their ancestors, elbowing the European couples returning from an exploration both fascinating and a little bewildering, to see if one could really live on the other shore,

"in the stretching out of hours with nothing on the horizon, the somewhat nauseated leisure where one indefinitely contemplates the waves, between two sittings of the movie, waiting for meals where one knows one will hardly eat in spite of the abundance of dishes,

"completely astonished by this silence that thickens inside them, like a white acid fog washing away a little of the miserable torment of their habitual preoccupations,

"by this talisman of silence scarcely touched by the cries of the gulls, the howlings of the wind, the gusts of raindrops, the beating of metal cables, the rumblings, the tremblings of the machines, which penetrate them through their feet, the clashes of dishes in the kitchens, the bells, the fragments of dance music crushed by the loudspeakers,

"and the trails of humming that the airplanes leave hanging very high up, usually on the other side of the clouds,

"where the most hurried, now most of them, squeeze the armrests of their seat a little anxiously, after having squeezed all the juice they could from a magazine or a novel now slipped in the open pocket in the middle of the back of the preceding row, look at their watch, calculate with difficulty the number of hours remaining before landing,

"the Ocean crossed by its river of warm waters where schools of fishes meet the trawl-nets,

"the archipelagos of ice come to melt in their driftings,

"and another ribbon of ports, enormous cities, swampy estuaries and sands,

"sounding with other cries of men and birds,

"then another countryside with apple trees and red barns, wooden villages, imposing cars,

"forests rising little by little in a long fold of lands split by the flowerets of highways,

"valleys spanned by their metal arches,

"and checkerboard plains, the immensities of wheat, corn, cotton, covered at this moment by snows or fogs, "drained by great winding rivers,

"and spots of deserts finally, reddish and fawn, becoming larger and larger, climbing slowly in furrowed plateaus up to the ragged mountains, Sandia among them, which I contemplate from my window."

Here appears the first of the thirty-six views of Mount Sandia, which I skip. Then, carried in its movement, the text returns a first time to Paris while continuing the circuit of the Earth:

"I am in the city of Albuquerque in America, in the middle of the state of New Mexico, in the valley of the Rio Grande, in the middle of the cowboys and Indians, and my house is eighteen hundred meters up, the sky is almost always clear; on the other horizon rise the cones of five extinct volcanoes, far beyond is Mount Taylor covered with blue snow, I know that the deserts and mountains continue a long time before subsiding among the vines and fogs of California all the way to the waves of the Pacific, almost complete liquid hemisphere, dotted with innumerable atolls, then what monstrous thickness of Chinese and Russian Asia, what concentration of hatreds and history in the Mideast, in Central Europe, before finding again the tiles of Burgundy, the slates of Ile-de-France, and the first suburbs of Paris spreading out!

"I fled.

"I breathe.

"I feel myself a little bit secure among the thorns, the screes, the canyons, in spite of this sputtering in my head, secure in spite of all that rises in my throat, for a little while, a very little while.

"I will try to explain to you.

"I have wanted to talk about it for a very long time.

"It is not here that I began talking about it. It was very near Paris, in secret, in one of the secret places in Paris.

"This is not at all what they asked of me. This is not at all what I thought I had to say.

"That is what I have tried to explain to you."

The whole first part of the book leads directly to this text, "Je hais Paris." At that time, before my first stay in New Mexico, we were living in the Parisian suburbs, at Sainte-Geneviève-des-Bois, just to the south, halfway between Orly airport and the gate of Orleans. Two voices speak to each other in the first and second person, one naively critical, the other sarcastic, describing with irony the former attachment, which is still present:

"I hate Paris. I am obliged to live near it, to go there several times a week, on the train, bus, or in a car, I form a part of these innumerable globules of suburban blood, which pumps without respite the urban heart."

And here is the second voice:

"Only a few years ago, I could not have imagined living anywhere but in the center, and, more precisely, on the left bank. To travel, certainly, to travel as much as possible, as far as possible and for a long time, but how could one have one's home port anywhere else?"

I isolate this dialogue among the other voices that are mixed with it:

"I hate Paris. I come back dog-tired; as soon as I leave for it a cloak of weariness falls on my shoulders. It will again be necessary to rush into the metro, the automatic gate will close just before I get through it; there will be so many people on the platform in the same hurry I am, counting as I will the accumulating minutes of delay; it will be necessary to dig a hole for myself in the solid crowd to manage to slip into the car, to let the doors close so the train can start up . . .
"As soon as I was far away, Paris was like a wound, I pined for my return, for my dear stations, dear platforms, dear churches, dear bookstores, galleries, cafés, and the look of the ladies, and the clouds. When the train or plane was approaching, what emotion!"

With these two principal voices are mixed, in fact, walks around various quarters of Paris, some of which are completely transformed today, trips in the metro with young girls of all races and colors passing by, and a kind of churlish litany. But I leave that all aside today:

"I hate Paris. I know there will be no taxis at the stands when I need them the most, when the buses are full, when the traffic lights insist on remaining green for cars just when as a pedestrian I would like to cross, that I will always be going in the wrong direction from the crowd on the sidewalks, going in, coming out of the studios, offices, and stores. I know I will miss one meeting out of four.

"Yes, remember: when you arrived you bathed in the movement of these avenues, the roar of the traffic filled you like a breeze. Yes, that still existed, you verified, you had then not been too imprudent in leaving, it had not all profited by your absence to disappear like a mirage, like a magician's trick.

"Now I hate its blusterings, its noise of the chicken-yard, its sickening smells of third-class restaurants, now I am beginning to free myself from this infantile attachment. I no longer have this hollowness when I live in another city, my heart does not beat so strongly on my return, I am no longer obliged to repress as before the sort of ridiculous song that wanted absolutely to burst out, I no longer plaster on my face that idiot air that surprised my comrades and made passersby ask questions. Oh, how I had to learn to hate you, Paris . . ."

That continues until the moment when I say to myself that if I hate Paris in this way, it is because there is indeed a visceral attachment, a badly cut umbilical cord, and it is appropriate therefore to make feelings evolve to an active equilibrium:

"Then when I come back, secretly, the most glaring and shrill days will be like a sweet night of relaxation, and all of Paris will finally be given back to me. I can quench my thirst again at its stones; the hands, the shoulders, the iris, the heads of hair, the crossed knees, the rainbows of lips will slip slowly along my eyebrows.

"And the whip of time passing lashes me and I go there.

"Then I shall taste you as if I were a stranger, as if I discovered you suddenly coming from the other side of the earth, and I said to myself: in another existence I must have lived here, I have known it all, the least doorknocker, the least geranium, the least fireplace, the least puddle of water or of blood

"—I set out again in the middle of the whistles, the balm of some beer at a café bar will attenuate these burns.

"I hate Paris, because it keeps me from seeing Paris, from being in Paris, from lying down there.

"I hate Paris because it forbids Paris to me."

The book ends, naturally, with the return to Paris, or, more exactly, to the Paris suburb where I was living at the time:

"I fled.

"I had to flee.

"At each moment that I spend here the countryside repeats to me: I had to flee. I had to put between it and me this ragged Mount Sandia, these steps of desert plateaus, these slow muddy rivers in the checkerboards of plantings,

"these trees, these furrows, and these beaches,

"this foam, these currents, and these migrations,

"these time changes and these reefs,

"these quais, these gardens, these ponds.

"But I am going to come back, it is no use insisting, I know very well that I will come back, you know I will not manage to resist you for very long.

"I am like a diver who takes a breath.

"There are only a few more months of space.

"O Mount Sandia!

"O lavas, pueblos, and trails, how I shall be devoured by impatience to see you again, as to see again so many other places studded in me!

"And, however, air, which I drink in big gulps, which enrapture me, deliciously spiced by the smoke from fires of pine cones, nothing, not even you, elixir, breathable gold, nothing, I know it, I lament it, I am resigned to it, nothing will be capable of keeping me back, I shall come back.

"With a sort of hatred and disgust in advance I come back.

"And I know well that an immense, deceptive pleasure will fill me and I will not even try to fight against it (not entirely deceptive, I know, I said that in a last burst of independence), and that exasperation, building little by little, I will soon have all my veins filled with your poison, Paris, and I will have to flee you, Paris, and I shall flee.

"But I shall come back.

"It is to make you drink that I shall come back.

"All the trips I make delineate your throbbing.

"And it is for you, for you that I breathe here.

"And it is for you, for you that I flee you here.

"And it is for you, for you that I hate you here."

. . . . . . **43 Southern Hemisphere**

At the very moment I published that book, I perceived a lack. Here is the little presentation that I gave on the flap of the cover.

"Sensitive to weather conditions, the narrator, traveling salesman in French culture, travels for a few years around the world giving courses and lectures. Coming from Paris without having been born there, he composes, on the occasion of a stay at Cauterets during which he hoped to improve the throats of his daughters, a few memories of a trip to the Far East for the attention of two professors at the University of New Mexico who had asked him for samples of narrative. Invited for an academic year to that establishment, he is lodged in a house whose windows look out on a high mountain.

"In the first volume of *Génie du lieu* his travels were limited to the Mediterranean area; in this one, more ample, they still do not go beyond the Northern Hemisphere."

I recognized that that was inadmissible and that I had to begin to prepare as quickly as possible a third volume, called *Boomerang,* in which, this time, I try to make the Southern Hemisphere appear also. Each time I have had a chance to cross the equator, I have seized it. I thus went to Brazil and Australia so that my sphere would be more complete. In *Boomerang*—the biggest book I have written, certainly the one that demanded the greatest effort, I shall never again make one like it—I travel a little throughout the whole planet, but still not enough.

To try to make things clearer, I used in it numerous interior signals. I needed a more complex system, but at the same time, if possible, one more striking, more immediate. That is why I decided to use three colors (and I succeeded by a miracle in persuading the editor): black (like ordinary books), blue, and red. Black is a color so usual in books that one does not notice it; it is as if the pages stayed white. The work, each time one leafs through it, will evoke blue, white, red, a certain number of flags: the French, but just as much the American and the Australian.

These three colors allow one to distinguish seven principal regions. Three can be characterized by a single color: one of them will be printed all in black, another all in red (Australia), a third all in blue (the United States of America). The one that is all in black is the exterior of the regions into which I go, those where I do not go, a mythic Africa, the preeminent black continent, in which one sees and hears animals swarming around a bird of particular concern to me, my totem, the bittern (*butor*). The combinations of colors will characterize other regions: blue and black for British Columbia on the west coast of Canada, red and black for the Pacific, other New World, other hidden face of the earth, red and blue for the musical exoticism of Rameau's *Indes galantes,* finally the combination of three colors will celebrate the carnival of Rio, responding to the one in Nice, where I lived then half the time, teaching during the other half at Geneva, on two borders, clearly farther from Paris than at Sainte-Geneviève-des-Bois.

The reader who has already looked around a little in the work knows in what region of the Earth and of the book he is when he opens to a page.

xi
travel

. . . . . . **44 Scansion**

My existence has been punctuated by a certain number of trips. I have already mentioned two that had a considerable influence on what I have written. First the voyage to Egypt: the discovery of another civilization, and especially of obscure regions in our history. It was after the trip to Egypt that I wrote novels. Another essential discovery: the first trip to the U.S., during which I had the impression of traveling in a possible future with both good and bad sides, with some things one could try to imitate, and others try to avoid. After that trip I never again published a book with the subtitle of "novel," which might seem strange, since one could say that today the U.S. is one of the classic lands of the novel, in the nineteenth as well as in the twentieth century.

Geometry originally meant the measuring of the earth. After a first *Génie du lieu* winding around the Mediterranean, the second winding around the Northern Hemisphere, the third, *Boomerang,* added a certain number of things concerning the Southern Hemisphere.

Two other countries have had a decisive influence on me: Japan and Australia. I have begun to try to give an account of this effect. As early as in the second *Génie du lieu* I alluded to Japan in those meteorological anecdotes concerning Seoul and Angkor. I have returned to the archipelago several times since. I spent a whole spring there two years ago. I went with

123

the intention of succeeding in writing something about this country. So it has been years since the first time I went there in '67 that I have been trying to talk about Japan. I have succeeded in writing a certain number of texts concerning Japanese works of art, classics of Japanese art. But that is not enough: I am therefore going to try again to give an account of this encounter. What is it that struck me so in this country?

Today Japan has become one of the principal items in the news. The development of the Japanese economy encourages businessmen to develop relations with it, and they travel there. What is fascinating is the link between an ancient culture, profoundly different from ours, and a modern industrial development that competes with ours. It is the most outstanding case of success of the absorption of Western culture by another. Until the present we had the impression that Western culture was destroying the others while absorbing from them just a little. Once they were destroyed, they were put in museums and studied in universities.

With Japan today one finds a culture that is both exterior to the West and successful in competing with it on its own turf. Thus many intellectuals are fascinated by the Japanese phenomenon.

Another country that has marked me also—less deeply, probably, but in a strange way—is Australia. When I went there for the first time I knew nothing about it. I knew only that there were kangaroos and tennis players. When I was invited to go there to give a reading, it was so far away that I could not resist. It was a matter of sport. The idea that they would pay for such a trip so I could read a text for an hour was almost fantastic. I took advantage of it to pass through the U.S. and give some lectures there, and I passed through again on my return to give others. At the time of this first contact, I stayed a week, naturally giving not only an hour's reading at the time of the cultural festival at Adelaide but a certain number of lectures in the two principal cities, Melbourne and Sydney. As soon as I found myself in this city, I said to myself: I must come back. There is something curious, bizarre there; I must try to elucidate it. Fortunately, I had the chance to go back twice for several weeks and to visit a large part of the continent.

First there is the question of geometry. Australia was for me the reverse of the Mediterranean. The latter is a sea around which, in antiquity, cities and cultures developed along a very narrow band. Australia, on the contrary, is a desert all around which, on the edge of the sea, which is this time on the outside, there is a band of development that in certain parts enjoys a climate similar to that of the Mediterranean.

Australia is inverted geography. And yet, it is a country whose nature is profoundly different from that of other continents. It is a kind of other planet in the interior of the Earth. It is this strangeness of nature, this challenge, that so impressed me. This is why in *Boomerang* it has an essential place. With regard to Australia, I believe I will not go back there very often. I believe I have written just about what I had to write on this subject in the section of *Boomerang* called "Mail from the Antipodes." As far as Japan is concerned, I have the feeling of being altogether at the beginning. Perhaps in coming years I shall succeed in finding the form that will allow me to advance.

I have been to many other countries that have also interested me. What I have done does not constitute a complete geography, not even a complete account of my own trips. There is another country where I hope to return soon, which has impressed me and which I am going to try to write about: Mexico, the America below the U.S., a level that I have already explored a little from inside the U.S. itself and Canada, in the second and third *Génie du lieu*. But Mexico is a window, a cellar window that is very vast.

. . . . . . **45 Absences**

What is strange in this collection is the absence of some regions of the Earth whose importance is nonetheless evident and has been decisive for some of my contemporaries. There are many places I would very much like to go—China, for example—and I hope that will happen. Many of my colleagues had the opportunity to go there at the time it was opening a little, before it closed up again. China had a considerable effect on them, but I have the impression today that this effect was superficial, that texts brought back from China (there was the genre "My Trip to China," just as there had been "My Trip to the U.S.") in the last twenty years have not succeeded in truly posing the Chinese problem. There was a certain fashion, long gone from sight now, of Maoism among French intellectuals, but that did not bring about true relations either with ancient China or with what could be really interesting in the China of these recent years, now under a cover, but which will open up again.

This absence within the ensemble of my texts is something I do not regret very much. I do hope that in the years to come it will be possible for me to discover this other world. I think the beginning of the third millennium will bring us extraordinary news from that side. I hope to be able to go there, and the sooner the better. It will be a prodigious adventure for me. But I do not think I have missed very much by not going yet. I have the impression that my colleagues, some very great, who went there did not succeed in piercing a certain propaganda that was offered them within the invitations they were given. I hope that invitations of another kind can occur in a few years.

There is another set of countries whose absence may appear surprising. These are the countries of the East. I have tried to increase the radius of my circles, my rings, my spheres. I have succeeded by choosing a certain number of regions that have especially summoned me. That has been possible only to the extent that there was some demand on the part of these regions, that there were invitations. The texts I have been able to write are the expression of a general relationship between numerous individuals. If I was able to discover the U.S., it was because there were numerous universities in the U.S. where French is taught. I give a representation of the Earth that is that of a Frenchman from the fifties to the nineties, of a Frenchman who writes within relationships that go beyond the international. The State is no longer what it was either, that summit of a pyramid such as Hegel imagined it and such as have imagined, following him, all the totalitarianisms. It is a matter then of intercultural relations that have developed all through these years or decades.

There is an almost complete absence in this representation of the planet of what was called, until very recently, the Eastern bloc, which was considered as half or almost half the world.

Realizing that the second *Génie du lieu* treated only the Northern Hemisphere, I had the feeling that the Southern Hemisphere was the hidden face of the planet Earth, in the same way there is a hidden side of the Moon, since the Moon always presents the same side to us; or rather, there was a hidden face of the Moon, since, for several years, the Soviet probes have brought us excellent photographs of this other side. One of the most beautiful moments in Jules Verne's novel *Around the Moon* is the one where one glimpses the hidden face.

· · · · · · **46 Hidden Faces**

The Earth also includes hidden faces. The Southern Hemisphere is one in many respects. It is gradually beginning to enter our consciousness of reality, beginning to enter into its own consciousness of reality. For the

Southern Hemisphere something is happening that is fairly comparable to what happened for the U.S. Until the last war, people in the U.S. considered themselves a cultural colony of Europe. The Southern Hemisphere still considers itself today a Northern Hemisphere turned upside down, bizarre, in which one is displaced. Within language this is vital. The seasons are reversed, but it is difficult to admit that the month of December is summer. It is a troubling term. The true summer for the Australian, Argentinean, South African, is that of the Northern Hemisphere. Instead of speaking of summer in December, they prefer to explain that the Australian winter is very warm.

The department stores, at Christmastime, when it is terribly hot outside, are full of artificial snow on which Santa Clauses dressed in furs slide along on sleds drawn by reindeer. The fundamental Christmas, the real Christmas, is cold. The twenty-fifth of December, in the whole Anglo-Saxon language and culture of Australia, is necessarily one of the coldest [days] of the year. It is hot there by mistake. It happens that by mistake in Australia it is the summer solstice, but language has not yet recorded that.

One can say that the Southern Hemisphere in general has not yet understood that it is in the South. Language has not yet succeeded in making its corrections, so one can find evidence of the most elementary astronomy. It is thus a face hidden to its own inhabitants.

Another hidden face: the Pacific Ocean. Indeed, it occupies almost half the Earth, but for us Europeans it is what is on the other side, what is the farthest, and there is no big continent in the middle to balance ours. That is why, when the navigators began to make the trip around the world more frequently and perceived that in going one way they had to set their watch forward, and on going the other they had to set it back, which gave birth to the notion of time zones, the astronomers decided it was necessary to fix that. Indeed, going toward the east one has to add hours and hours, and going west one has to take them away. After having changed the clocks twelve times on each side, one finds oneself in the Antipodes with a lag of twenty-four hours, that is, one day. Navigators who meet on the other side of the earth are thus no longer on the same date as we, which is intolerable. The English and French astronomers of the eighteenth century therefore decided to trace a line essential for our present-day life, the international date line, where the correction officially takes place, where one sets not only the clocks back to the correct hour, but also the calendar to the correct day.

They put it naturally at a place where they thought it would not disturb anyone, on the other side, in the very middle of the Pacific. It was a place where no one important, or with good sense, went. There was a navigator from time to time. Now that is no longer the case at all. Most of us have crossed the international date line. I crossed it myself, for example, to go from the U.S. to Australia and to come back. But back then, from the point of view of Western Europe, it was a region that, so to speak, did not exist. It was like those margins for the ancient Romans, which were so far away that it was not worthwhile to know too much about them, because from them could come forth only disturbing monsters threatening to destroy what they had gone to so much trouble to set up.

Today the Pacific is revealed as a sort of other Mediterranean, enormous this time, and the people who are all around it have more and more relations with each other and are in the process of inventing something new, echoes of which reach us gradually. The relations between the West Coast of the U.S. and Canada, on the one hand, and Australia, New Zealand, and Japan, on the other hand, are multiplying, and that is why atomic tests in the middle of this region—which, for a French government, is so far away that it could not bother anyone—will soon no longer be possible. To make them at Muroroa would be as if they were made in Sardinia or Corsica.

Another hidden face: the Eastern bloc, that other world that existed beyond the Berlin Wall, today in the process of very rapid transformation but which for years was so immobile. All this region of our planet has had considerable importance for some French intellectuals and writers, and for me too. I have never been politically militant for anything whatsoever, but I have never hidden my sympathies for the parties on the left. How does it happen that I do not, so to speak, mention them at all? Certainly the invitations have been less numerous. Yet there have been some. I have been to a certain number of these countries.

The first were Bulgaria and Yugoslavia at the end of the fifties. Then during the year I spent in West Berlin in 1964, I had occasion to go to the east of the city, which was not, incidentally, very agreeable, and I was invited to Hungary and to Czechoslovakia. The city of Prague overwhelmed me. It was before spring, the month of March. I speak of a mental month of March, because I no longer know the exact dates. All sorts of things were beginning to sprout, to bud. Then there was the brutal repression. I was also invited to spend ten days in the Soviet Union, three days in Leningrad, as they called it then, four in Moscow, three in Kiev.

I saw that this so-called Eastern bloc is also a hidden face, and that the usual representation we had was completely false, that it was in reality a mosaic of peoples who hated each other and who were held together only by a police regime, which only exacerbated the hatreds. In my Western naïveté I thought that they spoke Russian from one end to the other of the Soviet Union, that there were probably remnants of ancient languages here and there, as in France some old people still speak Breton or Nissard.[1] Going to Kiev I immediately realized that my charming interpreter from Moscow was unable to understand a word of Ukrainian and that the Ukrainians refused absolutely to speak Russian. Thus it was necessary to have an interpreter for the interpreter. The uniformity and understanding that we imagined was a pure illusion.

I have spoken a little about Prague in a special way, in accounts of dreams, but in the *Génie du lieu* series, nothing about these very superficial visits to the other side of the iron curtain, which has become a rusted curtain. Why have these countries not set off the same mental revolution as the U.S. or Japan? Why Australia and not Russia, since I had also visited a little of Russia? It would probably have been necessary for me to stay longer to penetrate the shell.

But I believe above all that what provoked this gap was profound disillusionment. In all these countries I was intrigued by all the evidence of the past, ancient or recent. But I found almost no sign of discovery, except in Prague in the period before the spring. I felt I was traveling in old-looking, out-of-date countries, which was catastrophic given the passionate hope that so many people and societies had lodged in them then, toward and against so many successive contradictions.

I had the feeling of a freeze. A story that had started fairly well had jammed, and the only thing to do was to wait until that changed. In Prague I had had the feeling that it was going to change, in other countries that it could change. But the brutal repression of the Prague spring smothered all that in the egg; now one could only wait for it to collapse. It was necessary to wait a long time, and in that respect it was useless for me to return to those countries until now. Just as well to wait somewhere else. Today, already, everything appears different.

The problem of Eastern Europe, of the former Eastern bloc, is comparable to that of China. I was still more intrigued by China because its immense cultural tradition and its great distance from the West mean that when it really becomes capable of absorbing Western technology (and we are really on the eve of that), it will bring prodigious discoveries. I shall go, as relations are changing; my trip will be an expression of that, and many others in addition to me will go, listen, and question.

It will soon become intriguing to travel also in the Eastern countries, because those people will find themselves facing such problems, with such disappointments, that they will be obliged to invent new ways to pose the problems. They will certainly not be content to imitate passively the West, to be helped by the European Community, the World Bank, or the United Nations. They will have to find sense in what they experienced during communism and before. I still have work to do.

The problems that I have been able to treat in intercultural relations are only a part of those with which French intellectuals and writers have been confronted in the second half of the twentieth century in their discovery of foreign lands. We are only at the beginning. More and more imagination will be required on the part of writers, more and more effort and patience on the part of the readers of these writers.

xii

the gift of languages

. . . . . . **47 The Tower of Babel**

We can use the word *language* in a very general way. We can speak
of "musical language" or of "pictorial language." But I am going to use
it today in its restricted sense: different languages—Japanese, English,
French . . .

When we travel we are often stopped by linguistic barriers. A Frenchman arriving in Japan encounters enormous difficulties because of the
profound difference between the two languages. Thus we dream of a state
of things in which there would be only one language, which would greatly
aid us in understanding one another. In the Christian religion the story of
the Tower of Babel is told. Formerly, the Bible tells us, men all spoke the
same language. Seized with audacity, they wanted to construct an enormous tower that would reach all the way to the sky. God was concerned
and pronounced this remarkable sentence: "Now man wants to become
like God," as if by constructing the Tower of Babel man would become the
equal of God. God then defended his privilege by punishing man with
what is called the confusion of languages. There in the midst of collectively
constructing this splendid work, men stopped understanding each other.
From that time on, instead of a common language, they have had many
different languages. They scattered, and since then have never managed
really to understand each other.

131

The writer depends a great deal on the language in which he writes. First, anyone writing in French has a possible public much less large than someone writing in Chinese or in English. Therefore, even for basic economic reasons, many of us would like to go back to a time before Babel. Shall we all then begin to speak the same language?

Today most countries in the world use English to communicate with one another. Specifically, it is English that has become the language of science. Scholars, whatever their origin may be, most often publish their results in English. Therefore in English-speaking countries there is a tendency to conclude that not only should the whole world learn English, but also that it should forget the other languages.

This point of view is particularly popular in the United States, a country formed of immigrants, of whom only a part were originally English-speaking. In order to survive, Italians and Greeks were obliged to learn English as quickly as possible. The need was so vital that in many families it produced a violent rejection of the native language. This is what is called the phenomenon of the third generation.

During the nineteenth century and at the beginning of the twentieth, immigrants often had great difficulty learning English. Thus they continued to speak Italian or Greek at home. Their children had the tendency to speak only English, but, as another language was spoken at home, they learned it even though they no longer wanted to speak it. Since this native language was considered the source of all kinds of difficulties, they tried to cover it up and used it less and less. So the grandchildren of immigrants, the third generation, no longer hear the language of their ancestors spoken at home at all. Hearing it sometimes at their grandparents' home, they reject it. It is only later that curiosity comes. The great-grandchildren know that they came from Italy or Greece; they want to know what those quasi-fabulous countries were like. They will thus relearn the original, lost language.

Those people who had so much difficulty making English their own language, or who remember the difficulty their parents had, want others to go through it too. In the United States they have seen English become the language of all prior nations. They therefore have a tendency to believe that that process will be generalized. It must be recognized that many aspects of the issue suggest that movement in this direction has been initiated very seriously.

But other languages will defend themselves against English, first of all for nationalist reasons. The Japanese language is a rampart against indiscreet foreigners. It is well known that Japanese industry and commerce draw considerable advantage from the difficulty of their language and writing for Westerners. In a business conversation, the Japanese person almost always has the advantage because, if he is capable of expressing himself only in an English that is not much worse than that of his French interlocutors, he is also capable of speaking with his colleagues in a language that functions as a secret code.

One of the problems of Europe today is defense against the control, the preeminence, of the American economy. If Europe is being unified, it is not because the European people want to be. Indeed, all Europeans have been taught in schools where it was explained to them that their nationality was the best and that they had hereditary enemies whom they must always mistrust. French children still learn today that they must mistrust the Germans, the British, or the Italians.

Electoral speeches mention the necessity of a European union only in driblets. For years all French political speeches had as their principal theme French grandeur, French independence; it is only slowly, because of external pressure, that politicians have allowed Europe into their programs. Only those French who have traveled a great deal realize the necessity of a European union; the rest do not suspect it.

In European institutions it is necessary to use common languages to communicate. The British believe that a common language is needed, which can only be English because it already almost is, to which the other European countries reply that the English language today is actually the language of the United States, particularly in the economic domain. Now, it is the American economic danger that has provoked the establishment of a federation in Europe; to adopt their language would be to renounce self-defense.

Then the French declare: We have the clearest language in the world, which not very long ago was that of diplomacy. Why not go back to that state of things, which was so advantageous for us? But it is certainly only in France that people imagine French could be the only common language of European institutions. It is the subject of interminable jokes among other peoples.

The solution can only be to conserve all the languages, and to use them; but that presents such difficulties and complications that European institutions have not yet succeeded in truly posing the problem. There are still too many living languages in Europe to be able to use all of them all the time. We must convey some languages via others. That is what happens today when we have the use of all national languages, though with translation into a certain number of languages that are considered common languages. The question obviously lies in knowing which languages are to have this privilege.

At the United Nations, the common languages are English, Chinese, Russian, and French, which does not cease to provoke discussion. Since communist China for a long time was not represented in the United Nations, the Chinese used there was primarily the language of Formosa, and Chinese was almost abandoned as a common language. This problem is posed in a very different manner today.

The conservation of national languages will increasingly require, on the part of the languages considered principal and which are used as common, the recognition of all the secondary languages. It will not be long before the Norwegians accept the use of German or French as the common language in a meeting only if the Germans and French make an effort toward the Norwegian side. This will require, after awhile, considerable reform in European education.

· · · · · · 48 The Teaching of Languages

Europe cannot be unified and maintained unless there is profound reform in the teaching of History in each of these countries, from the primary school up, because it is at that level that images are formed, the fundamental figures of the foreigner: what a German is for a Frenchman, an Italian for a German. Present-day education will not permit the Europe of 1992 to function appropriately. There is thus a great urgency, but there is as yet no project for serious educational reform in this regard in the different countries.

On the university level there must be a transformation of the teaching of law, and on all levels a transformation of the teaching of languages. Some young French students must learn Norwegian if they want enough young Norwegians to learn French.

But one cannot stop with national languages. In numerous countries several languages are spoken, even if only one is considered official. France, a very centralizing country, has made a great effort for the unification of language, which is a very efficient means of government. The person who knows well the language considered official and obligatory always has the advantage over the person who knows it poorly. When the language of the elegant neighborhoods of Paris became the national language, Paris strengthened its power greatly. Since the accent of a provincial is seen as ridiculous in Paris, he will try to hide it and to give himself as Parisian an air as possible.

It was not very long ago that several languages were spoken in France, some very different from French. Pursued in the nineteenth and the first half of the twentieth century to the point that children were forbidden to speak them when they started primary school, they have been gradually eliminated. It has only been for a few years that Breton has been taught in the universities of Brittany. The universities waited until it was virtually dead. Today, other than a few specialists, there are no longer any but the very old who speak Breton. The same process has eliminated little by little Basque, Alsacien, Provençal, and Nissard. Only the Corsican language still possesses some vitality. This point demonstrates very well the problem this island poses for French policy.

If Basque is no longer any more than a memory in France, it is still widely spoken in Spain; the problem posed in that country by Catalan was happily resolved with the collapse of the Franco regime. A romance language with a very large literature, spoken by a more numerous population than those of many independent countries, Catalan was forbidden in the time of General Franco, not only in schools, but in public places. People caught speaking Catalan in a café in Barcelona could be arrested for that reason alone.

Well before the collapse of that calamitous regime, I served on the jury of an international literature prize, which has long since disappeared, originally held in Spain but which, because it manifested very clear opposition to the ruling regime, after awhile had to hold its sessions in other countries. It was a prize organized by a group of editors from several countries. There was a Spanish editor, an American, an Italian, a British, a Norwegian, a Swedish, a Danish, and a French. I remember that at one meeting, when some Spaniards proposed a Catalan author, the Danish editor had the imprudence to say, "We cannot take an interest in these provincial languages." The Catalonians present stood up to retort, "Sir, you are fortunate that your country was separated from Norway a few years ago. As for us, we have the misfortune of living under a regime that forbids our language, but you should know that there are four or five times more people who speak and read Catalan than Danish. Aside from the flukes of politics, it is rather the Danish language, in spite of all its great writers, Andersen or Kierkegaard, which should be considered a provincial language." One can imagine the furor that would have broken loose if there had been a Belgian editor and if someone had referred to Flamand as a provincial language.

The problem that is posed to Europe is not only that of national languages but, increasingly, that of languages actually spoken, which are really "maternal" languages. One can say, indeed, that language is a womb or belly from within which we are born. It is language that forms all our first ideas, which brings us everything about which we do not question. Everything that seems to be a matter of course is what is inscribed in language. When someone is deprived of his maternal language, when he is forbidden to speak it, he is disabled. He will always consider the language imposed on him as artificial; he will never feel he is speaking it perfectly. There will always be a discord in his thought or imagination between what seems to be a matter of course and the way in which he is obliged to express himself. When we forbid a language, even gently, we deeply wound those who were born into it.

The plurality of languages cannot be uprooted. We must therefore think and work always within that plurality. This is something that was difficult for people in the generation before mine to admit. My parents or my grandparents certainly felt the close relationship linking language and personality, but the consequence they drew from it was precisely that it was dangerous to learn foreign languages. I have taught French myself in various countries, and I have seen numerous Frenchmen who lived there for awhile absolutely refuse to learn, even a little, the language of the country, saying that if they learned the language of those people they would do them no favor, for the most useful thing they could do would be to force them to speak French. They even declared in apparently scientific language that bilingualism provoked psychological disturbances.

More and more people are bilingual by necessity. We must therefore accommodate these disturbances, transform them into an advantage. The differentiation of languages at the Tower of Babel certainly produced much unhappiness, but we can no longer consider that a punishment. An immense advantage results from it. The plurality of languages brings us great richness, because each language is a different world.

Each language is a different approach to reality. Our personalities are born within one or several languages, and each literature is created within one or several languages in evolution. The work of Shakespeare is magnificent, but it is possible only because of English, a world richer still.

We are beginning to perceive that we are destroying our environment in a very serious manner. Beautiful species of animals are disappearing one after the other. At the moment of their extinction we try to get them to reproduce in zoos; we launch publicity campaigns to save the giant pandas. Certainly we lose a great deal when an animal species disappears, but when a human language disappears we lose something that concerns us even more directly. Many languages are in the process of disappearing today before anyone has been able to study them seriously.

We must therefore conserve the plurality of languages, not only from one country to another, but within a country, and within individuals. As soon as we travel with a little intelligence we take on a tint of the language of the country. Even if it remains superficial, it brings us new tools.

. . . . . . 49 Translation

The writer often envies other artists because he has the impression that they are not bound by linguistic barriers. We often say that music or painting is universal. This is an illusion precisely to the extent that these arts can be called languages. One learns little by little to listen to different music and to have a taste for different paintings. The boundaries are not the same and crossing them is often easier, which means that if we find difficulties in comprehension we do not have true problems of translation in these domains.

Translation is an essential given of literature today. I have written many books and have had the good fortune to see some of them translated into several languages. I would like there to be still more; I hope with all my heart that it is only a beginning, but already it has been essential for me. When the first translation of one of my books appeared—in German, I think—I had a feeling of victory; something was really beginning; I was going to conquer the world through the intermediary of translation and thus of my translators, for I am incapable of translating my work myself since I know only very few languages, and even someone who knows two languages very well has difficulty in translating his own texts. Samuel Beckett, whose maternal language was English (a maternal language at the same time both detested and adored by this Irishman who did not know Irish, thus a child stolen from his true maternal language), began to write in French, which he knew as admirably well as English. What an opportunity to translate himself his own texts from English to French, or the reverse! But he almost never did it. He preferred to ask friends to do it for him.[1] For the author the text is so attached to the language that the translation requires a complete remodeling. One might as well translate someone else's text, because one is then obliged to respect it; one does not feel one has the right to remodel it.

Translation naturally implies collaboration; the good translator develops an affinity, of an almost familial nature, with the original writer. Three levels in criticism can be distinguished: that of the journalist who talks about a book that has just appeared, who often understands nothing about it, and who has not taken the time to read or to engage with it; that of many commentators who have understood the text, know it well, but say only what I already know, do not bring me anything; and that of the one who reveals to me what I did not know in my books. This is the great critic; he often gives me quantities of new ideas. I do not know how to thank him.

The good translator is a critic in depth. He must bring to the text something profoundly new; that is his language, and all the more as this language is further away. He must thus question the text from his own language, exploring all sorts of aspects that remain unknown to the author himself. Certain translators know much better than I some of my texts, because I have forgotten them and also because they project on them a different light, which reveals for me tunnels and passages in myself.

Translators represent an irreplaceable relationship with reality for me. I have tried translation a little myself, to experiment somewhat with this research, but I have never dared translate a living author.

My texts are often considered difficult. One day my German translator said to me, "When you write, you ought to consider us a little, because there are moments when it is really too difficult." But if I tried to compose a text in such a way that it would not be too difficult to translate into German, that would change absolutely nothing in the difficulties of the translation into Japanese.

Toru Shimizu, who has translated several of my books into Japanese, including *La Modification,* found himself one day in Paris at the same time as a Chinese woman from Shanghai who had just published a translation of the same book into her language, and I asked him if he would like to meet her. He assured me he would be very happy to. Then, drawing back a little, he said, "But how can one translate such a book into Chinese?" I said to him: "But you certainly translated it into Japanese!" "Ah! That isn't the same thing at all; in the Japanese language there are aspects which . . ." I do not know Chinese at all, but I am sure that there must be some aspects that would allow certain passages to be easier to translate than into Japanese. Each language questions the text differently, multiplies it. That is why, far from attempting to facilitate the task of my translators, I try to use the French language in all its specificity, to exploit its possibilities to the limit.

One of the characteristics of French relative to most of the present-day languages that I know a little is the extraordinary arsenal of verbal tenses, the way in which conjugation works to show temporal succession. It is certainly very difficult to learn for a foreigner, but what a marvel! I do not want to allow any of the forms of the French verb to perish.

Young French children used to be taught much grammar, but only French grammar for the French. When I began to teach French in foreign countries, those languages questioned me about mine, permitted me, forced me, to learn anew my own language and to see it a little from the outside.

The translator will be obliged to find in his language a way to say something that is expressed in a particularly natural and simple way in French. He must thus transform his language. A great translator is an inventor, and all the more so the more faithful he is.

. . . . **50 Multiplication of Languages**

We can study the language of a writer in relation to ordinary, spoken language. He uses only a certain number of the words collected in the dictionary, often many more of those used in popular conversation, and he even alters the frequency of their use.

We can study the newspapers appearing during one year, and we can see that one word has been used a hundred times, another five thousand, some only once. In the same way, each writer has a vocabulary of his own, and within the common vocabulary he has frequencies that are proper to him; these, along with many other elements, will define his style. The translator is obliged to invent a new style inside his own language. He does work then that is somewhat comparable to that which the writer did in his original language, but the translator does it backwards in a way. The writer uses the properties of his language in relation to others, while the translator is obliged to twist his own language to force it to express what at first sight it could not. He brings about a fundamental transformation; he considerably enriches his own language. We rarely give the translator the respect and admiration he deserves.

Languages are and ought to remain different from each other; each offers a different point of view on reality, but they must integrate the points of view of other languages more and more. We must continue to speak Japanese, but we must also learn to speak English or French in Japanese. In the same way we must surely learn to speak Japanese in French.

People already often speak English in French, but it is a matter often only of introducing English words, which keep their foreign nature. These are technical terms especially, which spring up like little islands, ice cubes gradually trying to cover the surface of the linguistic ocean, strongly manifesting a dependence on American culture. We speak in French of "jet" and of "hamburger," and these terms are impossible to translate. But such colonialization is not at all satisfying. We must learn to use not only certain terms, but the riches of English grammar and expressions, which can be done only through the intermediary of the best translations, consequently those of great literary works. As of that moment, cultures will speak as equal to equal and something new will begin.

We must become multilingual and thus make our texts multilingual, even if for the most part they keep a basic language within which the others begin to carry on dialogues. It is somewhat like the relationship between the narrator and the characters in a novel.

This is less extravagant than it appears. Languages are historical edifices; one of the fundamental aspects of the literary text is the use it makes of several historical levels of language: into speech one hears in the streets today, the text mixes classic French as it was painfully taught us in the primary schools of our childhood, with its pomp and its elegance, and even its archaic terms or expressions. Time passes within the text, where it is already easy to reveal multilingual phenomena inside a seemingly single language. A certain linguistic school's insistence on synchronic phenomena, that is, on the study of the language as it is at a given moment, has neglected the very important diachronic phenomena. Fortunately, current linguistics is abandoning some of its presuppositions that were once useful but which today could only hinder it.

In literary language we travel from one moment of the language to another, and we can point out phenomena of translation within the same language. French of the Middle Ages is unintelligible to anyone who has studied only today's French. The average French reader cannot read *La Chanson de Roland* or the works of Chrétien de Troyes in the original. We are obliged to translate. But as the evolution is continual, the difficulty is knowing at which moment one should begin to translate. The text of Rabelais is so difficult to understand for some readers today that some editors now publish the text with a facing-page translation in modern French. There is a whole range: translation, notes, commentary.

In classical literatures we often find phenomena of historical multilingualism. I think of the presence of Chinese within Japanese, of Latin and Greek within French. Let us look at the author we may consider the most French of the French, the one who used ordinary Old French in the most extraordinary way: the text of Montaigne is stuffed with Latin, Greek, and Italian citations, which he kept on increasing in his successive editions. There the languages play with one another.

Latin was considered the mother tongue of French. Behind the "maternal" language there were grandmother languages, Latin and Greek; Italian was then rather like an aunt. One did not work in only one language, but in a whole family of languages. In Europe, beginning in the eighteenth century, French began to play a role somewhat comparable to that of Italian and Latin before. English has two fundamental layers: a German stage, Saxon, and a French stage, Norman. Some writers use one vocabulary rather than the other, succeeding, in this way, in sometimes writing Latin or French in English. In this respect English is a much more supple language than ours and could teach us something.

· · · · · · 51 Languages Travel

In the twentieth century, as the frequency of both business and tourist travel continues to increase, the intersections of languages occur more and more often. Some writers will be the writers of present-day travel, of this essential given of our contemporary life. One name comes immediately to mind: James Joyce. Some say that in *Ulysses* he tried to use all the words in the popular English dictionary. This is certainly false; it would require a much more vast work, but it does indicate a certain tendency. We know that it is a narrative in English of a day in Dublin, the capital of Ireland. The different chapters or episodes are closely related to the books of the

Odyssey. Thus it is a translation, in a very broad sense, of that poem into a language and a culture of the beginning of the twentieth century. Within this general translation we can see all sorts of parodies, as the style of one region or of one epoch is applied to another. Each chapter has a different style, and one of them follows the evolution of the English language through several of its great writers from the Middle Ages up to the period contemporary with the writing and the narrative.

These preoccupations reappear, are carried further in his last work, *Finnegans Wake,* a title that is itself fairly difficult to translate into French because of its pun. The word *wake* in English designates a funeral vigil, and there is a celebrated Irish ballad, but in the English language, on the funeral vigil of a certain Finnegan, entitled *Finnegan's Wake.* By omitting the apostrophe, Joyce puts the proper name in the plural: the Finnegans are awake or waking up. Thus it is a reawakening of traditional Ireland, which is shaking itself free of the English occupation. In the English of this work Joyce introduces words that come from all sorts of other languages—Irish, of course, but also French, Italian, Latin, and so on—and he constantly makes plays on words from one language to another. Naturally, this makes for very difficult reading, but everyone, in accordance with his culture, will find different ways through it. The reader from an Italian culture will first identify the Italian words and expressions; the French reader, those from his language. For the same reader things will change from one reading to the next. It is a text that swarms, in which everything stirs under our eyes, where the meanings are multiplied.

The text is structured by the use of very well known European legends, so we always know to some extent where we are, but the way the stories are told changes constantly. This was a decisive experiment in multilingualism. Certainly it is not written in all languages, but in an English that gradually becomes capable of adopting everything coming from other languages.

Samuel Beckett is an Irishman whose mother tongue is English. It is a mother, but a cruel mother admired and detested at the same time, a wicked stepmother. When he began to write in French he deliberately used a rather limited vocabulary, the meager language of an exile, admirably adapted to the narratives about unfortunate people, about the misery of those who talk all the time without ever managing to say what they mean. Beckett was a sort of student of Joyce; in addition, he took part in the first effort to translate a passage of *Finnegans Wake* into French. For Joyce, too, English is the wicked stepmother. They speak English in Ireland today, but the official language is Irish, which is almost never spoken anymore. Linguistic occupation subsists after political occupation. In the spirit of resistance and revenge, Joyce would have liked to speak English better than the English themselves; the ideal would have been to succeed in making them ashamed of their ignorance of their own language, the language they had imposed on others. This attitude is frequent in those who have problems with their mother tongue.

In France we have a very typical case of this kind, Apollinaire. The man we call Guillaume Apollinaire had a Polish mother; we do not know for sure who his father was; he, in any case, did not know. His mother admired the emperor of Germany immensely, and that is why the young Kostrowitski had the given name of Wilhelm, with Apollinaris as a second given name. Our poet felt it essential to change his name, to replace Wilhelm by its French equivalent, Guillaume, and his surname by that second given name, gallicized to Apollinaire, a saint's name, but also "Apollonian," solar.

This determination to choose French in his name, even over German, explains a certain patriotism, which may seem to us outdated in his collection *Calligrammes,* published just after the war of 1914. At the beginning of that war, even though Apollinaire had been writing only in French for a long time, he did not have French citizenship and had to join the Foreign Legion. He acquired French citizenship only at the end of the war, just before he died.

The French language represented for him a sort of forbidden paradise. It was absolutely necessary to him to prove his right to write in French; that is why he spent hours at the Bibliothèque Nationale[2] reading medieval texts, understanding French through its history and its regional particularities. He was especially interested in a region that is now in Belgium, but which at the beginning of the century was part of the Kingdom of Prussia, between Malmédy and Verviers. In this region of the German empire they spoke a very full-flavored French dialect, Wallon, which Apollinaire was to adopt and adapt in the writing of one of his most beautiful novellas.[3]

. . . . . . **52 Readability**

As we have the feeling when we read *Finnegans Wake* that a great part of the text is always escaping us, we have a tendency to set it aside, labeling it unreadable. But this only demonstrates more clearly a very general phenomenon. There are always words or aspects in a text that escape us, especially if we read them in a foreign language. We deduct a part of the text; another part remains foreign, especially as soon as a little time has elapsed. Then the part that was so evident we did not need to mention it no longer is at all.

Thus, on any page whatever of Flaubert, there are always several words that are not or are no longer part of the popular language, and which most of us do not know until we have done research or special studies on the subject. In general, annotated editions help us, but they are often disappointing; they explain the places we already understand and leave us stranded in many others. Of course, the context often gives us the general meaning. We know that a certain term must signify a carriage or a fish. We do not know exactly which, but we move on. In another reading, when we perhaps feel the need to know more, we consult one or several dictionaries, which perhaps uncover for us treasures we did not suspect, hidden under the veil of rapid reading.

We read words more or less. If we do not accord the text great value, we often skip whole paragraphs. These structures are so banal we know what is going to happen. We choose our path on the page. We dash from sign to sign. Even when we try to read with care, there are fluctuations in our attention, so that, for example, when we prepare a course on a text that we have already read twenty times, we discover something new. There are things we had indeed read but which we had forgotten, but there are others to which we had never paid attention, and it is the evolution of our own critical thought, of our reading, of our writing, that shows us their importance.

This is true on all levels. If we look for easy reading today, if we work only with the most obvious, material that goes without saying, which does not need explanation, we rapidly condemn ourselves to misunderstanding and to oblivion. To describe a character, for instance, I could compare him with some rock star, some leading man of the movies, some television commentator—the best-known personalities today—but in ten years, even sooner, they will be completely forgotten. Our environment is saturated with advertisements; certain big brand names are the easiest references. We make dates to meet under a certain Sony sign. But when the big business collapses, the reference collapses too.

We have never "read" a book. They are always there to be reread. But certainly rereading some books that we already know will reveal to us only commonplaces, while others will appear more and more rich. The difficulty of living literature is the very difficulty of our life.

Contrary to what advertising slogans tell us, life is not becoming easier and easier. All day long they repeat to us, "With this appliance, this refrigerator, this washing machine, your life will be easier." That may be true for washing clothes, and that is progress we must applaud, but this acquired ease implies a transformation of relations that are, without a doubt, going to be more and more interesting, but more and more difficult. Life becomes more difficult linguistically from the fact alone that our technology is more and more refined. Our environment includes more and more objects that we must name and classify.

Most of us today still have one mother tongue, even if it is sometimes a wicked stepmother, but already more and more parents speak several languages. Children are thus born into complex mother tongues, into languages in dialogue, which will give them richer and more varied personalities. More and more, each individual will have a different linguistic profile.

Every great writer has a different vocabulary, a language within language, but he only shows more clearly what already exists in anyone at all. This is in the process of developing greatly.

We need books in which the phenomena of translation and of citation play a larger and larger role. There could be texts in which foreign languages are heard or deciphered, in which words, foreign sentences, pass by. What place is more typical of our day than an airport? That is a place where all sorts of languages are heard being spoken, where announcements are made in certain languages, sometimes in several. People meet there who come from all regions of the world. In those waiting rooms, those restaurants, those long corridors one has to go through to reach the departure gate, how many conversations are overheard, how many worries, how many adventures, told in how many accents, dialects, verbal musics? I can describe an airport only according to the languages that I know. I can amuse myself by learning a little of a certain language expressly to put it in my description. I can use an elementary Finnish textbook in order to put a Finnish sentence on the lips of a passerby. A Finnish reader will immediately understand it, but for most of the others it will be only a mysterious foreign language.

Let us imagine an epistolary novel in which some correspondents write in Japanese, others in French or in English. Those who understand the two or three languages could read it all. For the others, differentiated translations would be necessary. Our linguistic situation implies that a radical transformation in all literary genres is near. We are at the beginning of the history of literature.

xiii

invasion of images

. . . . . . 53 Peoples of the Book

Among the problems that writers have encountered since the war is a whole chapter linked to the change in the situation of the book relative to the rest of reality. We have seen many problems linked to the change of France's situation relative to the rest of the world. Now it is a question of the way the book is changing place in relation to the rest of cultural activity.

The book has been our civilization's most important instrument until recent years. The Arabs say there are three peoples of the book: the Hebrews, the Christians, and themselves. Their three civilizations are founded on a fundamental book. With us it is the one called the Bible, which means the preeminent book. Everything is secondary to this fundamental instrument. Still today everything revolves for us around the written word, which is still generally presented in the form of the book to which we are accustomed, that sort of brick of white paper formed of superimposed pages that one can leaf through.

The book has not always existed, and certainly not always in this form. Within the three great civilizations it has passed through different forms. Books as we know them today appeared at the end of antiquity, in the first centuries of the Christian era. Before that time the book was a scroll, which is still used sometimes. The word *volume* comes from the Latin *volumen,* which means something that turns. Remember the famous expression from the Apocalypse about the sky disappearing like a book that is rolled up. That form gave way to what is called the codex. Today we find ourselves facing great transformations of this object. Throughout antiquity and the whole Middle Ages the book was written by hand. It was thus always considered a unique object. Texts were recopied from earlier books, yet each book had a different physiognomy. Therefore the book was worth a considerable price.

With the invention of printing the book was multiplied, certainly not to an unlimited number, but to one that is sometimes very great. Its cost diminished. The same text is reproduced in thousands or even millions of copies. It is then considered an interchangeable object. It is the prototype of the modern industrial object, the object in a series, each being considered equivalent to any other, which soon leads to considering men themselves as equivalent relative to others.

Still today we consider our civilization as starting from the written, and especially the printed, word. It used to be that the most important painting, what was called historical painting, was always subtended by a text. The essence of art criticism consisted in finding the text under the painting. The book had a preeminent importance relative to all other forms of expression.

Today book manufacturing has completely changed. And, most importantly, we are achieving means of recording word and thought that are different from the book and in some respects more effective in performance than it is. This implies great transformations for those concerned above all with books. But just as political transformations relating to old images of France are so deep that it is very difficult for the French to realize them and remain aware of them, changes having to do with the book are so fundamental that it is difficult even for most of the craftsmen to understand what is happening. They thus endure these phenomena without being able to control them.

. . . . . . **54 Illustration**

Books are no longer made today as they were at the beginning of the century, when the process was almost the same as in the time of Gutenberg. Our techniques are so different now that they permit us to create objects quite different from those that we are accustomed to. The discovery of processes of photographic reproduction allow us to include a great number of images in the book. In medieval manuscripts there were miniatures, but even in printed books of earlier days there were already illustrations—first wood engravings, then etchings, and then, as of the beginning of the nineteenth century, lithographs. But today, with the development of photography, the normal book is an illustrated book.

Almost all the books you see in bookstores include illustrations, particularly schoolbooks. These textbooks, through which children become accustomed to books, are always illustrated. All paperbacks of the classics have illustrated covers.

A book without illustrations is forevermore an anomaly, a remnant of an earlier form. That is difficult for some editors to admit and, naturally, for some writers. Of course one continues working on the text, but often illustrations are imposed on it without consultation with the writer. Often he is not used to attending to these things, and, more often still, publishers prefer that he stay in his little writer's room and not meddle too much with the rest.

Newspapers are also all illustrated. For years two great European papers tried to remain unillustrated. That was the mark of their tradition, of their class, of their seriousness. They were the *Times* in London and *Le Monde* in Paris. Soon economic necessity forced them to take advertising, and advertising was illustrated. Refusing illustration soon meant that they were letting their papers be illustrated by others. Finally, when there were so many photographs of cars and perfume bottles, they put in pictures of the news that went with the text.

The relation between the text and its illustration is no longer the same as it was in the nineteenth century. Usually very little thought goes into it. They make illustrated books as best they can, and most of the time the writer does not think about the visual aspects of his text and the relation it may have with the pictures.

Thanks to the illustrated book, we are able to know all sorts of things that were virtually hidden from us before. We now have the possibility of seeing distant countries, thanks to good-quality photographs in color. So we establish for ourselves a picture of reality that is of a different nature from that of our ancestors. We are finally beginning to be able truly to make art history. Until the last war, art books were very poorly illustrated.

First there were engravings, which we find very beautiful but very inaccurate. As it was difficult to transport paintings, the great art critics of the eighteenth or nineteenth century most of the time discussed paintings they had not seen and which they knew only through the intermediary of descriptions. Today we have great exhibitions. We can go visit museums here and there and, above all, we have at our disposal art books with reproductions that are becoming better and better. There is always a distance between the work and its reproduction in a book, because of the difference in scale, which becomes considerable when it is a question of big paintings. If we find Veronese's *Marriage at Cana* reduced to the size of a postage stamp, we do not see it in the same way. The colors play differently with each other. The contact is not the same.

That is why the practice of enlarged detail has developed. One sees not only the entire painting, but also such and such a part, which is isolated and which one can examine much better as the diminution of scale is reduced. The painting is represented by a whole collection of pictures that allow us to move around in it. We have means of exploring reality in a new way, changing the status of the text relative to what it was a few decades ago.

Some functions of the book are now fulfilled by other means. Developments in film and television permit us to have a new relation with reality, which in some cases is better than the one we had with the book. The latter is progressively being replaced by the televised spectacle or by videotapes.

The usual novel, the novel for popular consumption—sentimental, detective, medical, and so on—is giving way to the televised series. A large part of today's publishing will disappear before the end of the century, to be replaced by other "products," as they say now, which will be excellent for books, the Harlequin collection hardly being the glory of books. Undoubtedly far fewer books will be sold, but they will be read much better.

The illustrated book reminds us of the fact that the book is a physical object, and that its pages are usually white surfaces covered with signs that are generally black. These signs are particular drawings, letters. In the nineteenth century it was believed that these drawings had nothing to do with the ones students learned to make in the schools of fine arts. But we have changed all that. We know very well that numerous painters' drawings curiously resemble enlarged letters that are often scarcely readable, but not much less so than those of our rough drafts. The sharply defined distinction made in the nineteenth century between pictorial images and what we can call textual images no longer holds today.

Businesses and institutions are trying to make it last a little longer because of institutional premises. An art dealer is something other than a bookstore. A museum is something other than a library. A fine arts school is something other than a faculty of letters. All these institutions are trying to remain what they were and to defend themselves thus against what is threatening them. They have difficulty admitting that the distinction between what were called the different fine arts is now being called into question. There are differences among today's arts, but they are no longer to be found in the same places as before.

. . . . . . **55 Art Criticism**

Because of the evolution of printing and the picture within our society, the relationship between literature and painting is no longer the same as before. Literature finds itself faced with the necessity of exploring this relationship. It has, naturally, been a long time since writers got interested in painting and painters. Paintings are found in many novels. Many great writers were art critics.

Art criticism is the first relationship between literature and painting. It is a text about a painting. With Diderot, for example, it was a text about a painting that he had seen but which his reader had not been able, and would not be able, to see. The description he gives must in some way take the place of the painting. In his *Salons* he tells Catherine of Russia, Frederic II, the subscribers to the *Correspondance littéraire,* what he saw at the last exhibition. These princes could buy one of those works on the sight of, or rather on the reading of, the description. Other people could never see them.

For us, a text of art criticism is a text we read in conjunction with the work itself or its reproduction. The first readers of Baudelaire's *Salons,* which are practically catalogs, read them or held them in their hands while walking in front of the paintings described. With the development of illustration, art criticism is confronted with reproductions of the work. We can verify if the description is exact. But if the painting is under our eyes, one might ask, why describe it? We again find the problem that we mentioned relative to the descriptions of the *nouveau roman.* For Diderot description was absolutely necessary, and even for Baudelaire, since once the *salon* was closed the text would help people to remember. It is still very useful, as is shown by the fact that most painters working today who have exhibitions ask critics to write texts for the invitations or the catalogs.

Thus there is considerable production of texts about painting, often very vague, as it is sometimes difficult to describe contemporary painting. It used to be easy to recognize the represented objects, to identify a tree, a woman, a house, or, for Historical painting, St. Sebastien, Charlemagne, or the Rape of the Sabines. Today there is still representation, but in a different way. One has to use another vocabulary—for example, that of geometry. One can speak of squares, of triangles, of circles, of stripes, or the vocabulary of the activity: the gesture, the scar, the dripping, the flowing, and so on.

We know these texts help us a great deal to look at works, because we have texts in our eyes. We look at everything with literary and pictorial glasses. That is why we need new paintings and new figurations. Without them we could not manage to see what is around us. Without descriptions we could not manage to talk about it all. It is not enough to have the painting before our eyes to see it. It is very useful also to have someone talk to us about it, even if it is so we can say that the text is stupid and that this critic has understood nothing. In order to contradict, we set about saying what he should have seen. We become able to explain to others why this painting that they find absolutely nil is worth the trouble of looking at.

The description of a painting proposes to us a route for looking. One cannot speak of all its regions at the same time, especially if the painting includes many of the details that can be isolated in an art book. The discourse, passing from one detail to another, traces an itinerary within the image. We are made to look at this first, that afterwards. The text animates the painting that illustrates it by detaching objects from it, by returning to them their mobility, by telling the story of which it is a moment or a combination of moments. What we read is a text with a new grammar, in which certain images play the role of paragraphs or clauses or words.

. . . . . . 56 Reading and Writing Painting

When a writer—and we are all here a little bit writers—finds himself in the presence of a painting, he naturally feels a desire to talk about it, to write about it. Some works, to tell the truth, will provoke an impression, a thrill, to the point of leaving us mute, but that only emphasizes the viewer's normal propensity for discourse. Leaving an exhibition, we might declare, "It is so beautiful I can say nothing." It is nostalgia for the glimpsed but inaccessible commentary that makes us sketch it thus.

The first relationship between painting and writing is criticism, a multiform discourse full of gaps. With Diderot, for example, it is a matter of finding the text that is at the source of the painting, or could be, or ought to be, not only to uncover the prior text but to improve it, transform it, invent it. It is thus perfectly normal to write criticism of painting, since it is so often revealed to be criticism of a text. What was called historical painting presented itself as the magnified illustration of, or commentary on, a moment taken from a historical or mythological work. It was therefore a "citation," as in justice, the witness text summoned under the interrogating lights of the painting: a citation or a montage of citations. The art critic examined the cutting in the unrolling of the narrative: Was it really this moment, this passage that should have been retained? Would not some other one have made the rest that was left out more perceptible, and thus the whole more striking? Often Diderot reads the painting he is considering in this way, often he does it over, replaces it with an imaginary painting that he describes to us, inviting a future painting, useless to the ultimate degree.

In the *Salon of 1763*, for example, seeing a landscape by the young Loutherbourg, he interprets it as a pause in a stroll that he imagines is with a companion:

> Ah! my friend, how beautiful nature is in this little canton! Let us stop here; the heat of the day is beginning to make itself felt, let us lie down beside these animals. While we admire the work of the Creator, the conversation of this shepherd and peasant girl will amuse us; our ears will not disdain the rustic sounds of this cowherd, who charms the silence of this solitude and overcomes the cares of his service by playing the flute. Let us rest; you will be beside me, I will be tranquil and safe at your feet, like this dog, assiduous companion of his master's life and faithful guardian of his herds; and when the weight of the day has passed, we will continue our way, and at some later time we will still remember this enchanted place and the delicious hour we spent here.

A talking movie. Two years later the sight of a landscape by the same artist provokes this command:

Courage, young man, you have gone farther than is permitted at your age. You must not know poverty, because you work quickly and your compositions are valued. You have a charming wife, who ought to settle you down. Do not leave your studio except to go consult nature. Live in the fields with her. Go to see the sun rise and set, the sky coloring with clouds. Walk about in the fields among the herds. See drops of dew on the shining grasses. See the haze forming in the evening, stretching out on the plain and hiding from you little by little the summit of the mountains. Rise with the lark in spite of the charming young wife near whom you rest. Go before the return of the sun. See its disk obscured, the limits of its orb effaced, and all the mass of its rays lost, dissipated, stifled in the immense deep fog that receives from it only a feeble and reddish tint. Already the cloudy mass begins to sink under its own weight; it condenses toward the earth; it dampens it, it soaks it and the softened sod will cling to your feet. Turn your eyes toward the summits of the mountains. They are beginning to pierce the ocean of mist. Hurry your step; climb quickly to some high hill; and from there contemplate the surface of this ocean which undulates softly above the earth and detect, as it sinks, the tops of the steeples, the summits of the trees, the peaks of houses, towns, villages, entire forests, the whole scene of nature lit up by the light of the star of the day. This star is hardly beginning its career; your charming companion still has her eyes closed; soon one of her arms will seek you at her side. Conjugal tenderness calls you. The spectacle of animated nature awaits you. Take the brush that you have just dipped in the light, in the waters, in the clouds; the diverse phenomena with which your head is filled ask only to escape and be attached to the canvas. During the burning hours of the day, while you are busy painting the coolness of the morning hours, the sky is preparing new phenomena for you. The light becomes weaker; the clouds move, separate, assemble, and a storm is brewing. Go see the storm form, break out, and end; and two years from now let me find in the Salon the trees it will have broken, the torrents it will have swelled, all the spectacle of its ravages, and let my friend and me, leaning one against the other, eyes fastened on your work, be frightened again.

The painting gives impetus to a literary painting, which replaces it. But writing thus pictorialized will untiringly continue to seek out this sensual and critical excitement. So Diderot, after having in some way digested one Salon, waits for the next with avidity. An ogre of images.

Diderot returns the painting to its story, but all the texts on painting, even very different from his—descriptions, commentaries, appreciations, interpretations, sociology, psychology, and so on—introduce or reintroduce time into the image. Even if I have the painting or its reproduction under my eyes, the text that accompanies it will draw my attention successively to its details or aspects. Thus during the guided tour in the museum, whether the guide be of flesh and blood or present only in the form of a recording, the thread of discourse in our ear will oblige our eye to travel at controlled speeds. The text will transform the painting into a film; I think, for example, of those of Luciano Emer.

The simple description of a painting changes it, and after having repeated even for pages that it is indescribable, one must always reach the point of beginning a description, if it be only for practical reasons: identification, classification, advertisement. The axiom of modern physics, that observation transforms the thing observed, is particularly applicable here. Indeed, the text starts from vision, but from a vision already entirely penetrated with words; the label on the frame, or next to it, in the museum is only the hanging up, in extreme simplification, of this tumultuous cloud. Indeed, the text always leads to a "look," but the silence it demands is always temporary. The author dreams of abolishing himself in contemplation, of having only served to clear the atmosphere or the pane of glass, but he dreams at the same time of being undetachable from what he detaches, of being its very frame. "See with me, see me with it."

The discourse about the painting is inevitably followed by the one that is affixed next to it, juxtaposed to it. However discreet it may try to be, it acts upon it none the less; however active it knows it is, it will always allow something unconsumed to subsist in this sort of fuel, which it devours like a flame. The painting produces a hole in the discourse, which bathes it and assails it from all sides—a window, a breath. The more the text manifests its activity on the painting, the more the latter will defy it—an interminable dialogue not only between the ear and the eye, but within the eye itself.

· · · · · · 57 Litanies of the Virgin

A text about a painting at first sight with no "local" relation to it; at first sight only, for this text is always also next to it: on the frame, right next to the frame, a little farther away, fixed relative to the frame, as in a classic illustrated book, more or less mobile, as in a work that includes a separate volume for the plates. From the frame on, all the space is more or less traversed by the lines written about it, haunted by the words about it. Is the painting then always the only space in the inhabited space where it is not spoken of? The discourse concerning it becomes more dense up to that limit. Does it stop there brusquely and totally? In any case this would be only to be sent back to it, reflected, maintained. The frame is a mirror, but is that all it is?

This limit, whose hermetic seal some would like to guarantee, is porous on all sides. One part of the label nearby on the wall only reproduces the signature that, most often, more or less legible, is already found on the painting. This separation—which our culture, for mythological, ideological and especially institutional reasons, has wanted to maintain—is ended. Within the sacred rectangle the profaning word has already soiled everything. It is revealed to be already a painting, with its particular properties, animated as it is by our codes with an extremely powerful movement—from left to right and from top to bottom, for example, for the West.

The forms of writing within the painting greatly transform it. When I look at a Japanese inscription, I may first of all not suspect that it is an inscription, seeing in it only a drawing that I may, incidentally, find admirable. From the moment that I am capable of identifying these signs as being Japanese, I understand that a meaning gives them life, that my eye should follow them, usually from top to bottom. If my knowledge becomes more polished, I become aware of the fact that within each character there is a dynamic, that the strokes composing it are always traced according to a certain order. The drawing comes to life with new dimensions. A whole other adventure begins when I become capable of identifying some of these characters, of linking them together in sentences with all their connections, their grammatical twists, which introduce still other movements, new drawings superimposed on the others, when finally the true reading of these words sets before my mind a painting in some way concurrent with the one I am seeing.

Words in painting also reveal innumerable other objects or structures which function more or less as they do. I am thinking, for example, of Zurbarán's *Immaculate Conception* in the museum in Barcelona: not only do the cherubs in the two corners on top carry tablets on which can be read "*quae est ista*" (who is this?) and "*aurora consurgens*" (dawn rising), not only from the lips of the two young people kneeling at the bottom do the words rise, "*monstra te esse matrem*" (show that you are the mother) and "*mites fac et castos*" (make us sweet and chaste), whose ascending curves would merit a whole analysis, but the presence of all these inscriptions obliges us to interpret the pictorial words as words of another type, not just the isolated objects that appear in the niches of the clouds: the star, the mirror, the ladder, the door, as terms from litanies of the Virgin, but also those we could first take as accessories of a delightful realism: the lily and rose in the cherubs' hands, and especially the landscape with all its details—tower, house, fountain, well, palm, and so on—in all its light. Each of these "titles" could replace "*aurora consurgens*" on the tablet at the right or again "*matrem*" in the speech on the left. Everything in it is thus a way of naming or praying to the central Virgin, a creation of a paradisiacal ideographic discourse.

Such linking together of pictorial forms through the words they more or less openly contain can continue indefinitely. Painting, if it is capable of bringing to life around it an immense text, succeeds also in absorbing it, in transmuting it. Nothing in it is sheltered from the text, but there is produced in it also a kind of flight from the words. If there is no limit at which one can say that their power stops here, neither does one exist for their powerlessness. Invaded painting invades the text in its turn, to the extent that no text can exist, however abstract or "pure" it may be, which does not give something to be seen, which especially does not give the desire, the passion, to see. They say that Homer was blind; a formidable calling passes through his closed eyes.

Words in painting cause another work to spring forth from this work. The icon of Zurbarán is not only the representation of the prayer of the two young men, but is itself prayer. It is not only representation of a dawn, or of a fountain, it is itself dawn and fountain, not only representation of a virgin, whom one of the young men wants to show herself as mother, despite the warning of the other, who wants her to render them chaste, she is the passing from virgin to bride. The hieroglyphic language of the litanies is not only description, but establishment, exploration, weaving of a paradise where the opposition between chaste and nonchaste, pure and impure, will never cease transcending each other.

But in the same way that there is no need for words to be actually on the painting for them to act upon it, the painting has no need to be below the words to penetrate or bathe them. Among the imaginary works of art that surge from within the contemplative reading of every real work, the discourse causes others to spring forth that will have an influence just as great on future painters. All the museums of the world are necessarily incomplete because they can never present to us the works of Elstir.[1] Thousands of painters will try to fill this gap, thousands are working at it without being clearly aware of it, trying to fill that gap and other gaps formed through the same circumstances; the gap will always remain. The great imaginary works of art in literature bring us the certainty, as if we needed it, that the history of painting will never be finished. The destruction of an ancient work, which we no longer know except by description, causes it to function in the same way. Thus, starting with a text of Lucian, Botticelli gives us his fascinating reconstitution of the *Calumny* of Apelles,[2] which of course does not reproduce it for us but carves out its absence very differently.

. . . . . . **58 The Artist's Book**

We have seen text and painting approach each other progressively while still keeping their independence. The painting does not change in the physical absence of Diderot's text. But as the text animates the painting and the painting illustrates the text, we arrive inevitably at the illustrated book, in which we have before our eyes an image made up of the juxtaposition of a work of art and of a text. In the same rectangle of the page or the double page, we have at the same time both pictorial images and textual images. These two kinds of images react relative to each other. The most successful illustrated book is the one in which the image is necessary to the text and vice versa. There is a true marriage that produces something new. An artist and a writer working together create a child that has a certain independence relative to his two parents.

The artist who begins to work regularly with a writer will soon suggest to this writer images that are different from those he ordinarily makes. Similarly, in order to animate these images, the writer will perfect a vocabulary and grammar different from those he used before. This will permit him to open up new roads in his imagination. That is why collaboration between painter and writer is so fruitful. Each time this has been an extraordinary adventure for me. It has multiplied my imagination so much that many have had difficulty following me, appreciating what I did with or for a particular artist, but not what I did with or for another. The ideal is to succeed in creating an object in which the components react so much with each other that separation would be almost impossible.

But as soon as the object is finished and satisfies me I have only one desire, which is to reply to my own challenge, to see how I can detach my text from the whole, which is necessary to be able to live outside the images that gave it birth. Separated from its symbiont or companion in development, it must often be transformed. In the books called *Illustrations,* where there is only text, certain parts play relative to others a role similar to that which the pictorial images or engravings played relative to the blocks of text in the original editions.

First we have a neutral distance between the text and the image. In principle there is no obligation to see both things at the same time. That is text about painting. Then we have the illustrated book, whose most interesting forms are the artists' books, which represent a cultural level much higher than art history books. The text is next to the painting, enclosed in the rectangle of the double page. Most often it is a rectangle of text next to a rectangle of image, but it can be much more complex. This leads us to a third relationship: the text within the painting.

. . . . 59 Words in the Image

When text is put inside a painting, fascinating phenomena are produced. The painting is still something sacred for us, hence its liaison with the fundamental rectangle of our culture, the form of the sacred enclosure, the form that indicates to us that we must not come in: "You have to stay on the outside to look. Keep your distance. Don't come putting your impure hands inside this magical world, which we authorize you to contemplate from the other side of a pane of glass or barrier."

In the museum the catalog is a mobile element relative to the hanging pictures; but we also have on the frame and the wall beside it labels with sometimes several pieces of information, a whole rectangle of text glued beside the rectangle of the painting itself. Entering within the frame is terribly troubling for the writer. All sorts of ancestral taboos are awakened.

But if the double page of the open illustrated book is an image, it already functions like that enclosure, that *templum.* One need only leaf through textbooks to see that we can have several pictorial images on the double page, which may in reality form a single one when we have details of the same work. We have diptychs, triptychs, or polyptychs. As soon as we detach a detail the painting moves about on the page, where the text includes different genres according to the regions. There is the running text, the speech or lesson of the art historian, and there is the legend next to the reproduction itself, like the label on the wall or the frame in the museum. Surreptitiously the text enters within the image. It can enter an engraving or a painting.

It has happened that I have had to write texts on the engravings of my friends. The first time, I trembled. From the moment that my text enters the rectangle, which until now has been reserved for the artist and is his privilege, my writing evidently appears like drawing. What I write will transform not only the significance of what I am looking at but also its plastic balance, even its composition. In the work there are, for example, plumes on one side, little squares on the other; between the two I introduce lines of writing. There is the risk that they will unbalance what was perfectly balanced. One must then twist one's pen or pencil twenty-five times before daring to intervene. One must not destroy the work; on the contrary, it must be more beautiful after the intervention. The writer thus discovers himself to be a painter.

The writer paints with words; that is an expression we use all the time, the tradition being even *ut pictura poesis,* according to Horace; you see that it can mean many different things. It can be taken very vaguely or very precisely on all sorts of levels.

Painters themselves, particularly since a certain period, are faced with this problem of writing because of the signature. A signed work is worth much more than one that is not. The signature is a drawing, and painters sometimes encounter great difficulty in signing appropriately so the signature does not destroy the work they have just finished. The adventures of signatures in Western painting make up a whole novel. Obliged to confront words and letters, painters teach us much about them. To know what words are, it is not enough to read the linguists, it is not enough even to read writers, one must also look at the painters, for they have worked for centuries on rendering words visible. Since the last war, words are one of the fundamental themes, a veritable obsession in modern painting.

xiv

toward discovery

. . . . . . **60 Before the Wave**

The role of the United States in the evolution of contemporary French literature and the role of painting leads quite naturally to an examination of our French relationship with American painting.

In this fifth centennial of the first voyage of Christopher Columbus, forerunner of so many crossings, it is important to remember again the immense variety of people established on the American continent and the cultures they had developed before the European colonizations.

The encounters often destroyed the original inhabitants, and always transformed them; however, their immense inventiveness has survived until our day. The introduction of the horse, for example, brought to the plains completely new ways of life, and thus of expression, to certain tribes.

But of course what became the art of the United States in no way took American productions as models. Only some marginal trappers adopted the local dwellings, teepees or wigwams, causing them to evolve. The colonist properly speaking, from the Pilgrim on, took the type of dwelling he had left behind to imitate any way he could and gradually adapt.

Even in the centuries that followed, if the Indian's teaching was considered basic with regard to hunting or fishing techniques, to botany, to tracking, or even to political organization, as far as what was then called

160

the fine arts is concerned he was sometimes considered a subject of choice, as for George Catlin or Edward Sheriff Curtis,[1] but never a master. This is equally true for the earliest European waves into certain regions, for example, the Spanish settlements in the Southwest. The new occupants brought with them their Anglo-Saxon traditions, and it was only much later that the Hispanic fashion would spread through California.

As for the wave of population brought much against its will from Africa, they were specifically forbidden to practice any plastic arts. Certainly blacks had the right to become painters or sculptors, but only provided they submitted entirely to the white school. We see nothing in painting, sculpture, or architecture that is comparable to what happened in music with the invention of blues and jazz.

. . . . . . 61 Inventive Colonists

The colonist who landed at Plymouth brought with him his whole aesthetic. His departure had already been a declaration of independence, but founded on a basis of loyalty to the Crown and to tradition. What these colonists wanted was a New England, as in other regions a New France or a New Spain. To accomplish this nostalgic ideal they tried to make a clean sweep of everything previous; they wanted to erase the board to restore there the image of what they had left behind.

But if in New England what was initially essential was that England that they missed despite everything they reproached it, "newness" would take on more and more importance. An England, indeed, but an improved one, one delivered of its rust and corruption. An England where they would start again at zero, an England more beautiful, more sunny, more bountiful.

While they continued to hold that European art was the absolute model, they surreptitiously transformed it in two ways: First, the mere fact of their successful survival in this different sort of nature made it the virtue of generosity. The new continent was harsh; only heroes or saints could manage to take root there. But at the same time it was vast; for a long time it seemed unlimited. It was the place of the sublime. However naive the landscapist, he would always try to capture the immensity. Second, the fine arts themselves were held suspect in the puritan condemnation of luxury. They did not reject the portrait, for example, and they knew that painters who came from overseas practiced it in a superior manner; they condemned, however, the "embellishments." They in no way regretted that local artists exhibited a certain inflexibility. Their "naïveté" was the mark of their "honesty."

In this period, if the European artist was still considered the norm of "taste," they in no way sought to compete with him. They imported a few to render certain settings or ceremonies comparable to those from overseas, at the time of governors' receptions, for example. Local production was in no way destined for export; it responded to local needs and in so doing brought into question some of the accepted ideas of the academies of the Old World.

· · · · · · · **62 Gradual Independence**

The Declaration of Independence did not touch the cultural domain. The new United States remained in a state of artistic dependence, which outlasted the colonial situation by more than a century. The ideology of the Revolution, like that of the French Revolution a little later, advanced Roman Republic standards. All the vocabulary, all the imagery, referred to the Republic. The Empire was not far away.

Here, for example, is a letter from Jefferson, not only one of the founding fathers of the American republic, but also one of the greatest artists of its beginnings:

> In 1785, in Paris, I received a letter from the contractors appointed to direct the construction of a capital at Richmond, asking me to advise them about the layout, to which a plan for a prison needed to be added. Thinking that this was a favorable occasion to introduce into the State an example of architecture in the classic style of antiquity, and that the Maison Quarrée [Square House] of Nîmes, an ancient Roman temple, was considered the most perfect model of what is called cubic architecture, I asked M. Clérissault, who had published drawings of the antiquities at Nîmes, to make me a model in stucco of the building, changing only the Corinthian order to Ionic, given the difficulty of the Corinthian capital.
>
> I agreed, against my better judgment, to Clérissault's taste, who preferred Scamozzi's modern capital to the more noble capital of antiquity. This was executed by the artist whom Choiseul Gouffier

had taken to Constantinople and employed, during his ambassador-ship, to make the beautiful copies of Greek architectural remains which can be admired only in Paris.

During the nineteenth century and the greater part of the twentieth, the American artist had to go to Europe to be trained—to London, to Rome, and soon especially to Paris. This need for a model soon brought not only a taste for copies of all the famous examples of European styles, which culminated in the International Exposition of Chicago in 1892, for the fourth centennial of the first voyage of Christopher Columbus, but also the establishment of enormous collections and magnificent museums. One had to be able to study at home, to bathe again in the fountain of youth of the great masters, without having to make the entire trip every time. The Metropolitan of New York and the National Gallery of Washington, fol-lowed by so many others, are Europe at home.

I have before me the catalog of the San Francisco World's Fair of 1915, when Europe was already at war but before the United States got involved in it: "The only complete and fully illustrated book of the exhibition of LA VILLE-JOYAU, its conception and realization, its architecture, sculpture, symbolism and music; its gardens and palace; as well as samples by Ben Macomber, with a frontispiece in color, two maps and more than 75 other illustrations."

From the chapter on the Fine Arts Palace, I excerpt this description of art in the United States:

Of very greatest importance for a citizen of this country is the art of the United States. It can also be of great importance for foreign visitors for the expression "American art" no longer provokes incre-dulity. It is finally recognized that the American has something of his own to offer the world, a style developed in the last two decades. The principal characteristics of contemporary art being daring, brilliance, and indifference to detail in representation, the art of America, as has been seen in this exhibition, shows them without exaggerating them. If one keeps in mind that the Palace contains little American art before 1905, the American artists show marked individuality, even in their interpretation of common precepts. The virile artists of today love luminosity; it dominates everything else and sheds sunlight on their canvases; they calm the too audacious brush strokes of the radical impressionists, but firmly underline the forms to the extent that the details are more easily imagined by the viewer, even when the expected line is absent. Even the older artists, although marked by an earlier tradition, show a style which profoundly distinguishes them from their English, French and German contemporaries.

· · · · · · 63 The Conservatory of Modernity

Just before the war of 1914, the famous exhibition called the Armory Show struck with a sort of thunderbolt in the aesthetic sky of the United States. The arrival of modern European works, completely different from those that French officials of the period would show in San Francisco in their pavilion, an exact copy of the Salm mansion, naturally scandalized some a great deal, but made the most perspicacious art lovers feel that here was an art made for them, all the more because it was encountering so many difficulties in gaining acceptance in Europe itself.

Modern art accorded admirably with what was most original in the art of earlier centuries in the United States: puritanism; a (if not deliberate at least proudly claimed) naïveté; the sublime in the landscape; and, naturally, the imagery of technical progress. Even the discovery by the Europeans of that period of the so-called primitive arts allowed consideration of Indian traditions from a different viewpoint. Thus at the Barnes Foundation, near Philadelphia, to the splendid impressionist and modern collections, not only Spanish ironwork but a beautiful series of ceramics from New Mexico were added.

The avant-garde movements in the first third of the twentieth century succeeded each other with such extreme rapidity, without omitting some neoclassic episodes, that it was very difficult to follow them. Fashion pounding on the new nail drove the old one out. The American art lover had the advantage, not only of his fortune, but of his distance. Modern art appeared to him almost in a block, and, distance taking the place of time, he much more easily put things in their place.

It is thus that, after having collected ancient art without hope of seriously rivaling the great European museums, the United States set about financing and accumulating modern art in such a way that it has gradually become indispensable for the European art lover or young artist to cross the Atlantic to see the famous works there. The Museum of Modern Art in New York is the archetype of the new generation of museums.

There remained one stage to get to: the making of modern art on the spot.

64 Reversal of the Current

That is what happened with the war of 1939 to 1945. Not only did the American artists who were working in Paris go back home, but some of the most important European artists left to take refuge in New York. Everything, under National Socialism and then the Occupation, was slowed down. On the other side of the Atlantic everything went right on. Gradually not only the old masters but the new came back. The current had reversed.

Certainly young Americans came, and still come, to Paris, but no longer as students; they were a little like prophets. Everything in their attitude, in their way of speaking, of seeing, or of painting raised the adjective "new" like a banner. The young European intellectual or artist, in the same way that his ancestors had wanted to make the pilgrimage to Italy, wanted to discover America. They knew they would come back all "up to date." For some years we had been out of touch, been behind. I myself went for the first time to the United States in 1960, and I was well aware of the kind of lead it gave me.

After the war, the United States, which had certainly already produced first-rate works in all areas, and had been doing so for a long time, suddenly asserted itself as a transmitter of culture. It was from then on not only the first power economically and militarily, but the laboratory of a new way of life with expressways and supermarkets; and it is there that all the pictorial movements of the avant-garde succeeded each other for about thirty years with extreme rapidity, being diffused fairly quickly over a good part of the earth, filling the new museums with a harvest that can be compared for its richness and variety only to the one produced in Europe during the first thirty-some years of the century.

65 The New Deal of the Cards

The city of Paris, uncontested capital of painting in the first half of the century, felt itself painfully deposed. New York, a city swayed for a long time by imperialist temptations (one might think of the Empire State

[Building] or the Chrysler Building), believed during these auspicious years that it was Paris's sole heir. After having for a long time and in vain fought against what it considered usurpation, Paris more or less resigned itself to vassalage, hoping thereby to be recognized as in second place. But can the one who was sultan become vizier? Or, if you prefer, how can a president accept his predecessor as deputy? At the same time, candidates began to flock in for this post of vice president, and the presidency itself showed signs of vacillation.

It was already too late. While French art in the first half of the century was concentrated in Paris, which greatly augmented the attraction of that pole, American art counted many secondary but very active centers spread out over the whole of the United States. The situation was somewhat comparable to that of German art until its occultation.

For a number of years, in the midst of upheavals that jolt the Earth and which we have so much difficulty not only in leading but even in following, the forefront of artistic activity has been spread among a number of transmitting centers of very varied size, among which pass waves of influence, of recognition, and of fashion. This new deal of the cards has not yet really found institutions or even concepts to suit it. Let us say that, for years, the museums of modern art, which were made uniform "in the American way" by being made into sorts of supermarkets of culture, each one proposing samples of the same products, have been seeking, like the places where they are located, a new originality, each one wanting to be different from all the others and obviously admitting their difference.

Formerly Americans came to Europe to admire there what they did not have at home. Then Europeans went to the United States to see, among other things, what had been made in their home but was no longer there. For several years one saw about the same thing everywhere. With the upheavals in the painting market, it was neglected artists who were then to be discovered, one here, another somewhere else. From then on the influences would be much less constraining. One no longer had to be "with it," because there were too many "it"s. It was a new consciousness of the history of art that was being put into place and which was looking for a new geography.

It is thus that the United States is beginning to discover the buried links that attach it not only to Europe but to all continents, Africa as well as the Far East and, particularly, to the continent on which it developed. And the art of the Indians, which has so evolved in the margin, in reserve, can show itself in an entirely new way and carry on dialogue in concert with others.

After the temptations of a unifying imperialism, the crisis of present-day art, in the United States and elsewhere, is paving the way for a growth and flourishing as yet undreamed of, from the federative seeds inscribed since its origin within its very name.

. . . . **66 Prestige**

Let us profit from this to meditate a little on the role of the museum in our culture. The Parthenon, transformed into a powder horn by the Turks, blew up; the marbles were collected and deposited in London, where they are sheltered from pollution and vandalism. But protection is only one aspect of the question: the museum permits us to see the object differently. If I see a coffee pot in a place of this kind, I will perceive the one in my kitchen differently, and that is true also for a Greek statue. The museum is an optical instrument.

The word *museum* comes from the temple of the nine Muses, which corresponded to nine poetic genres. The Greeks had no museum of painting, and the first "museums" were libraries. Collected there, around the manuscripts, were geographical maps, curiosities, plants and animals brought from distant regions. (That is the "museum"; there exist representations of botanical gardens from the time of the pharoahs.) In the Acropolis at Athens, a room called the pinacoteca[2] housed a certain number of celebrated works of art. The Romans established great collections of Greek works—statues and paintings. In the Middle Ages the cathedrals had their treasuries, and then the kings accumulated sumptuous objects, often gifts from other kings.

Francis I, whose collections would constitute the nucleus of those in the Louvre, not only had works of art brought from Italy, but the artists: two great mannerists, Primaticcio and Il Rosso,[3] who decorated Fontainebleau; and the old Leonardo da Vinci, who died at Amboise. Ferdinand of Aragon and Isabella the Catholic, the one who financed the voyage of Christopher Columbus, had works of art brought from their possessions in Flanders. The dual passion of Philip II for Venetian painting and Flemish fantastic painting explains the richness of the Escurial and the Prado. The greatest part of the work of Hieronymus Bosch, for example, is found today in Spain. When relationships between royalty, the nobility, and the rest of the population deteriorated and the notions of ownership and utilization were modified, a new concept appeared: that of the public collection.

The function of the great museum-like institutions of the nineteenth century (British, Louvre, Pergamon, and so on) is double: to accumulate and to educate. At first it was a question of supplying models: works of Greek and Roman antiquity, then of the Renaissance. Young artists who could not afford the trip to Rome or Athens admired the classic works in London or in Paris, and copied them. The prestige of the museum depended on the number of works it assembled. The often beautiful engravings are rarely faithful: once the young Frenchman who, in 1830, wanted to know Raphael or Titian, had consulted the works in the Louvre, he was obliged to make a trip to cities that held others, choosing first those richest in this area. Thus competition arose quickly. The Pitti Palace is a perfect illustration of the nineteenth-century museum conceived as a place of accumulation: the walls are covered up to the very high ceiling with magnificent paintings that, for the most part, cannot be studied in detail. People copy the ones down below; the others are there to swell the crowd.

• • • • • • 67 Modernizing the Museum

Toward the beginning of the twentieth century, the museum again became a place for education, but in another direction: it was a question of lighting the object, bringing it out of its darkness. No more accumulation in the presentation; on the contrary, one isolates what is shown, introduces spaces and resting places, and multiplies the number of rooms. The present-day museum requires a great deal of space; it eats up its surroundings. When we leave the tumult and confusion of the city to go look at paintings, we want to find calm, to be alone with the Cézanne or the Renoir. We must have a place of meditation, as the church or temple was formerly. This is in flagrant contradiction with the characteristic tendency of our era, which is to judge the value of an exhibition by the number of entries, or that of a television broadcast by the number of viewers. The problem of space has preoccupied many architects, among them Le Corbusier, to whom we owe a beautiful project for an expandable museum according to the spiral principle. It is a little like the Guggenheim, which could climb higher indefinitely.

It is now necessary to be able not only to transform the buildings but also their interior arrangements, to change the exhibits constantly. It is necessary also to be able to send the works of art traveling from one end of the world to the other. A great museum today is one that transmits and diffuses its works of art, the point of origin of a whole network of exhibitions. In this way the Turners of the Tate Gallery travel about. The architectural concept of the museum determines our relationship with the object it presents. If there is a sole entrance with an obligatory route, we cannot have the same impression as if we have multiple entrances at our disposal, if the different sections are conceived as so many little museums that we can wander through independently of the others—a much more attractive formula, but naturally more costly.

Lighting becomes an essential problem—if the function of the modern museum is to make the object come out of the darkness where it had been kept—and its solution has not ceased to evolve. The museums of the nineteenth century were made up of large rooms lit by stained-glass windows in the roof. Later, lateral lighting was preferred, more like that of private collections. The number of projectors was increased, and the entirely artificial lighting of some American museums, which sometimes provokes claustrophobic reactions, was achieved. At the Beaubourg[4] the Museum of Modern Art section had to be entirely reorganized in an attempt to improve it in this respect.

Buildings exist that were from the beginning conceived as museums: the Guggenheim, the Museum of Modern Art, or the Museum of la Villette. Others were first something quite different: places of worship or of power, churches, palaces, train stations (like the Musée d'Orsay), or even former places of creativity, like the studios of Rodin, Bourdelle, or Brancusi. Most of the time the interior is rearranged, but a shell subsists that bears witness to an epoch, transports us to the time of the Crusades or of the Revolution. Other museums are like snares for the past: some parts of the Louvre pay testimony to their own eras (foundations, the clock, the colonnade, and so on); others go after much more ancient periods: Assyro-Babylonian or Egyptian. The museum thus collects echoes of a distant past and, introducing them to young Parisians, plays an essential role in the formation of their historical consciousness.

• • • • • •   68 Generalization of the Museum

To pronounce the word *museum* without further precision irresistibly evokes painting. The museum is like a machine transforming the world into painting. It is taking part in a general evolution of our civilization, tending toward the replacement of the oral by the visual, the written by the image.

The development of museums is only one of the means of this tendency, manifested also in television, illustrated newspapers, cinema, and so on. The nucleus of the museum is what has traditionally been called the fine arts—painting, sculpture, engraving—but the boundaries between these disciplines and many others are being called into question more and more, and what would not have been considered painting fifty years ago may very well be so today. The notion of "museum" has expanded so much that anything whatever can be displayed in it. We want museums for everything. And we are awaiting a museum of museums.

Specialization in education: scientific, technical, historical museums. These last play an essential role in the national consciousness: to be French means to speak French, but it means also to entertain a sentimental relationship with a certain number of people and places, a relationship that is nourished by pictures, such as those of [Hector] Berlioz or [Eugène] Delacroix on the banknotes. Another classification of museums may bring into play the aspect of the object that they bring to light. Let us take the example of the automobile: one can show it as a work of art, show the signature, the style of a great carriage maker; or as a landmark in a historical evolution; or as a technical object whose functioning we unveil in cross-sections, diagrams, and scale models.

If the museum is by definition conservation and exploration of the past, how can one put the present day in it? Because time passes differently according to where one is, on the Earth or in our society, History does not have the same thickness everywhere. In the United States, for example, Western History does not have the same duration as in France. An American art museum deals with a shorter period. Americans have felt this to be a lack and have put forth a gigantic effort to compete with European museums; they have succeeded in acquiring so many ancient works of art that, from now on, young Europeans cross the Atlantic to go admire these Italian, French, Flemish classics. It is the United States that invented the idea of a museum of modern art, with the one in New York, whose influence was and remains great. Conceived as the antechamber to the classic museum, it functioned as intermediary between the latter and more audacious creations, introducing this new relationship to the present, which centers of contemporary art here and there are trying to explore.

Through the museums of modern art, the museum is changing its function. It is becoming not only the place of conservation and education but of activity and animation, revitalizing the classic museum by multiplying lectures, films, concerts, sales of reproductions, books, art objects around the preserved works. Some daring institutions even engage in rental. One can try out a painting, show it at some gala, put it to the test, thus experimenting with novel solutions to the problems of financing our culture. The museum is transformed into a motor for art and civilization. Heir to sacred places, it must indeed preserve, but if it closes too hermetically its bronze doors, it risks just as grave a destruction of its treasures as if it had left them in the street. It must make air circulate inside.

xv
literature and music

. . . . . . 69 **Divide and Conquer**

In Western Europe, and especially in France, the different arts correspond to different professions, different lives, different educations. One does not learn to play music in the same institutions as those where one pursues literary or linguistic studies, and it is difficult to pursue both at the same time. So, too, there are special institutions for learning to paint. They are like parallel corridors whose walls have thickened over the course of centuries, so that relations between them are rare and little encouraged.

Indeed, interdisciplinarity is talked about a lot in France at this moment, but it is only a theme for a campaign speech. It always remains a project and is accomplished only outside teaching and its institutions.

Today, still, French society does not encourage mixtures. For anyone to paint while writing books or practicing medicine is scarcely approved. There are only a few individuals who succeed in imposing this crossing of boundaries, and with great effort. In other countries or in other times universality was considered a matter of course. It has happened that I have seen people be astonished by my interest in painting and music, not only that as a writer I am interested in one or the other, but especially that I am interested in both. I have been treated almost as a meddler.

I have eyes, I have ears. For me the world is not only visible but audible. As a result, what seems abnormal to me is not being interested in both

172

painting and music. Whoever is not interested in painting is blind, in music, deaf, and I would like to do everything in my power to cure these illnesses. What is normal for a painter is to read books, for a musician also; what is normal for a writer is to be interested in music and in painting.

But a whole economic system produces a preference for containing people within their specialty, because, in a very short-term view, it is a way to exploit their production better. When one writes books one needs, still today, a publisher to bring them out. Since I am very much interested in the visual aspect of books, I have often asked my publishers to go to the printers of my books to study certain techniques, to invent things with them, to help them if necessary. In most cases I have come up against absolute refusal. The encounter of writer and printer risks creating relationships such that after a certain time the publisher himself no longer has so much importance or advantage. It is Machiavelli's famous maxim, "Divide and conquer."

Yet, even if people want to maintain these activities separately, it remains true nonetheless that most of us read, listen, look. Even if they try to forbid us, more or less nicely, sooner or later we cross the barrier and enter the forbidden territories.

. . . . . . **70 Weeks**

The fact that the access roads run parallel to each other leads to the notion that the relationships between these activities are themselves parallel. Although it goes back much further, this was a very important theory in nineteenth-century art, designated since Baudelaire as the theory of correspondences.

One can imagine that a musical work evokes the same thing as a literary work does. This idea is based on a concept that is very important in all cultures, which is that one can organize the universe through the intermediary of a certain number of groups in which the elements correspond to those of other groups. If you prefer, we can consider the universe a language. The fact that there is language in the universe shows us that we can relate groups of objects that are very different from each other, for example, the object "moon" with the word "moon," the object "fire" with the word "fire," the object "tree" with the word "tree," the word "water" with the object "water," and we can continue thus with "gold," "earth" and "sun." It is because we can establish this type of relationship that we can express ourselves.

If I have chosen these seven elements, it is because in Japan they relate to the seven days of the week, which came from the West. This is a good example of a group of correspondences. In each culture there are thus correspondence operators; and one of the great difficulties in approaching another culture is the adopting of new rules for the imagination.

In traditional Western society we have numerous correspondence operators, the most important of which are the numbers seven and twelve. To see this kind of operator function, one need only ask the question, "What goes by sevens"? Immediately the Westerner will reply to you, "There are seven days of the week, seven colors of the rainbow, seven notes of the scale," and so forth. We can set up a whole table of correspondences by seven. One can set up others for other civilizations—Japanese, Chinese, and so on. One can try putting these groups in parallel columns, in such a way that an element in one corresponds to one and only one element in the other. One can in this way try to know which note of the scale corresponds to which color of the rainbow. Baudelaire states, "Perfumes, colors and sounds correspond."

A painter will quite naturally ask himself "What goes by sevens?" if he is asked to decorate a collection of seven panels. If he is a minimalist painter and wants to make seven monochrome panels, he will immediately think of the rainbow. Now, it is obvious that the rainbow does not have seven colors. We know that the spectrum appearing in the rainbow is continuous, that there are, therefore, an almost infinite number of nuances; on the other hand, it is easy to distinguish three primary colors—blue, yellow, red—and three secondary ones obtained by their mixture—green, orange, violet. We see very well that in our rainbow there is an intruder called indigo. We say there are seven colors in the rainbow because we need to have seven to make them work in our table of correspondences.

The correspondence between the rainbow and the scale is a literary theory fundamental to many writers of the nineteenth and twentieth centuries. It can be seen, in particular, functioning full force in all sorts of expressions, figures, and scenes in Proust. In *À la recherche du temps perdu* this metaphor plays a fundamental role. One need only think of the great description of Vinteuil's septet. Study of the manuscripts shows that Proust hesitated for a long time over the number of instruments. He first thought of a quartet, then a work for ten instruments, but given the way the work appears to us today, with its seven parts, the Vinteuil piece could only be a septet.

The number twelve is just as important for us: the twelve months of the year, the twelve signs of the zodiac, the twelve apostles, and so on.

We can try to relate more and more vast elements and ask the question, "Can a musical work correspond to a literary work?" Officially, one would tend, given institutional separations, to reply no; but, going more deeply, the tendency would be to reply inevitably yes; it suffices to situate one's work within cultural ensembles. This is immediately evident if we replace works in their historical context. If we consider musical and pictorial works of the sixteenth, seventeenth, and eighteenth centuries, we see that the date forms a common element that connects them to the same "world." The people who composed these works, or for whom they were composed, who painted these others, or for whom they were painted, sat in the same chairs. They send us to the same region. Japanese literature, music, and painting all have something Japanese in them, and their relations are not the same as those of their correspondents in classical France. They are not the same in the France of today.

. . . . 71 Correspondence Operators

I spoke [in chapter 5] of correspondence grids; within these one quite naturally arrives at the question of number symbolism. In Western civilization the numbers seven and twelve are very important correspondence operators. But if one asks, "What does the number seven mean?" one risks receiving all kinds of contradictory replies. We are better off asking, "What goes by sevens?" We can then accumulate answers that do not cancel each other out: the days of the week, the colors of the rainbow, the notes of the scale, and so on. It is tempting to put all that in columns. For example:

1, violet, Monday,
2, indigo, Tuesday,
3, blue, Wednesday,
4, green, Thursday,
5, yellow, Friday,
6, orange, Saturday,
7, red, Sunday.

Immediately a question arises: "Was I right to put violet on the same line as Monday?" Depending on the writers, the works of art, the time periods, we can have different arrangements within this matrix. We often use numbers to designate days of the week. In France and in England we make Monday correspond to one. In other countries, other languages, it is Sunday that will be one. So if someone asks what the number seven means, I am obliged to reply, even as far as the days of the week are concerned, that in one country it is Sunday, in another Saturday.

This can have great cultural consequences. Indeed, in Christianity it is said that God created the world in six days and that on the seventh he rested. That is the basic week. That is why it is normal to consider in Christianity that the number seven represents Sunday. But this idea of the creation of the world in six days comes from Genesis, a Hebrew text; now with the Hebrews the day of rest is the Sabbath, which corresponds to our Saturday. Thus it is Saturday that is naturally designated by the number seven.

I could develop that with the number twelve, but let us take for example the number four. If we have a room to decorate with four walls, whether they be walls of stone or movable partitions of paper, the fusuma,[1] what themes will the painter use? One of those that come immediately to mind in Japan as well as in the West is the four seasons. If I say "winter, summer, autumn," even a little child feels that something is missing—the fourth term, spring. With the seasons, as with the days of the week, we have an obligatory order; we know which element always follows which other. The difficulty lies in knowing which one comes first. Given the way we have organized our calendar, it is winter that comes first in a year. But we have the habit of relating the course of the year to that of an individual life. We prefer then to relate spring to childhood, winter to old age, as in the series recently painted by Jasper Johns;[2] it is therefore spring that is put first.

Operators used in the West are not very high numbers. We have no difficulty naming single objects or collections of two, three, or four terms. The number five gives us more difficulty, but we can use the five fingers of our hand, the four directions in horizontal space plus the center, and so on. With six we have the six faces of a cube, the four directions of horizontal space plus the up and down, or, if one prefers, the four cardinal points plus the zenith and the nadir.

Seven offers great richness. Eight is much more difficult; I suggest the eight edges of a cube. For nine, the nine inspiring Muses of classical poetry or the nine choirs of angels in medieval theology. I forgo for the moment proposing examples for ten and eleven. With twelve I have as many as you could want. But beyond that it is very difficult to find numbers that serve as operators in our daily life. In other civilizations there are much larger operators. Thus God is named in the Koran by ninety-nine different names; they are learned in Islamic schools, and in all Muslim countries it is believed that this essential number is inscribed in the lines of our two hands.

The child just mentioned knew the seasons, that there should have been four and not three. He therefore immediately interpreted the three as an incomplete four. In other cases we have the feeling that a disturbing element has joined a group that, without it, would have been perfect. That is what happens with us for the preeminently evil number, thirteen. You know that in American hotels there is never a thirteenth floor or a room thirteen. The thirteenth element disturbs the harmony of the twelve. Popular Christianity links this feeling to the fact that on the day of the Last Supper there were thirteen people at table, the twelve apostles plus Christ. The twelve apostles were perfect, but on that day there had to be the wicked one, the traitor Judas. Once Christ was dead, they replaced Judas by Thaddeus in order to have twelve again.

I have studied the functioning of numbers in French literature, particularly with regard to the work of Rabelais. You know that *Gargantua* ends with the description of a paradisiacal place, the Abbey of Thélème. Everything in it goes by sixes: it is a building in the form of a hexagon, with six floors whose steps are so wide that six horses abreast can pass on them. In the library there are books in six languages, and so on. But that is not the end of the work. The *Fifth Book* brings us to the oracle of the divine bottle, where, this time, everything goes by sevens. We can easily see that the six can be interpreted as an as-yet-incomplete seven, but Rabelais suggests also all kinds of other interpretations. Six is the number of faces on a die, thus for him the symbol of chance; there is also a pun on the female sex organ.

A supplementary element can be either disturbing or amplifying. Thus Rabelais uses the number eight (seven plus one) to indicate the ocean, the departure toward something new. One of the greatest works of Arabic literature was translated into French at the end of the seventeenth century, and from there disseminated throughout the world: *Les Mille et une nuits* (The Thousand and One Nights). A thousand is considered a very round, very clear number. With 1,001 something begins again; it is thus the equivalent of an infinite number.

Awhile back I wrote a little essay on the *Thirty-six and Ten Views of Mount Fuji* by Hokusai. Some years later, in the second *Génie du lieu, Où* (Where/Or), which discusses the Northern Hemisphere, I tried to describe Mount Sandia, which overlooks Albuquerque in New Mexico in the United States. This mountain is indescribable, and it is because it is indescribable that it is indispensable to try to describe it. So I wrote *Thirty-Five and Nine Views of Mount Sandia.* It is an homage to Hokusai, with the "minus one" of modesty.

. . . . 72 The Musical Ceremony

In the life of an individual, musical instruments or song play a certain role. There are moments of the day, feasts when a certain type of music is made, when a certain category of instrument is used, a certain kind of text is read. In a great cultural ensemble, such as the liturgy of the Roman Catholic Church, we have a close relationship between times of the year (for example, the feast of Easter or of a saint) and texts (those of the breviary or mass) and music (that of the Gregorian chant collected in what today is called the *Liber usualis*). This ritual can be considered a gigantic theatrical production that varies subtly all year round, with elements that move in relation to the others from one year to the next.

With regard to any society, we can ask the question, What role do texts play here—conversation, of course, but also texts that are recited, written, read, played, and so on—what role do music, song, instruments play, in the church or the temples, in the popular feasts, the feasts of the nobility, fairs, love relationships? The more we know about that, the more we see differences between the equilibriums of other times or of other places and those of our own society, which become apparent little by little. All sorts of prejudices are thereby abolished. Lessing[3] believed that painting addressed the eye and organized space, while music addressed the ear and unfolded in time; like a Frenchman, he mistrusted mixture; literature, however, obligatorily mingles it all.

But certain aspects of language and thus of literature underwent a curious occultation in Europe in the nineteenth century. We know, we are obliged to know, that speech is sound. I speak to you, you listen to me. We know also, but we know it almost in secret, that writing is drawing; this is much more evident in Japan than in France. In France it has been possible to try to hide that from us. In Japan it is quite impossible.

Language is something both visual and auditive. But, for various ideological or political reasons, the message is made to be perceived as rapidly as possible, thereby hiding the signifier, specifically, these auditive or visual aspects. In the army an order must be obeyed as quickly as possible. It must be clear; the soldier must immediately do what the lieutenant or general has commanded. The quicker the transmission, the more chance the army has to win. First obey, then ask questions if you are still there. It is thus forbidden to pay attention to the form itself of the message. One cannot imagine a soldier in an army replying to an officer who just gave him an order, "What a beautiful voice you have!" There would be immediate punishment. The same interdiction applies to the visual aspect.

But we are obliged today to find again all these latent forbidden aspects of language, which are linked to everything that is forbidden in our society, in our conduct, and are thus linked to the transformation of that society. In general, people who have power try to hold onto it, and will therefore do what they can to keep society from changing, at least in this respect. If they sense that some people want change, they will protect themselves against those people; the prohibitions will become more violent or more subtle. Fortunately for us, all societies end up by changing, power changes place, royalty is little by little divided up. The activities of the avant-garde, in painting, literature, and music, are linked to these transformations.

Even music, if we look more closely at it, is not addressed only to the ear. There is a great difference between a sound that one sees being produced and one whose production is hidden from us. The sound that we do not see produced seems to us to be a revelation come from another world; hence the importance of hidden musicians in some performances or festivals. The musician is hidden to draw attention to another element, the prince dancing, for example. To draw attention to himself, the musician must become visible at a certain moment, hence the ceremony that has become so important in Europe during these last centuries: the symphony concert. It is a special kind of theater, generally given in theater halls of Italian style, with two principal characters who stand out: the orchestra conductor and the soloist.

The orchestra conductor is the one who unleashes the tempest and calms it. With a sign of his finger he summons the thunder; with a movement of his hand he makes the forest murmurs undulate. He is the romantic hero par excellence. Some conductors seem to be kings or emperors manifesting their sovereignty over a whole people. Passion, emotion penetrate them to the extent that they conduct not only with their baton or hands but with their hair.

The soloist is the second star, who also sometimes plays the role of conductor, but most of the time we see these two stars in dialogue or combat in front of a background of the choir, which is the orchestra.

The theater, properly speaking, is also a ceremony, which always includes, by the way, a certain number of musical aspects. Even in the most "realistic" plays there is this essential musical phenomenon: the establishment of silence. In the symphony concert, as well as in Italian-style theater, nothing can begin before a certain degree of silence is obtained by a certain number of coded calls. For example, the orchestra conductor comes on, he is applauded, he taps a bit on his podium with his baton, sometimes shows a little impatience until the moment when he judges he can begin. Even before his entrance there is that whole prelude of tuning up; the oboe plays his A, which is taken up by the first violin, who passes it on in some way to all the others. This kind of sonorous fog gives way to true music and to its silence.

It used to be believed that music was added to a silence, conceived of as an essential, very rich and nuanced sonorous background, which nature offers us. What appears to us as silence is indeed very different depending on where we are, to the extent that when recordings are made for radio or film, besides the words or noises desired, several minutes of silence are captured. The world has become more and more noisy. Music thus can no longer be something added to a noise that is already present, often to the saturation point. Music must dig out a silence in this noise to be able to be heard. That is why silence plays a much more important role in twentieth-century music than in earlier music.

In the most naturalist theater we also need to establish silence, which is commanded in the West by the three knocks. It is only when a transformation of the sound level in the hall has responded to them that the curtain goes up. The three knocks are part of a language.

· · · · · · **73 The Music of Words**

The word *language* is often used now in a very general sense. Even music critics who thunder against "literary" music do not hesitate to speak of musical language. It is not only a very pregnant metaphor, but an inevitable one. When musicians talk about Liszt's works for piano, for example, they say "Liszt's literature for piano."

Language in the restricted sense of the term is obviously sound, and I can focus my attention on this sonorous aspect, work on it. You listen to me, I speak at a certain pitch, I can make my voice move, I can make it go up, down, speak more loudly or more softly, more quickly or more slowly. Depending on the accents I want to give my sentence, I create different melodies.

If I am speaking to people who know French very well, I go fairly quickly. If I sense that there are people in my audience who do not follow very well, I slow down and separate the words or groups of words from one another to obtain as much intelligibility as possible. If there are words that are a little long or rare I detach the syllables: in-tel-li-gi-bil-i-ty. The same text can be spoken *allegro, andante,* or *presto.* The language of musical technique quite naturally serves us in specifying the delivery of an oral text.

To set a text to music consists of working on the musical phenomena already present there. If I increase the length of the syllables, I pass from conversation to recitation or declamation. If I work on the pitches, accenting the ascents and descents, imposing new rules on them—for example, those of the classic scale—I reach song. There are all the intermediaries one could wish between the most codified song of opera and that marvelous music that occurs in the briefest conversation. Even if I do not understand what is said in a foreign language, I can enjoy the music of that language. It is even easier in some respects if I do not understand it; I will then hear it only as music. In addition, to appreciate this music better and better, not only must I become accustomed to it, but also I must feel it as meaningful.

One can find all the intermediaries, but sometimes one wants to mark boundaries and even to raise walls. In some cultures the difference between song and conversation is also a difference between social categories. The singers of baroque opera represented kings and queens. If the people sometimes sang, it was thought that they sang differently. The very rich popular song in eighteenth-century France, still fairly current in the nineteenth, scarcely exists at all any more in twentieth-century France, or it is replaced by listening to the star vocalists of the music halls or on the radio.

Languages have different musics, and in the West their relations with classical music, as it was codified in the eighteenth century, are not the same. Thus the musicality of the Italian language relative to that of French is characterized by the presence of heavy tonic accents on words, while in

French these are distributed throughout the sentence. These accents concern not only the intensity but also the pitch. Finally, the difference in length among the syllables is much clearer than in French. The result is that it is easier to notate spoken Italian expression than French with the classic musical system. There is certainly melody in French, but it uses very subtle differences of pitch and length, which it was impossible to notate with musical writing of the time. On the other hand, Italian and German lend themselves to it admirably.

Great musicians definitely felt this difference in the relationships between languages and the musical system of their time. Mozart changed his musical tools according to the language he used in his operas. In the operas in Italian there are two regions of song: the arias and the recitative, which is notated to be spoken. In the latter, it is the spoken voice that is clarified musically and which must remain perfectly intelligible, whereas in the arias it is not essential to catch all the words; meaning often hangs on a few words detached and repeated at will. The only faithful interpretations of the author are those in which the recitative is intelligible for those who know the language; thus it must not be too hurried. The spectator of today who does not know Italian is often impatient on hearing the recitative; therefore the singer and the record maker or the theatrical producer tend to make it move as quickly as possible.

Other operas use German libretti. Mozart keeps the spoken voice for some dialogues, but he keeps a certain kind of recitative to link the arias to this conversation. In operas with a French text the opposition is total. At the end of the eighteenth century, it was believed that French was not very susceptible to musical notation, which did not keep Lully, Rameau, and many others from creating remarkable examples in this mode, but they were by then out of date.

This makes us understand the importance that a certain number of aesthetic quarrels were able to assume at the end of the eighteenth century, the most famous of which is that of the Bouffons [Jesters] between Italian and French opera. Rousseau, for example, thought that Italian opera was the domain of the natural, the French that of the artificial, and he tried with his *Devin du village* (Village Seer) to invent a new French opera that would rediscover the natural. This difficulty continued throughout the nineteenth century until Debussy tried to reinvent a French recitative, pushing his audacity to the point of writing an opera without arias.

But musicians can teach still much more to the linguist or writer. I have been speaking until now only of a single voice that can be modulated, modeled by the musician in all sorts of ways by stretching syllables and intervals, that which gives the word not only a new expressivity but also a new grammar. Musical formulae play the role of grammatical signs, superimposing on the primary grammar of the sentence another that naturally brings out aspects simple conversation would have left hidden. This is translated in particular by the multiplication of words within the musical phrase, a phenomenon well known in opera. By cutting the sentence into a certain number of elements that are only heard bit by bit, one can progressively change their meaning.

. . . . . . **74 The Grammar of Noises**

The musician is a supergrammarian, an analyst of language. But, people will ask, if that is true for vocal music, what about instrumental music? First of all, it must be pointed out that the greatest part of known music is vocal music, even if certain song parts are often replaced by instruments in modern executions of ancient music to obtain more clarity of sound. Many instruments represent a sort of translation of the word into an already existing instrumental world; but it must be added that this instrumental world has also existed from the beginning, that music comes from noise as well as from the voice.

The study of noises—like the three strikes of the bass bell in naturalist theater—is first of all the study of their meaning, and it can organize them into a more and more precise language. Let us come back to the army since it is, alas, the world of clarity (a world that claims clarity, of course, and refuses to allow its abominable obscurities to be revealed); the fanfares, the trumpet blasts have a meaning that no one is supposed not to know.

Noise is closely linked to dance, to all gesture. There is a language of dance, and within music for dance are some instruments that play the role of speech with respect to others. Hence the violin is an instrument felt as particularly "human." That great form of classical music, the string quartet, is the instrumental transposition of a structure already well known in vocal music, with two masculine and two feminine voices. Today's technology provides us, by the way, with all sorts of transitions between vocal and instrumental sounds.

In the phonemes we use there are two large categories: consonants and vowels. Vowels are the timbres; they designate the difference in form between two vibrations that for a certain length of time are not modified: the difference between a note held by the flute and one held by the clarinet. Consonants are the attacks, that is to say, the way in which the volume and even the timbre change, particularly at the beginning of a note. We can record a song and save only the series of volumes; if you like, we save only the consonants. We then pass the sound of a violin through this screen of consonants. If the operation has been well done, the phrase of the violin remains perfectly intelligible.

Moreover, especially in Western music, not only has the word been multiplied horizontally, but also vertically, which is to say that several voices can be heard at the same time. In a dialogue between lovers, the words "I love you" can be repeated a great number of times in succession, but the singers can sometimes sing together at the same pitch or at different pitches.

The combination of these horizontal and vertical redoublings produces all sorts of obliques. A phrase begins; the same phrase begins a little later at another pitch. These are canons or fugues. Horizontal multiplications allow the words of the text to be clearly heard, the verticals also: let us imagine within a phrase sung by a single voice a word sung by four voices; it stands out in a remarkable way. As for the oblique multiplications, they produce new encounters between different parts of the original sentence. The structure of the spoken sentence is subordinated to a polyphonic scaffolding.

The rules of classic polyphony are made in such a way that the voices can be distinguished from one another, and thus, in choirs or ensembles, the words and sentences can remain distinct. Music thus permits us to hear several words at the same time. This is obvious in the music of the opera duet, but it can go much further. Medieval music developed a polyphony of texts whose intelligibility does not always appear on the first hearing. It is only little by little, often with the aid of reading, that the work is heard in all its richness.

Music is not content to multiply intelligibility. It plays with it, it arranges it in gradations, it renders this part clear by leaving some other part obscure. Sometimes we feel there is language, but we do not understand it. Even if it is in our own language, we can recognize it but we can no longer understand; it is a lost language. Only a few words survive that, in a sense, carry to us the summoning of this lost text that we may find again elsewhere, if it already exists, or that we can dream of. On the basis of ancient texts, music asks of us and promises us future texts.

The writer also can gradate the intelligibility of performances in a theater or on television, in public readings or on the radio, and, naturally, within his text itself. Some writers of the twentieth century—[Paul] Claudel, [Antonin] Artaud—foresaw a theater that would completely renew the habits of Western theater relative to music. As I have just taught a seminar on Villiers de l'Isle-Adam, I borrow from him an older but remarkable example of the musicalization of theatrical text. This is a passage from his anniversary piece on the American Revolution, *Le Nouveau Monde* (The New World). In a tumultuous scene leading up to a riot, there is a moment when, he tells us, "everyone talks at once." He gives us in detail the words of each of the "instruments" of this verbal orchestra. Then he summarizes the auditive impression that is to result from it: "This 'ensemble' must not last half a minute on stage. It is one of those moments of confusion when the crowd itself has the floor. It is a sudden explosion of tumult in which are distinguished only the words: 'dollars,' 'psalm,' 'late!' '*Babylonis*,' 'let him speak!' 'Boston!' 'meridian,' etc., mixed with barkings, children's cries, the squawking of parrots. Monkeys, frightened, escape from branch to branch, birds cross the theater from one side to the other."

. . . . . . **75 The Score**

He wants to make noise with words, handle speech with other sounds. He treats the text as a musician would. Here we come to the problems of the score. The musician addresses the ear, but he addresses the eye also. His text, his "literature," in which words sometimes play a very important role and whose signs are transformed words, permits us to create a phenomena of sound. The professional musician reads a score as we read a book.

When we learn to read we are first asked to read aloud, then in a whisper, then to get to meaning without even listening to our own interior voice. The musician can first read with his instrument; then he no longer needs it. The orchestra conductor is able to read at a single glance a score containing twenty or thirty superimposed staffs, which he grasps as a single phenomenon. As for the analysis of music, it takes place, above all, on the basis of scores or transcriptions. Musicians are also draftsmen.

We are all draftsmen. Writing is a series of drafts, drawings, usually black signs on a white background, but there can easily be other colors. The composer also draws signs on a more or less striped white page, signs to which his hands communicate the same expressiveness. We are impressed by the differences in the handwriting of a [Victor] Hugo or a [Stéphane] Mallarmé. We are amazed at writers' rough drafts, at the plastic qualities we see there. It is the same for musicians. All the power of Bach passes through his strokes of the pen, all the distinction of Webern through his.

As soon as a writer wants to work with the phenomena of sound, he encounters comparable problems. The classic example of a literary score is the late work of Mallarmé, *Un Coup de dés jamais n'abolira le hasard* (A Toss of the Die Will Never Abolish Chance). He tells us that in creating this work he did nothing more than recover the good things from music. Everything there is of language within music returns within poetry of this kind. It is a long, very complex sentence whose principal clause, written in very large type, moves through all the rest. Around the smooth recitation of this "tenor," clauses, circumstantial phrases, are written above, below, in more or less small type, ascending or descending. The height of the word on the page corresponds, Mallarmé tells us, to the intonation, that is to say, the pitch; the size of the type corresponds to the volume.

In the theater, we listen to, but we also see, the actors, like the instrumentalists in the concert. Today we have sound productions without a visual part. These are, notably, those offered by the radio. When I listen to a text being broadcast I completely detach the spectacle surrounding me from what I hear. I experience the state of the blind man. The world for me becomes sound. While still seeing what is in my room or my office, I no longer accord it the least attention. The text is set in [sound] waves.[4]

Since radiophonic art has difficulty finding a place in the institutional corridors I was talking of earlier, the texts used for radio are usually those serving some other purpose. We hear music, opera, theater on the radio. But we all know that in the theater heard on radio there is something essential lacking, and that although it is convenient to fill up programs, it is in fact very poorly suited to radio transmission. On the other hand, reading aloud suits radio admirably. The best is to create texts especially for radio, as has been done in Germany for years. These are especially conceived for the ear, and the writers have to provide for the way they will be produced. They therefore write scores, and the inventions of musicians in this area are very useful to them.

The idea of the text as score leads to a new conception of literature.

Literary production today revolves around one essential genre: the novel. The preeminent literary ceremony today is the solitary reading of a novel at home. This form implies a certain linearity. The detective novel, for example, must be read from one end to the other. As soon as the novel becomes more literary, the reading becomes more independent of the thread of the action: one goes back, delays on certain passages; the text becomes a score, the reading explores a surface.

We can arrange the signs on the page in such a way that one can and must read rather as the orchestra conductor reads his symphonic score, each reader having in detail the different routes. This distresses the classic literary journalist and the typical professor, since it is necessary to invent a new vocabulary for analysis, a new principle of criticism. Really modern works obligatorily encounter great resistance, but they are the only ones responding to our needs.

Scores for the radio, scores for the theater, for imaginary radios or theaters—polyphony teaches us a new literature. But listening to music teaches us a new way to read the novel itself, reveals to us a certain number of fundamental aspects of this literary form, so rich but so evasive today in its twilight.

. . . . **76 The Round of Voices**

In the theater the characters are embodied by actors, who bring their physical presence and the difference in their voices. On radio, since we do not see the actors, the difference in voices becomes still more important. But when we read a dialogue in a novel we no longer have the help of actors; we are ourselves the actor, more or less good, who embodies all the characters of the text. If we are a good reader-actor it is because there is in the text itself something that allows us to obtain this difference of tone or of voice, which allows us to distinguish the characters from one another. This is what is called the novelistic presence.

The great novelist is the one capable of giving presence to his characters, that is to say, each of whose characters has a voice. This is very clear in Balzac or Proust, who, by the way, admirably showed in his *Contre Sainte-Beuve* (Against Sainte-Beuve) that this was one of the principal virtues of his great predecessor, with the result that most of the criticism ordinarily made of him missed the mark completely. Each of Balzac's characters has a different style, which means that the style of Balzac is not that of the narrator but a superstyle, an aesthetic entity much vaster and richer than what is ordinarily called style. With Proust, also, all the important characters really have different voices. These writers give us in the text itself the music proper to each character; this is possible only because the writers were capable of isolating within the conversation the discourse surrounding them, elements that carry with them a certain tone. It is these expressions, these turns of phrase, that are the very origin of the characters.

The great novelist is not the one who first has characters about whom he later asks himself, How he will make them speak? He is the one who constitutes characters and the events that happen to them based on ways of speaking.

When we read in our theater at home, we can be good actors because we have in the text what we need to give to Françoise, to Charlus, or to the Duchess of Guermantes[5] different voices and attitudes, that which allows them to compete with real people.

The great novelist is a sociologist far superior to the professional sociologist. No nineteenth-century specialist has been able to make an analysis of the essential phenomenon of the department store, of the transformation of commerce during that period, whose consequences are still developing today, comparable to that of Zola in *Au bonheur des dames*. No linguist has been able to make an analysis of the language of the years 1910 to 1920 in France comparable to the one Proust empirically made to accomplish his work.

We can distribute tones and timbres in space, horizontally, vertically or obliquely; we can superimpose novel and theater in a new type of literary score. I have written novels myself, and through this experience, and that with all sorts of other texts, I have come to attach more and more importance to the phenomena of timbres. In the music of the Vienna school they speak of the melody of timbres. Instead of a single instrument playing a melody, it is distributed among several. With Webern, for example, the piano plays one note, the oboe the second, a violin the third. Each of these notes is articulated in a different way. One can naturally have transitions of great subtlety; that happens especially with the great interpreters and with some great soloists of jazz music.

I like classical music very much, and it is easy to see in my books what lessons I have drawn from it; but I have tried also to make use of the music of jazz, of the way dialogue appears in it, of all the work on articulation of the instrument. I have in this way tried to create texts in which the "score" is transcended, in Mallarmé's sense, in which the novelistic experience attempts to pass through the whole poetic experience, texts in which the tone and timbre can change from one sentence to the next and even within a sentence. This presents huge difficulties because the more one succeeds with the detail, the more difficult it becomes for the reader to restore this color or articulation. But it is because it is difficult that we must hasten to begin it. Others will succeed where I have failed.

xvi

school for dreams

. . . . . . **77 Language Basements**

We have looked at certain aspects of the hidden face of the Earth. Today I would like to take up the hidden face of ourselves, what psychoanalysis calls the unconscious, that which in ourselves escapes from us. It is a hidden face of our language. We play different roles in society, characterized by discourses with distinct vocabularies. The words we use most often have several meanings. To make ourselves understood, we have to eliminate a good many of a word's meanings in order to retain only one or a few.

Science is a language utopia where words have one unequivocal meaning. Literature, on the contrary, is established in ambiguity, in the plurivocal nature of words. In daily life we need constantly to drive away some of the meanings of the words we use, but they resist; in spite of the needs of the moment, they conserve all their plurality. And they take revenge for the treatment we subject them to.

We spend our time driving away some of the possibilities of our language, and they come back to haunt us. It is this haunting that we call the unconscious. In psychoanalysis it is especially the haunting of sexuality that is addressed. Indeed, in our societies we need to separate our activities in this area from most others. It would be too disturbing to let them mingle. Therefore, there is major repression in this area. But there are many others. There are many other emotions we have to hide, at least at certain moments and for a certain time. There are many meanings of words that we must leave in the dark.

These repressed meanings accumulate and constitute a kind of resistance inside ourselves, as in a society controlled by a central power, a police; parallel organizations are constituted to trick them. One often finds these organizations as mirror images: there are counterpowers and counterpolice. An entire part of the literature of the sixteenth and seventeenth centuries, what is called the picaresque novel, is based on this consideration of an upside-down society within the very interior of our own, the underworld, which itself has a language: slang. The themes of the picaresque novel have continued to develop up until today. In the nineteenth century one of the fundamental themes of the novel was the secret society. This is especially evident in Balzac. Within ourselves we have secret societies.

We all belong to different groups within society. Most of us, as of a certain age, choose one or several functions. One is the father of a family and a banker. Another is a bachelor and a professor. These are well-recognized roles that correspond to established behaviors and languages. There may be many more delicate things. Each of us belongs to manifest societies and to secret societies. Any book at all original gradually establishes a secret society around itself. Its readers are endowed with a language and with common references; they thus have ways among themselves of recognizing each other. In 1900 the mere fact of having read Mallarmé was a sort of talisman that—within all sorts of groups where something completely different was spoken of—permitted these individuals to be distinguished from the others. We recognize the mention of a book, the use of a word; we say to ourselves that this person is aware of certain things and that, consequently, we can carry on with him a conversation different from the one we have with the pompous imbeciles who make up the collection of people invited to this party, with the members of this club, or with the functionaries of this administration.

Different functions and discourses, with special vocabularies, correspond to all these official or clandestine groups. You know to what extent we must pay attention to what we say in certain surroundings. We must not talk with these people as we would talk with those people; you know to what extent improprieties of language are punished by ridicule or exclusion.

All that is thus repressed lurks in the shadows and wants to be called up to consciousness. A whole part of ourselves, a whole treasure, provisionally eliminated, continues its life in secret, without our being able to control it. In this way other discourses are born without our knowledge. The meanings we repress join the desires we repress. This is manifested particularly in dreams. What bores us, what risks disturbing us in the daytime, we set aside, but it remains; and in the evening we are tired, we do not want to think about it anymore. That will be for tomorrow, for later. Another time. We do not have time. We are too hurried for that. We need to sleep. But, precisely, certain worries prevent us from doing so.

Mechanisms within our brain and our personality permit us to manage to sleep just the same. The most important of these is the dream. We are marvelously capable, while still continuing to sleep, to tell ourselves stories, to experience extraordinary adventures, and this does not trouble our sleep unless we encounter particularly horrible difficulties. Then we wake up with a start. A nightmare. Fortunately it was only a dream! A surprising expression, since in popular language there is an equivalence between the dream and what we desire: something is as beautiful as a dream, a dream woman, a dream city. Advertisements use this word constantly: a dream washing machine, dream vacations.

· · · · · · 78 Knowing What One Wants

Popular language itself teaches us that dreams manifest to us a certain number of our desires. The dream is therefore particularly important, for we have a great deal of trouble knowing what we want. An adage from antiquity tells us that when the gods want to make sport of someone, they answer his prayers. At that moment he recognizes that that was not what he wanted at all. This is our drama. In all our politics, for example, we do not know what we want. We believe we want something but we are unable to express it appropriately. The mechanisms that in principle serve our expression of will function badly. We know what difficulty we have organizing our existence in such a way as to be happy.

A dream indicates to us what we want in a generally confused and circuitous way because it has all sorts of obstacles to overcome, and it indicates also what we fear. Both are always there at the same time. Our representation of the future is always bipolar. For awhile the United States represented the future for Europe, an ambivalent future, at the same time things we desired and others we feared, which were difficult to untangle.

What we want and what we fear are manifested through the intermediary of everything we have been obliged to eliminate during the day, in the nighttime dream, and in all sorts of more or less daytime activities, in particular literature, which furnishes us a waking dream that we can somewhat control. A book can propose dreams to me. If they are too dark or too black I can close the book. If they are too rich I can read more slowly, a little at a time. To refuse a nocturnal dream I have only one solution, which is to wake up with a start.

Fortunately, a dream ends most often in a fairly satisfactory way; it dissolves agreeably in our sleep, and when we wake up we want to tell it. The nightmare sometimes pursues us and we would prefer to drive it away, while what persists of our dream we often want to retain. At breakfast someone says, "Last night I had a very bizarre, very funny dream." Sometimes the person is still laughing about it. Everyone says, "Tell, tell." The person tries. Usually, after two or three sentences, it is over. The mere fact of wanting to tell it makes it vanish.

The dream is an essential part of reality. We have the habit of opposing dream and reality, or fiction and reality. If we look at things more calmly, what we dream at night is an integral part of what we are, and what we tell about our dreams is a fundamental document. We cannot simply oppose reality and imagination, reality and fiction, because what we take for reality is often revealed to be only fiction. We only know certain aspects of the people we spend time with, and we are always obliged to imagine something about them. We imagine to a great extent what we are ourselves. Science itself offers us a representation of reality, but what makes it science is that it can make progress and thus demonstrate at a certain point that what one believed before was false. Thus one approaches something more and more closely, but without ever reaching it.

The way the ancients represented reality to themselves appears to us now a fiction. They first believed that the Earth was flat and the sky was a vault above. Others came along and succeeded in showing that that was illusion. Ptolemy gave a new picture of the world with the Earth as a sphere in the middle and planets, Sun, and Moon revolving around it. Then Copernicus found that if one put the Sun in the middle calculations could more easily be made and things better predicted, that the Ptolemaic system was an appearance.

Reality is in great part made up of fictions. We partly see the world as we want it, as we fear it. These fears cause us to have to mistrust what we want. There is constantly something or someone saying to us, "You must not take your desires for realities." The only thing we have to do is to succeed in making our desires our realities. But we are mistaken not only about what we take for reality, but also about what we take for our desires. The dream is thus an irreplaceable source of knowledge. Everything that allows us to clarify it, to manifest it, will therefore be very useful to us; painting, for example, will allow us to recount, to show dreams. Let us take, for instance, the character in Dostoyevsky's *The Adolescent*, who is found in a landscape similar to that of Claude Lorrain's painting *Acis and Galatea*.

Painting permits us reveries; literature is a machine that allows us to penetrate into the dreams of others and our own. Since the last war this concern for the dream has been manifested in literature in connection with efforts to elucidate, among which psychoanalysis is the best known. Between the two wars, with surrealism, the dream had already taken an essential place. It could not lose that place. If we want to write a realistic novel we cannot forget half of our characters' time. They have activities during the day, and they dream during the night. There are dreams in most of my novels, and I have continued to explore this "material."

Studies of medieval literature speak of a certain number of themes or "material," the best known of which is the "Brittany material," everything that concerns King Arthur and the knights of the round table.

I have also dealt with dreams in certain texts on painting by taking the paintings of such and such a painter as snapshots of a dream that I invented, because they seemed to me to be in communication with what I dreamed myself and which most of the time I had great difficulty recounting. Then I tried to work on the dream narrative, starting with the fact that the dreams we have are only very rarely original.

• • • • • • • 79 Stage Fright

We have the impression that our dreams are our own. In that gathering at breakfast there was only one person who had a dream that he tried to tell the others. But this dream is often recognized by the others; the elements are usually very banal. We almost all have the same dreams. That is normal since we have fairly comparable existences; therefore, because of the form of our society, we all need to eliminate the same words or the same meanings at the same moments. Hence it is approximately the same constituents that accumulate in the wings, in the back of our minds.

We say someone has ideas in the back of his mind. That expresses precisely the feeling we have when we have the temptation in society to use a word in a meaning different from the accepted one. We have the feeling of hiding it behind our back. That shadow will come back when we are incapable or almost incapable of protecting ourselves against it. Sleep surrenders us to our dreams.

I have noted that I myself often had the same dreams with only a few variants, that they were almost inexhaustible variations on certain fundamental themes. Given that I am a professor, that I give lectures, and that when I arrive in the hall I am obliged to do away with all sorts of preoccupations that I might have, and might have been nourishing the instant before, I am obliged to silence them. The sun has finally come out, and I would perhaps like to take a walk in the Bastions Garden. But I must not do it, not even say it, unless I take a roundabout way like this one: literature, oral in this case, allows me to speak of a desire I would normally have to eliminate in my discourse.

There are also things I fear. I enter the hall. There are people there before me, waiting for me to talk, and I am not very sure about what I am going to say; I do not know if it will please them, but too bad, I am there, I must speak and, consequently, I must quiet all the anxieties. They stay in the back of my mind. It is easy to overcome partly this fear by reading to one's audience a text entirely prepared in advance. This is a way of diminishing the stage fright. Not completely, because however prepared a text may be, one never knows exactly what effect it will have. Plunged into one's text, one no longer thinks of the people out front, which is a pity. That is why you have seen me during these years improvising before you, giving myself up to trapeze exercises, flying with very little net.

The effort to overcome the stage fright forces me to a great mobilization of my attention. I am forced to multiply my activity tenfold. Crossing this kind of wall of fear, I am obliged to repress what produces it and therefore all the fears I might have relative to the foolishness I risk saying. After every lecture I remember certain sentences I have said, and I perceive that that was not at all what I should have said, or that I have made an enormous blunder, a historical error, taken a name for another, made a mistake in a date, stammered over my sentence. Thus I risk doing it again and worse the next time. But since I am entering the hall, I have to repress all that.

One of my most frequent dreams is that of a failed lecture. I have it almost every week when I am in the process of teaching a course. I felt the need to tame it by writing it down. I did not want to write down only one version; it had to be tamed in its multiform, proteiform character. It was the theme that it was essential to grasp, while showing at the same time all the metamorphoses it could undergo. That is what I attempted in *Matière de rêves* (Stuff of Dreams). These are invented dreams, dreams of dreams. The first is based on very precise memories of my stay in the United States at the University of Santa Barbara, which is also the source of a passage in the second *Génie du lieu*. I dream that I am strolling in the evening after a lecture on the admirable campus, on cliffs just above the Pacific Ocean, and that I go down to swim. But there has been a black tide and the beaches are covered with oil. Then all sorts of obstacles keep me from taking part in a reception, where I am replaced by a particularly antipathetic double.

"I am on the beach; it is evening. A line of hills descends toward the left. Overhead an orange bar, with the gray trail of a climbing jet plane. There must be an airport not very far away, but I hear no motor noise. The wind pushes me. The waves lap softly at my feet. I am wearing long, black business shoes. That is because I gave a lecture just now. Then there was a little cocktail party: congratulations and canapés. I escaped by the service door, came down the steps, pushed open the white gate of the garden, took the path that went down among the flowering lilacs. The party must be continuing. They are no doubt waiting for my return. Then there will be a dinner at another professor's house; but I have several hours before that. My feet sink a little in the sand. In each footstep the water filters in. It forms a little pool. I turn, I make out the house on the cliff."

The narrator reaches this house, where he perceives that he has been replaced by someone else:

"Here I am again staggering along the dark and deserted road; I recognize on the right the villa where I ought to be, slip into the garden, glue my face to the window. The conversation still has a fairly animated air, but I hear nothing. The disappearance of Michel Butor in any case has not caused much concern. Black waiters pass whiskeys and canapés. I go around the house. Here is the kitchen entrance. Frying odors. Flurries. Several white coats. I recognize my last companion in the car, at his wrists cufflinks with snakes' heads. He welcomes me pleasantly, helps me get into the sleeves of a white coat, which fits me fairly well, places on my hands a platter of glasses. I slip among the guests, recognize some who smile nicely at me while serving themselves. The first Bernard arrives. Sensation. 'But where did you disappear to, my friend?' 'I walked a little by the sea.' His suit is impeccable, but he has not shaved. The guests are astonished. Murmurs: 'New Novel . . . 'Structuralism . . . 'Words in Painting . . .' He is holding forth. Now he tosses me a glance, makes a sign. I act as if I have seen nothing, but the hostess catches me, saying, 'Bernard!' and motioning me to go serve a glass of whiskey to the imposter."

. . . . . . **80 Judgment**

In another dream in the same book, things are going even worse. It begins with an airplane crash. I fall into a tropical forest, am rescued. I arrive on a stretcher in a dazzling big city.

"I seem to recognize Lisbon, but that is not possible. Cargo ships, sailing ships, cranes, stairs licked by waves. I end up a little farther on a beach covered with parasols. Balls and swimmers, children's cries. They run towards me. These are only blacks in gold briefs. The women have no bras. They speak French with a singing accent. The piece of wing sticking out of my chest is covered with emerald butterflies, which fly away at the approach of other humans. A single cry comes from twenty chests: 'The lecturer, the lecturer, it is surely the lecturer!' A jeep arrives out of which come black nurses in white jackets. We travel miles on the sand, then along avenues bordered by palm trees. The traffic becomes heavier. We are nearing the center of the city. They stop in front of a palace with a neoclassic facade, big corinthian columns, ornamental front. They take me along corridors with pipes running through them. They are the wings of a theater. They have me go on stage. Applause. The hall is full; all the spectators are white. The blacks set up my stretcher with the air mattress. They fasten me with big rubber bracelets so I can stay upright. An academician in full regalia—two-cornered hat, sword—demands silence: 'We ask you to pardon the slight delay completely beyond our control. I have the pleasure of presenting to you now M. Michel Butor, whom we have invited to come confess his sins.'

"I do all I can to move my lips, but no sound comes from my mouth. Various movements. The academician comes back, murmurs in my ear:

'Come come, sir, say something; they have waited long enough for you.' I begin to drool; it dribbles down in long strings on the prepared podium. A laugh bursts out, another; an enormous gale of laughter takes over the whole hall, which becomes wild. Insults begin. People stamp. Hands crumple the invitation leaflets and throw them at me. The stage is covered with balls of paper.

"The academician comes back; with a gesture full of unction he reestablishes calm: 'Well, since the accused manifests no repentance, let the judgment begin! Let the first witness come to the stage!' Cheers. There are steps on each side. The whole audience gets up and forms a line. It is an uninterrupted parade. I do not understand half of what they say. Each declaration is greeted by howling from the crowd, then a witness spits in my face, and the spittle mixes with the drool that is still dribbling, runs down the stage into the orchestra pit in long filaments. 'He stole books, soiled our museums, he never brushes his teeth, he lusted after his mother, deceived her, deceives his wife, desires his daughters, deceives them, sought his father's death, endangers the public order, was a dunce in Latin translation, disappointed the hopes we had in him, poisoned our wells, propositioned not only our daughters but our wives, even our sons, but also our landscapes, a single one of his glances is enough to inflame our families, a single one of his words brings dissension to our schools; as for his books they could succeed in corrupting fire; and now look how he is drooling! It is a torrent of slobber that he pours out in his dotage, which will burn everything in our city if we do not succeed in punishing him.' It lasts for hours. I did not know I had so much drool in me. It was true that something would have to be done."

It all ends up being settled naturally in a rather bizarre way. It helped me a great deal in taming my nightmares, but did not get rid of them. From time to time I still dream that I am making a mess of a lecture. Or a musician friend asks me to direct an orchestra in his place and stupidly I accept. Naturally the result is lamentable. Inexcusable. But now when I wake up I recognize this kind of dream and it is no longer the same anguish at all. It is an old acquaintance. "Well, there it is again, that one!" It is labeled. Thus literature helps us live with our dreams, look them in the face.

xvii

to change life

81 Preservation

Generous writers tend to consider that the function of literature is to change the world in which we live, and indeed literature can do so to a certain extent. But writing literature in the usual sense is not enough. On the contrary. A great part of literature is created so that the world will be preserved, so that the society in which we live can continue in the same way. We tend to consider that only literature that produces change is valuable, and we can say this is true for today. But if we consider great literature of the past, we are obliged to admit that some of the most important works are works of preservation, works created so that society could continue.

Sometimes it is so difficult for society to continue that one is obliged to change it to preserve at least something. Besides, if we need texts to make society continue, it is because it is already in the process of changing, in a way that might be catastrophic. We can envisage three cases: first, a society that is deteriorating, and for it to be preserved we need a certain number of texts (thus a certain change); second, a society that is preserved thanks to the texts it produces; third, a society that is being transformed in a positive way, and the texts are playing an eminent role in this transformation.

If we feel this need to transform society in a positive way, it is because the preservation is not produced appropriately and, therefore, that we have an inevitable deterioration.

The great works of classic literatures are often texts of preservation. First they are religious texts, or politico-religious; for example, all the ceremonial that exists around power, whether or not the king or pharaoh is officially considered a god. The pharoah was recognized as a god. Louis XIV was not; and yet, in the chapel of the castle of Versailles the entire public, the entire court, looked at him seated on the raised platform at the back, and only he looked at the altar; that is to say that in that place all religious efficacity passed through him as intermediary.

The poems of Homer were indispensable to the cohesion of Greek society. We have there something going beyond "politics" in the strict sense. Homer's poems were one of the references linking all the little states of ancient Greece, making of them not a state but a culture. In the Muslim countries they say the Koran is the dictionary of the poor; it is the fundamental linguistic reference. Even if the Arabic spoken today in the different regions is very far from it, they always come back to it. In the same way, they came back to the Homeric poems, and that is why Pisistratus, the Athenian statesman of the sixth century, decided to have them written down, whereas before they had always been recited by the bards or rhapsodists.

Traditional societies, whether of antiquity, the Middle Ages, or the classical period, functioned for a certain number of centuries and more or less held their own, thanks to preserving texts. These societies had great problems to resolve—in particular, great inequalities. A certain number of ceremonies and festivals permitted them to compensate in a fictitious way. This is what is called the carnival in Western Europe. We have phenomena of this kind in all societies, and naturally in our modern societies.

• • • • • • 82 Carnival

Carnival is a collective dream that can occur in full daylight. For a few days a number of rules are suspended, and individuals can try out other roles for a little while. In classical societies clothing not only served as protection from the cold but also played an essential classifying role. Its language covered three areas: first, it indicated geographic origin—each province, each region of the world, had its particular costume; second, it indicated work, function; third, it indicated rank, power.

In normal times changing costumes was forbidden. Disguise was one of the fundamental features of carnival. Today we still have clothes that classify us. We all have a sort of neutral clothing to which we have the option of adding the variations of fashion. Sometimes these variations are very limited. For quite awhile the only change possible in male attire was the tie, and in certain circumstances a black or white tie was obligatory. Fortunately these variations have become more extensive today: men can even depart from the old range of fundamental neutral, which was limited to black, navy blue, or gray. Now we can conceive of a man walking around in a green suitcoat, which a few years ago was still quite unusual. For women variations in fashion are much wider, but they are still subject to very complex and rigorous seasonal rules.

In addition, there is the very important classification by clothing, and we are forbidden to usurp that of others. This is clearest in the most hierarchical part of society, the army. A simple soldier is not allowed to dress as a general. He can do so only on a carnival day.

Formerly all ranks—kings, dukes, counts—had their semantically very rich costumes, which were summed up in their coats of arms, which themselves summed up what was called colors or livery, often worn by the whole household.

Another region of classifying clothing is the hospital. Everything must be regulated there; it must be possible to recognize instantly who is who and who can play which role. The same is true in aviation companies.

This is why today we need carnival moments when someone who is not in the military and might dream of it (this still happens with some children) can dress up more or less in the costume. One could also take on the disguise of a bishop or police officer. A few hours or a few days are thought to be enough to make us want to regain our own position and habits. Once the carnival is over, everyone returns to his place and society continues tranquilly.

But not always. Sometimes society is so shaken up that the carnival takes on another function: it becomes the image of the world turned upside down, whether for worse or better. At the beginning a carnival tries to furnish proof that society is properly arranged because, you see, if you try to change the rules, everything becomes ridiculous; but sometimes it becomes proof that society is badly arranged because, if you change the rules, things begin to get better. Then carnival takes on a revolutionary value. It becomes the prefiguration of the transformation of society.

Carnival can be prolonged in certain people, certain functions. Some societies institute carnivalesque functions, which endure within more or less secret societies, more or less closed locations. The clearest example in the Western world is the theater, where on the stage disguise is possible all year long. During carnival anyone can put a royal crown on his head; all year long (or almost) actors can do so when they are onstage. In the same way that in classic society carnival had to come to an end and everyone had to know it was over, so the theater had to be restricted in space. It had to be made crystal clear that the actor who played the role of king was not a real king. When he left the stage he was not only like everyone else, but he had a negative mark on him, which compensated for the positive mark he had dressed up in; he had to be less than everyone else. This ostracism was at the same time a mark of mistrust and a mark of respect. The actor was applauded, praised, but held apart from society, condemned by the official church.

Certain individuals could maintain a carnivalesque function all by themselves all year long and almost anywhere. These were the buffoons, the court jesters. Identified by a very special costume, the court jester had some unique privileges. He had the right to tell the prince the real truth, which no one else had the right to do. On the other hand, everyone had the right to insult him, to laugh at him, even to beat him. He was not permitted to resist, to fight back. Often not only his costume marked his difference, but his physical appearance: look at the famous dwarfs of the Spanish court so magnificently portrayed by Velásquez, or those for whom the Estes constructed a special apartment in the palace of Mantua.

The theater, the buffoon, lead us to reflect on what the artist is today. Some people today succeed in obtaining rules that are different from those obeyed by others. They produce a region of tolerance. From the seventeenth to the nineteenth century, the painter was the only person in society with the right to look freely at nude women or men. Even in the specialized houses the girls wore clothes.

Nudity too can be considered a term in the language of clothing: to be nude is to dress up in a particular sign indicative of certain situations or functions. Gradually our societies have conquered regions of nudity, but they vary according to the country, which can provoke many misunderstandings.

The painter thus enjoyed a privilege that for others was out of the question. Some painters acquire a type of celebrity, which gives them a role comparable to that of the buffoons of former times. Through a certain freedom of behavior and language, they give society some fresh air. Through their intermediary people can say things that ordinarily they could not. Take, for example, a character like Salvador Dalí.

Our society does not satisfy us; it is full of contradictions, and yet we have no desire to go backward. We find ourselves in a sort of chaos, looking for what should be done. We no longer know what we want. The individual dream or these institutionalized, collective dreams that spectacles and festivals are allow us to discover it bit by bit.

You see what I am getting at; political literary genres as they function today show their insufficiency more and more. They succeed neither in preserving society nor in transforming it. We can no longer manage to figure out what we want, and when we do have some idea we cannot manage to accomplish it through the intermediary of our present political system. We therefore need a complement to this system, a generalization of carnival, which is offered us, with more or less success, by the art and literature of today.

. . . . **83 May 1968**

Some have used the word *carnival* to designate the events of May 68. Certainly there was an aspect of carnival in the most serious sense of the term. It was a moment when many writers felt that it was truly impossible for them to remain in their studies, that they had to go into the street to talk with the others, for the others, through the others.

The primary importance of these events was their unexpected nature; the fact that they took the political institutions completely by surprise clearly shows to what point those institutions were functioning badly. A month earlier, no one suspected that anything was going to break out in this way and that because of it the government would come close to falling. We were within an ace of a kind of chaos, of civil war—a rather cautious one, but after which a reorganization would have been all the more difficult because no model had been provided in advance. The institutions succeeded in reforming themselves over this turbulent base, in which, later, some beginnings could be perceived, without the forms of government being fundamentally shaken subsequently. A problem was posed to which no solution has yet been found. It is imaginable that one day an even stronger and just as unexpected shock will occur, since successive governments have taken precautions only against the "symptoms" of events of this kind. They have arranged for things not to start up again in the same way at the same place, but those things will begin again differently somewhere else. We know neither where nor how because we have not really made the effort to study the problem.

Another important point is that these events and their reappearances—for example, the demonstrations at the Sorbonne in 1987, which were just as unexpected by the government and by the union organizations, the latter showing themselves to have been totally overwhelmed—stemmed from problems in education. Before the war France possessed an educational system it was proud of. In the forties the system began to deteriorate. This does not mean there were not excellent professors and also excellent institutions, but the uneasiness has only continued to increase. French education is no longer adequate for contemporary society. Since the end of the war we have observed a number of efforts at educational reform, but it is very difficult to reform education in France, for the very reasons that formerly assured its high quality. France is the most centralized of all countries, the one whose educational system is the most centralized. Aside from some safety valves, which are rightly called "free" education—not because one is more free there, but because they allow for a certain freedom of movement in the whole—it is an enormous and extremely unwieldy unified enterprise.

It is easier to transform smaller enterprises. Educational reform is less difficult in Japan, in Germany, in England, even in the United States, because in these countries there are units separated from each other that enjoy a fairly wide freedom to maneuver. They can thus experiment, try something in one place, something else in another.

They have indeed tried pilot high schools in France, different experiments on university campuses, but even when certain governments have evinced a sincere desire for reform, administrative sluggishness has always gradually reduced the changes to almost nothing. The only reforms that have had some staying power are those imposed violently from the outside by competition that became too great; too serious a breach had to be warded off.

Incapable of reforming itself, French education will be reformed bit by bit from the outside, ending up with a floating structure comparable to that of the big multinational enterprises with numerous centers that are sufficiently autonomous relative to each other to allow exchanges of ideas, proposals, experiments. At this moment it appears that it is the new Europe that will reform our education.

Faced with the student demonstrations, the surprised governments said, "We do not know what they want," and as the students could only demonstrate their refusal, the governments said next, "But they do not know what they want," and that is true, but they did know at least what they did not want, and they have not yet succeeded in eliminating it. They will need, we will need, years to know what they want, what we want. Professors are there for that purpose, but it will require years.

. . . . . . **84 Murder and Truth**

From a financial point of view, one of the most important genres in publishing is of course the novel. We can state that big businesses in the book trade have great difficulty publishing what we call "literature" in the strict sense. It is rather the little publishers who take that risk. The big ones, which have high costs, are obliged today to look for a best-seller and therefore favor the genres that provide quick and certain sales. Thus the novel today includes a certain number of subgenres, each of which obeys very strict rules. The novel written in view of a literary prize constitutes one of these subgenres; it is not very sure at all. The detective story, on the other hand, usually allows the editor to cover his expenses and also permits our society to continue.

The first rule of the classic detective story is that it must be readable in one evening. As soon as it exceeds a certain length it becomes something else: literature playing with the detective story. Among the great ladies of British detective literature, Agatha Christie wrote real detective stories, sometimes so well done that they became literature, but Dorothy Sayers invented a new genre: a distinguished, sophisticated, admirably literary parody.

If the detective story has to be read in one evening, it is because it plays the role of a pharmaceutical product. We all have difficulties in our daily life. We feel stress. We are squeezed into hierarchies obliging us to obey superiors who have their good qualities and their faults. If, fortunately, we most often are aware of their good qualities, there are days when it is above all their faults that appear to us, and when we would be very glad to be rid of them. Now not only are we forbidden to do away with our colleagues, but we are forbidden to say we would like to.

On a day when I have been particularly irritated by one person or another, if I have trouble going to sleep, I go to my literary medicine cabinet and get a detective story. I am sure to find a murder story, which, far from being abhorrent to me as it is supposed to be in everyday life, on the contrary, profoundly satisfies me. But something in us disapproves of such satisfaction; it is then that the machine of the detective story furnishes us a second murder, that of the assassin by the detective.

The detective often has superhuman aspects. He is the supreme decoder of signs. At the end of the book he creates light. In the classic detective story he often brings together all the characters and obtains a confession from the murderer. Once light is created, the merciful detective opens a door and the murderer commits suicide in a corner; he disappears. From that point on we can close the book again and go peacefully to sleep. The next day we again begin our workday with a smile on our lips; something happened during the night that allows us to tolerate the superior or colleague who irritated us so much the day before. If tension of this sort accumulated from day to day, there would come a time when everything would explode. The detective story is thus closely linked to the functioning of our administrations and businesses, and it is perfectly clear who is the public for the detective story.

We could make analyses of this kind with all the popular kinds of novels. The science-fiction novel, for example, is linked to our technological development. We are fascinated by the technological progress offered us, but all sorts of delays annoy us. We know such progress would be possible, but we are told by newspapers, reports, or speeches about the needs or rather the special interests, economical and political, that cause it to be given up for the time being. The science-fiction novel describes to us a world in which some of the technological progress that we believe is near has actually been achieved; what happens in the novel is not very important. The essential is the description. Often it is the destruction of this imaginary world that we need in order to return more easily to our own familiar world of frustrations. That is why the science-fiction novel so often leads us to a catastrophic end, and we find we are after all not too unhappy in our world of today.

The sentimental novel, the novel of the Harlequin collection, for instance, often offers us a young salesgirl noticed by the big boss. They have an affair and end up getting married. There are admirable novels on this theme, for example Zola's *Au bonheur des dames*, which includes, obviously, many other facets. These rosewater novels, administered in a dose of one evening's reading maximum, correspond to a female public suffering grave frustrations. The future of this type of novel depends on the technological evolution of a country. Those reading such works do not yet have television and want it. As soon as they (male and especially female readers) have a set, reading is replaced by the consummation of television serials.

· · · · · · 85 Active Leisure

Each of these genres is governed by laws that, manifest or not, permit its function as a preserving factor. The importance of such a need leads to thinking that it is possible to transform these genres, all the current genres, in such a way that they will acquire functions of transformation.

It is a question then of a positive carnival linked to all textual or artistic functions. In literature, the most efficacious work is the transformation in depth of language and literary genres. This is what ends up little by little by renewing even political discourse in the usual sense. It is necessary, obviously, to have a certain leisure at one's disposal to give oneself up to this laboratory research. It is thus obligatory, within our very crowded society, to make for oneself, to carve out for oneself, little islands of freedom. The writer must be able to make a difference for himself comparable to the one that the painter enjoys in his studio, which is very difficult.

It is fairly easy for the writer to enjoy a kind of approval from society when he is working on functions of preservation. If he works at transformation he necessarily implies the abolition of some of the privileges of those who are powerful within this society. With regard to this the powerful will have a remarkably fine sensitivity. The writer will thus have to establish for himself a carnivalesque region that is transfigured in some way, to disguise his disguise. Today each one is obliged to conquer by himself this place in which he is free to carry out research in depth, thereby transforming the equilibrium of literary or artistic genres, and thus the whole of social function.

This transformation is inevitable because of developments in technology that cause our society not to function in reality as we believe it does. We always lag behind. There are more and more numerous cracks and holes from which we must profit, whose value we must reverse. It is evident that no government, no administration, can decide to whom these zones of leisure will be allocated. Governments, directors, the powerful will always try to recapture that decision and control it, but in the long run it is the artist or writer who must manage to find a way within this game to fortify the unique place he occupies.

In peacetime, society, in spite of all its problems, functions more or less and disposes of a certain leisure as a result. In other circumstances the shocks are such that it is usually necessary to let the storm pass, to maintain oneself in reserve. At the time of wars, revolutions, political or even natural upheavals—earthquakes, for example—it is as difficult for the writer as for the scholar to give himself up to work in the laboratory. But that, however, is what is the most useful. It is the esoteric work of physicists, astronomers, mathematicians, biologists that in the long run changes our daily life in a much deeper way than all the politicians' speeches.

So long as one can work on a transformation in depth of society, that is what one must do. When one can no longer do it, one must work with the others so that a provisory state is brought back as quickly as possible in which one will be able to work at this transformation. What we can seek more and more today is to persuade administrations and governments that our society does not function well, that they do not function well, that it is essential to seek and to prepare something else, thus to bring about acceptance for the idea that it is appropriate to institute a sort of permanent carnivalesque region, to respect as much as possible all the activities of painters, musicians, writers, and scholars.

When a government admits that, it tries hard to encourage the arts, but it itself wants to decide what it is appropriate to encourage; the government wants to make the choice in order at least to profit by good publicity. A good part of the literature of socialist countries formerly was a literature made to order, directed by governments that understood very well that they would receive in return a glorification of themselves or of what they were doing, all of which helped to hide what was not working. These functions rather resemble those of the official poets of certain royal courts. Princes had literature valets. The prince was the preeminent speaker, but as he had many other functions, those of language had to be filled by others in his name, poets laureate, whose principal role was to sing the praises of the one who supported them. All present governments produce an official art that gives birth to an art of counterquestioning.

It is a matter of managing to obtain the respect of governmental or other enterprises for a region from which they have not a superficial need for publicity but an absolute need for their own transformation and, sometimes, disappearance. It is necessary, therefore, to manage to go beyond, little by little, the opposition still so often in place today between preserving and transforming, to understand that one cannot preserve except by transforming, and, inversely, that one cannot transform except by preserving in a certain way, and even in reanimating a past perpetually at risk of being forgotten. So let us hope that many writers will be true seekers so that even the idea of politics will be profoundly transformed.

There are many things I would have wanted to talk to you about, but I have no more time and am therefore obliged to repress them. That will certainly produce dreams for me, and I hope that it will produce some for you, too. I would have wanted to talk with you about my next books, those I dream of. It only remains for me to write some of them, dreaming of those who will write the others.

. . . . notes

Butor on Butor: An Introduction

1. As Butor indicates on the back cover of the French edition of *L'Écriture en transformation* (Paris: La Différence, 1993), "During my years of university teaching, it was understood that I should keep my hats separate. Professor and creator of literature should not be confused. My colleagues could talk about my books in the neighboring room or amphitheatre; for me, it was forbidden, even for my critical works."

2. Samuel Beckett, "Dante . . . Bruno. Vico . . . Joyce," in *James Joyce/Finnegans Wake: A Symposium. Our Exagimination Round His Factification for Incamination of Work in Progress*. 2d ed. (Norfolk, Conn.: New Directions, 1957), 1.

3. Jean-François Lyotard, "What Is Postmodernism?" in *Postmodernism: A Reader*, ed. Thomas Docherty (New York: Columbia University Press, 1993), 45.

4. Marcel Duchamp, *Salt Seller: The Writings of Marcel Duchamp (Marchand du sel)*, ed. M. Sanouillet and E. Peterson (New York: Oxford University Press, 1973), 141. Cited in Sidney Feshbach, "Marcel Duchamp or Being Taken for a Ride: Duchamp was a Cubist, a Mechanomorphist, a Dadaist, a Surrealist, a Conceptualist, a Modernist—and None of the Above," *James Joyce Quarterly* 26, no. 4 (Summer 1989): 544.

5. For a more in-depth consideration of the congruence of Butor and Duchamp's "anesthetics," see my "Animation of the Work of Art: Michel Butor's *L'Embarquement de la Reine de Saba*" in *Modern Language Notes* 109, no. 4 (Fall 1994): 741–52. Also, my "L'Anesthétique de Michel Butor" in *La Création selon Michel Butor: Réseaux-Frontières-Ecart*, ed. Mireille Calle-Gruber (Paris: Nizet, 1991), 247–57.

6. Michel Butor in Madeleine Santschi, *Voyage avec Michel Butor* (Lausanne: L'Age d'Homme, 1982), 162.

7. Critic Lucien Dällenbach has argued most convincingly for a number of points of convergence between Butor and Balzac, the writer most often targeted as the victim of the new novelists' attack. See "Une Écriture Dialogique?" in *La Création selon Michel Butor: Réseaux-Frontières-Ecart,* ed. Mireille Calle-Gruber (Paris: Nizet, 1991), 210–11.

8. Cited in ibid., 210.

9. Cf. Dällenbach's comparison of Butor to Balzac: "Même optimisme, enfin, quant à la vertu thérapeutique et je dirais politique de la littérature" (The same optimism, finally, as far as the therapeutic and I would say political virtue of literature is concerned) (ibid., 211).

10. Butor is currently completing the fifth volume, *Gyroscope,* in the *Génie du lieu* series.

11. Mary Lydon, *Perpetuum Mobile* (Edmonton: University of Alberta Press, 1980), 244.

I: The Cold Night

1. This fair, Expo '92, took place in Seville from April 20 to October 12, 1992.

2. The Colonial Fair took place in France in 1931.

III: The Road of the Novel

1. Paracelsus was a Swiss physician and philosopher of the sixteenth century.

2. Statius's twelve-book Latin epic poem on the Seven against Thebes. Also, the district around Thebes.

V: Glimmers in the Fog

1. Antonio Gaudi y Cornet (1852–1926) was a Spanish architect considered a leader in Catalan artistic revival.

VII: Railway Consciousness

1. Webster's defines the mathematical term *asymptote* as "a straight line always approaching but never meeting a curve; tangent at infinity."

2. This used to be a common reference to an automobile, namely, a larger Citroën model, which was practically always black.

VIII: Transatlantic

1. This text was published in the now defunct journal *Les Lettres nouvelles* (Paris: Gallimard) in December 1960.

XI: Travel

1. Nissard is an Italian dialect formerly spoken in Nice.

XII: The Gift of Languages

1. Despite what Butor says here, Beckett nearly always translated his own work from French to English or vice versa. It is true that he was helped in certain of his translations by others: Alfred Peron worked with him on the translation of *Murphy;* Richard Seaver helped him with the early stories; Robert Pinget assisted him on a couple of the radio plays; and Ludovic Janvier worked with him on *Watt.* Nevertheless, it was Beckett who was responsible for the translations. One can cite, in this regard, Beckett's comment to his American director Alan Schneider: "I have nothing but wastes and wilds of self-translation before me for many miserable months to come" (cited in Ruby Cohn, ed., *Disjecta* [London: John Calder, 1983], 108). And critic Leslie Hill has written: "Beckett began translating *Molloy* in collaboration with Patrick Bowles, but finally assumed responsibility for translating it and the rest of the trilogy himself. Since that time, bar a few joint versions (such as *Tous ceux qui tombent, Cendres,* or the French *Watt*) done in conjunction with other translators, Beckett himself has been responsible for all the translations of his own work to appear in English or French" (*Beckett's Fiction* [Cambridge: Cambridge University Press, 1990], 49).

2. The national library in Paris.

3. "Que Vlo've?"—which in Walloon, the language of the area of Belgium in question, means "Que voulez-vous?" or "What do you want?" This novella figures in the collection *L'Hérésiarque et Cie.*

XIII: Invasion of Images

1. The fictional painter in Proust's *À la recherche du temps perdu.*

2. The Botticelli painting, which dates from 1495 and hangs in the Uffizi Gallery in Florence, is entitled *The Calumny of Apelles* and depends on texts of the ancient Greek satirist Lucian. Apelles was an early Hellenistic painter of the late fourth and early third centuries B.C.

XIV: Toward Discovery

1. George Catlin (1796–1872) was an American artist and author devoted to the study of American Indians. His series of Indian portraits and Indian sketches are found in the National Museum in Washington, D.C., and in the American Museum of Natural History in New York. The work of photographer Edward Sheriff Curtis (1868–1952), best known for his photographs of Indians, is published in twenty volumes of *North American Indian* and *Indian Days of Long Ago.*

2. The original *Pinakotheke* was a gallery of the Acropolis that held the tablets or pictures honoring the gods.

3. Francesco Primaticcio (1504–70) was an Italian painter and architect called to Fontainebleau by Francis I in 1532; there he would succeed Il Rosso eight years later as chief artist. Appointed court architect by Catherine de Médicis. Giovanni Battista di Jacopo Rosso, called Il Rosso (1494–1540), was an Italian mannerist

called to Fontainebleau by Francis I in 1530 as head artist. His ornamental style exerted international influence.

4. Le Centre Beaubourg, also called the Centre National d'Art et de Culture Georges Pompidou, was created in 1977. It consists of a number of different cultural areas: the Musée National d'Art Moderne, the Institut de Recherche et de Coordination Acoustique/Musique, a children's center, a major public library, the Centre de Création Industrielle, a theater, and exhibition halls.

XV: Literature and Music

1. *Fusuma* is a Japanese word designating a sliding door, framed and papered, used to partition off rooms in a house.

2. The series entitled *The Seasons* was painted by Johns in 1985 and 1986 and first exhibited in 1987 at the Leo Castelli Gallery in New York.

3. Gotthold Ephraim Lessing (1729–81) was a German dramatist, critic, translator, and editor of his own dramatic journal.

4. Butor uses the expression "mis en ondes" in the French edition, which is a play on the expression "mis en scène," or "staged." The pun could not be kept in translation for "waved," as in radio waves, would have no meaning in English.

5. Characters from Proust's *À la recherche du temps perdu.*